Humor in the White House

Humor in the White House

The Wit of Five American Presidents

by ARTHUR A. SLOANE

McFarland & Company, Inc., Publishers
Jefferson, North Carolina, and London

Library of Congress Cataloguing-in-Publication Data

Sloane, Arthur A.
Humor in the White House : the wit of five American presidents /
by Arthur A. Sloane.
p. cm.
Includes bibliographical references and index.
ISBN 0-7864-0949-5 (softcover : 50# alkaline paper) ∞
1. Presidents—United States—History—Anecdotes.
2. Presidents—United States—Biography. 3. Presidents—United
States—Humor. 4. United States—Politics and government—
Anecdotes. 5. United States—Politics and government—Humor.
6. American wit and humor. I. Title.
E176.1.S615 2001
973'.099—dc21 2001030087

British Library cataloguing data are available

Manufactured in the United States of America

*McFarland & Company, Inc., Publishers
Box 611, Jefferson, North Carolina 28640
www.mcfarlandpub.com*

To Louise,
the very best

ACKNOWLEDGMENTS

As I am to the almost three hundred printed sources listed in the bibliography and notes sections of this volume, I am indebted to the many people who shared their thoughts on humor, on a specific president, or on a combination of the two topics in personal interviews. It is impossible to acknowledge all of them, but the following definitely deserve special mention: Dave Barry, Art Buchwald, Thomas R. Carper, Richard J. Cronin, C. Douglas Dillon, Sam Donaldson, Barney Frank, John Kenneth Galbraith, Annette Goodheart, Joel Goodman, Martin G. Mand, Bob Orben, Robert L. Paretta, Landon Parvin, Sanford S. Pinsker, Michael F. Pohlen, Arthur M. Schlesinger, Jr., George P. Shultz, Caspar W. Weinberger, and Paul M. Zall.

Equally worthy of my thanks are several other people. Rita M. Beasley not only typed every word of the manuscript but continued a tradition that, after the publication of three other books with her help, I have now come to expect: she contributed many suggestions that make me look better. Myrt Werkheiser and Nancy Sanderson each cheerfully and competently provided a variety of secretarial services. Mark E. Girardi, my graduate assistant during the early part of this project, was of great assistance in bringing much of the source material together.

Most of all, I appreciate the support that Louise P. Sloane, my wife, gave me throughout the process. Everyone else will have to be satisfied with the acknowledgments; she alone may also share in the royalties.

CONTENTS

INTRODUCTION

"Never make people laugh," Senator Thomas Corwin once advised James A. Garfield. "If you would succeed in life, you must be solemn, solemn as an ass. All great monuments are built over solemn asses." America's twentieth president apparently took this counsel to heart: already convinced that he was marked for greatness, he was nothing if not humorless as leader of his country, giving the appearance of a man who, if told a joke with a double meaning, would understand neither one of them.

Most of the nation's chief executives, in fact, have been seen by the citizenry as rather grave individuals. And, perhaps operating on the principle that levity amid the problems of their White House years might be viewed as fiddling while Rome burned, they have often preferred it that way. Grover Cleveland more than once remarked that it was "a solemn thing to be president of the United States." Woodrow Wilson, who believed that God had ordained that he should be president, said, "I'm not here to amuse the newspapers. I'll be damned if I will." Dwight D. Eisenhower was so conspicuously devoid of a light touch that when he responded to a reporter's request to name any contribution to his administration on the part of his former vice president, Richard Nixon, by declaring, "If you give me a week, I might think of one," his comment was widely accepted as seriously meant (despite Nixon's insistence that his old boss was "only kidding"). Jimmy Carter once opined, "If the American people wanted Bob Hope for their president, they should have elected him."

Few of these leaders have gone all the way without exhibiting any humor at all, of course. Even the virtually humorless Nixon was capable of saying, after listening to the inaugural address of his victorious 1960 opponent John F. Kennedy, "I wish I had said that," and of announcing (in a not-so-hidden projection of one of his own problems) that he didn't trust Lyndon Johnson "because of the way

1

he looks on television." Ulysses S. Grant, not by any means a barrel of laughs, either, turned to an aide three days after Appomattox
and declared, "On to Mexico," and often told admiring postwar
audiences, "I rise only to say I do not intend to say anything."

Cleveland, his statement about presidential solemnity notwithstanding, once remarked (as ex-president) to an excessively tenacious
interviewer, "That, sir, is a matter of too great importance to discuss in a five-minute interview, now rapidly drawing to a close." The
austere Quaker Herbert Hoover, who regularly removed anything
that remotely resembled wit from his already stern speeches in a
belief that it was entirely inappropriate to be funny given the economic conditions of his time, observed wryly, "I'm the only person
of distinction who's ever had a depression named after him." And
the earnest, self-absorbed Carter—despite his remark about Bob
Hope—once told an enthusiastic audience, "It really is a pleasure to
see people waving at me with all five fingers."

A few presidents, moreover, have by all informed accounts possessed excellent senses of humor but for whatever reason put these
on display quite sparingly—perhaps most notably Harry Truman,
who on one occasion declared, "Any man who has the job I've had
and didn't have a sense of humor wouldn't still be here." Truman
was capable of droll, understated wit, as exhibited in his observation, when confronted by one of the many huge challenges that faced
his administration in the months immediately following World War
II, that General William Tecumseh Sherman had been wrong: "I find
peace is hell." Truman also once announced that he would very much
like to have a "one-handed economist," since all of the economists
who were currently advising him tended to say, "On the one hand
... but on the other...." In retirement, he said that the Republican
presidential candidate Nixon was "one of the few men in the history of this country to run for high office talking out of both sides
of his mouth at the same time and lying out of both sides."

William Howard Taft apparently also could be quite funny when
he wanted to be; it's just that he didn't, from all of the evidence, want
to be very often. Destined to become, at some 332 pounds, the heav-
iest man ever to preside over the nation, as a young lawyer he wired
the stationmaster in a small town at which a train he wanted to
board did not regularly stop, "Will No. 7 stop here for a large party?"
When the train did stop, he climbed aboard and told the conductor,
"You can go ahead. I am the large party." During his presidency he
is also believed to have replied when his wife awakened him one

night and told him, "I think there's a burglar in the house," "My dear, there are probably several and at least as many in the Senate." When he ran a disappointing third in his 1912 attempt to retain the presidency—trailing not only Wilson but also former chief executive Theodore Roosevelt—he declared that there was some consolation for him in realizing that no one in U.S. history had ever been elected ex-president by such a huge majority.

Whether due to lack of a funny bone or reluctance to utilize it, the moments of jocularity for America's presidents have been conspicuous by their scarcity. Generally, to paraphrase Fred Allen's comment about sincerity in Hollywood, you could take all of the genuine humor ever shown by most of the forty-two chief executives of our country, put it in a flea's navel, and still have room left over for six caraway seeds and a media consultant's heart. Anyone bent on an exercise in futility might be well advised to sift through the often staggering blizzards of words autobiographically or biographically devoted to U.S. commanders in chief—not an impossibility in this age of the computer—in search of amusing quips that they tossed off or funny tales that they related at least once in a while over their entire lifetimes. The record is, for most of them, surprisingly barren.

On the other hand, five White House occupants—Abraham Lincoln, Calvin Coolidge, Franklin D. Roosevelt, John F. Kennedy, and Ronald Reagan—have displayed exceptional senses of humor, and in all cases that humor has served them well. The dividends to some extent varied with the president: for Lincoln, self-therapy was a key result, while Coolidge derived considerable self-amusement from the process. FDR was a master at diverting attention from his debilitating physical condition through humor, while both JFK and Reagan relied heavily on their abilities to amuse to defuse potentially awkward issues. But all augmented their popularity greatly through the use of their talents, and, as will be shown, each of the five derived many other advantages as well. The poet Marianne Moore could have drawn upon any of them as case studies in support of her often quoted opinion that "humor saves a few steps, it saves years." Had he lived several decades later, Mark Twain could have been referring to these presidents as he rendered his dictum, "The human race has only one effective weapon, and that is laughter."

A certain amount of solemnity comes, of course, with the presidential territory. But if we can learn anything from the experiences of these five holders of what has become the most awesome and

responsible job on the planet, it is that a marriage of sobriety and
levity can be a winning formula.

What is humorous to members of one generation can, of course,
seem quite unfunny and even tasteless to members of another. It is
hard to believe that, as relatively recently as 1969, the popular host
of a widely watched late-night television show announced in his
opening monologue that "tomorrow is the first anniversary of the
assassination of the Reverend Martin Luther King and in honor of
it Mayor Lindsay [John V. Lindsay, the liberal chief executive of
New York City] has declared a day of looting" and received much
laughter rather than immediate attack for his effort. Or that this
same entertainer not long thereafter referred to "Gay Lib, or United
Fruit" without suffering loss of life or limb.

Lincoln himself, typically for his times, used the word "darky"
frequently and included it together with a strong Negro dialect in
the handful of black-related jokes that he told. He had a much larger
arsenal of anecdotes that involved other ethnicities—especially Irish
tales, which he spun off with an especially thick brogue. Nor did he
seem to have any compunctions about publicly reciting to essentially
male audiences anecdotes so bawdy (a close friend once said that his
love of the lewd was "something akin to lunacy") that it is impossible to imagine any politician of today offering them, if at all, any
place except behind closed doors.

The puritanical Coolidge and the elegantly mannered patrician
Roosevelt are not open to any such indictments, even apocryphally.
But Kennedy, not so much a storyteller as a quipster, was known to
toss off more than a few off-color lines; these served him well in the
early 1960s but might have caused him trouble in the more politically correct early twenty-first century. He was also, as both the first
Catholic president and an Irish American, given to joking about both
his religion and his ancestry to a degree that might not have been so
welcomed had he done the same thing today.

Reagan was a master of political incorrectness who, in his early
presidential years, frequently told jokes, generally heavily larded with
dialect, about Japanese Americans, Italian Americans, Polish Americans, and his fellow Irish Americans without discrimination to all
kinds of audiences. He remained a fertile source of sometimes quite
irrelevant Irish-related humor to the end. Once, intending to gain points
with his listeners, he said to a group of professional women, "If it
weren't for women, us men would be walking around in skin suits
carrying clubs." He also did occasional imitations of stereotypical

gays and at times showed a Lincolnesque proclivity for telling rib-ald stories. Both of the latter behaviors were almost always demon-strated away from the public eye, but with his irrepressible urge to be funny his advisors worried that he might perform similarly when not among trusted intimates and also, with some justification, that some of the intimates might prove not to be so trustworthy. The obvious absence of malice in his humor, combined with his constant willingness to amiably poke fun at himself, spared him any real prob-lems on these counts while his many other displays of humor reaped for him enormous dividends.

The Gipper's success with his humor, indeed, could serve to illus-trate a fundamental principle applying to all five of the featured pres-idents: much depends on the set of circumstances underpinning the use of the jocular. All of these men were viewed by significant por-tions of the electorate as likable, down-to-earth White House occu-pants who took neither themselves nor their exalted positions overly seriously and who, when they essayed their humor, generally did so with an obvious good will and an empathy for their audiences. It didn't hurt, either, that each injected a sizable dosage of self-depre-cation into the mix or that, when they did tell stories about others, there was a visible sympathy for their characters in the telling.

In contrast, Reagan's own Interior secretary, James Watt, a man who demonstrated none of these attributes (at least in public) and whose views on cultural diversity were not known to be especially pos-itive, tried to be funny in the fall of 1983 by commenting that his coal-mining advisory committee was very balanced, being made up of "a black, a woman, two Jews, and a cripple." Following a large public outcry and with some evidence that the U.S. Senate might pass a res-olution urging that he be removed from office, he resigned. In so doing, he met the same fate that had been suffered seven years earlier by Ger-ald Ford's agriculture secretary, Earl Butz: also with no offsetting fac-tors, he told an insensitive and seemingly mean-spirited joke about "coloreds," and his long public career was abruptly terminated.

Mark Twain once reported how his strait-laced wife had tried to break him of his constant usage of strong profanity by repeating word-for-word a large number of obscenities that he had just uttered. He listened to her without showing an iota of emotion until she had finished and then said, "You certainly know the words, my dear, but you don't know the tune."

Each of the five presidents in this book, as dissimilar as one was from another, seemed instinctively to know the tune.

A word about authenticity. Famous people, especially those who are colorful—as by definition all five of the featured chief executives were—often have words that they never uttered thrust in their mouths by others. Thus, without any persuasive evidence at all, Yogi Berra is credited with many statements that reflect his brand of questionable logic (e.g., "That place is so crowded that no one goes there anymore," "When you come to a fork in the road, take it," "If people don't want to come out to the ball park, nobody's going to stop them"), but that he most probably never voiced.

The same goes for movie mogul Sam Goldwyn, who often seems to substitute for Berra when attributions for this kind of thing are sought. Goldwyn may actually have said, "An oral contract isn't worth the paper it's written on," "That atomic bomb is dynamite," and "Anybody who goes to a psychiatrist should have their head examined." But this is about as likely as Al Capone's having really announced, "You can get much further with a kind word and a gun than you can with a kind word alone." The lines have to be delivered by somebody, and these famous people are obvious candidates.

Lincoln especially was said—at times by his supporters and on other occasions by his detractors—to be the author of numerous remarks, witty and otherwise, which he probably never made. The most conscientious scholarship, for example, has been unable to establish any convincing linkage between the Great Emancipator and such statements that are inextricably associated with his name as "You can fool all of the people some of the time and some of the people all of the time, but you can't fool all of the people all of the time" and "Better to remain silent and be thought a fool than to speak out and remove all doubt."

Much mythology also surrounds the deadpanned Coolidge, whose legendary taciturnity and frugality were tailor-made for counterfeit Coolidge quips.

Even the more recent chief executives, although they have operated under increasingly intense media scrutiny (making it easier to separate what they have said from what they have not), have sometimes been unjustifiably connected to words.

Except where otherwise indicated, the humorous remarks and anecdotes relayed on the following pages are probably authentic. In many cases, they were reported verbatim (or more or less verbatim) in writing, by one or more listeners, either immediately or reasonably soon after they were voiced. In many others, the particular president himself—in personal correspondence, memoir, or other form—

was the source. In the bulk of the others, an official record—of a press conference, legislative proceedings, a campaign speech, or a banquet speech—is the testimony. The permanent sound and visual records allowed in modern times by the advent of radio and television serve as a further avenue of documentation. Only what is documented by such sources as these has been incorporated here, and consequently, while there can be no guarantee that everything apocryphal has been removed, the chances of much fiction remaining have been greatly reduced.

Even where there is little doubt, on the other hand, that the focused-upon member of this small presidential population actually uttered or signed his name to words attributed to him, the question of actual *authorship* must often remain open. But this consideration is really irrelevant for our purposes. All five men were, as will be noted, capable of much spontaneity. But each one also, with the possible exception of the consistently wry Coolidge, borrowed—in many cases quite explicitly—from the work of others. The point is that each was a successful *user* of humor, a leader who didn't hesitate to draw upon the jocular as a powerful tool for both professional and personal success.

CHAPTER 1

ABRAHAM LINCOLN

Carl Sandburg called him "the first authentic humorist to occupy the Executive Mansion in Washington, his gift of laughter and his flair for the funny being taken as a national belonging."[1] American folklore scholar B. A. Botkin said that he "raised the wisecrack to the level of scripture."[2] When in 1860 Stephen A. Douglas learned that Lincoln had been nominated by the Republican party as his opponent in that year's contest for the presidency, he lamented to a fellow Democrat, "I shall have my hands full. He is the strong man of the party—full of wit, facts, dates—and the best stump speaker, with his droll ways and dry jokes, in the West."[3] (Every one of his adversary's funny stories, Douglas had complained two years earlier when the two men, in competing for a U.S. Senate seat had held a series of debates, "seems like a whack upon my back."[4]) And a London periodical once enviously observed, "One advantage the Americans have is the possession of a President who is not only the First Magistrate, but the Chief Joker of the Land."[5]

Abraham Lincoln was, of course, far more than a humorist. But humor was an important facet of the personality of this most admired of all of our presidents. And he used it adroitly and entirely naturally as both a raconteur and a quipster to achieve a number of significant purposes.

As noted earlier, Lincoln frequently employed humor as a potent form of personal psychological therapy to, as a close friend of his once observed, "whistle down sadness."[6] Prone to massive bouts of depression—one of his colleagues in the Illinois Legislature claimed that Lincoln once said that the depression was at times so intense that he never dared carry a pocketknife,[7] and a former law partner wrote of the sixteenth president that "melancholy dropped from him as he walked"[8]—Lincoln asserted, "I laugh because I must not weep—that's all, that's all." He had no doubt that, as he once told an associate,

9

"most people are about as happy as they make up their minds to be."
And he guided his efforts, although not with complete success, in this
direction.

When a visiting congressman from Ohio who called at the White
House during the bleak Civil War days of 1862, was told a funny
story by the president, and complained to Lincoln that "it is too
serious a time" to hear stories, the latter courteously responded,
"You cannot be more anxious than I have been constantly since the
beginning of the war; and I say to you now, that were it not for this
occasional *vent*, I should die." On another wartime occasion, Lincoln declared, "I am not simply a storyteller, but storytelling as an
emollient saves me much friction and distress." On still another, he
said, "Some of the stories are not so nice as they might be, but I tell
you the truth when I say that a funny story, if it has the element of
genuine wit, has the same effect on me that I suppose a good square
drink of whiskey has on an old toper; it puts new life into me."

Nor was Honest Abe alone in believing in the therapeutic value
of humor for himself. His secretary of state, William H. Seward, one
of the president's two closest friends in the cabinet and a man whose
own well-developed sense of humor made him particularly attractive company for Lincoln, fully shared this belief. Lincoln, Seward
once pointed out, "had no notion of recreation as such" and "found
his only recreation in telling or hearing stories in the ordinary way
of business." He "often stopped a Cabinet council at a grave junc-
ture, to jest a half-hour with the members before going to work;
joked with every body, on light & on grave occasions. This was what
saved him."[9]

"At age 175," a Lincoln scholar observed twelve decades after
his subject's death, "Lincoln still is living witness to the power of
humor to hide the pain, heal the hurt, sustain the spirit."[10]

But his humor did much more than merely let the sixteenth president whistle down sadness. It also paid off handsomely for him as
a politician. As his ample possession of the trait—so rare for a public figure in his era of Victorian sobriety—became more widely known
(books such as *The Humors of Uncle Abe*, *Old Abe's Jokes*, and *Wit
at the White House* were major sellers in the Lincoln years), he
increasingly emerged in the public consciousness as a particularly
down-to-earth occupant of the presidency, who refused to take either
life or himself overly seriously. To historian Webb Garrison, the "perceived gulf between the chief executive and ordinary citizens" was
"perhaps shortest" in Lincoln's case because of his use of humorous

stories and remarks.[11] Lincoln's contemporary Horace Greeley believed that his ability to amuse "allied him intimately, warmly, with the masses of mankind."[12]

It probably helped Lincoln that his material generally related to plain people with whom his constituents could readily identify in an era when most people lived either on farms or in small towns. He told stories about the farmer who claimed that he wasn't greedy, explaining, "I just want the land that jines mine!"; the rustic owner of a pathetic parcel of rocky, nonproductive acreage who told a visitor, "I'm not as poor as you think I am, I don't own this land"; the small-town preacher who wrote nothing but long sermons because he "got to writin' and was too lazy to stop!"; and the villager who was fined ten dollars for his outburst in court, handed over a twenty-dollar bill, was informed that the court was not able to make change, and thereupon declared, "Never mind the other ten dollars. I'll take it out in contempt."

In this uncomplicated approach, the Great Emancipator stood in favorable contrast to the florid orators who dominated the political life of his time. But Lincoln did not tell the jokes and stories just to get laughs. "I have found that common people—common people—take them as you find them," he said, "are more easily influenced by a broad and humorous illustration than in any other way."

And Lincoln's jocularity almost always had a point. The greed-denying farmer who merely wanted the land adjacent to his own, Lincoln asserted, was a good analogy to the supporters of the Mexican War (Lincoln had opposed it) who had said that the conflict was not an aggressive one. The tale of the man who didn't own the barren property illustrated Lincoln's "things could always be worse" philosophy. The president was reminded of the lazy preacher by a lawyer who had written an overly long brief (Lincoln took to verbose people about as happily as a fish takes to land and once said of a gentleman who tended regularly to run off at the mouth, "He can compress the most words in the fewest ideas of any man I ever met"). The individual who wanted to take out half of his fine in contempt of the court was meant to underscore the president's abiding belief that his own former profession of law was no less susceptible to error than any other.

"It is not the story itself, but its purpose, or effect, that interests me," Lincoln once calmly informed a drunken major who had slapped him on the knee and asked him to tell one of his many stories, "I often avoid a long and useless discussion by others or a laborious explanation on my own part by a story that illustrates my point of view." That the stories were so often funny ones was, however, a significant further dividend.

As a result of Old Abe's entirely warranted reputation for telling such tales almost at the drop of a hat (he said, "That reminds me of a story" on so many occasions that one historian has suggested that the remark "might well have been Lincoln's by-line"[13]), large number of anecdotes were credited to him that he had never even heard, much less relayed.

He once told a journalist friend that he had actually originated only "about one-sixth" of the stories for which he had generally been awarded authorship (although on another occasion, he took responsibility for "about half"). Sometimes, tales that he had never told were attributed to him by his political enemies with the object of showing that he was a man of insensitivity, grossness, or other defects not flattering to those in the political arena. At other times, words and anecdotes were placed in Lincoln's mouth on the flimsiest of evidence in an intended compliment to the humorous president but without anything resembling real proof that he had ever uttered them.

But even in the really-told-by-Lincoln category, the stories were most often not created but simply passed along, although by a superb raconteur with considerable comedic talents. P. M. Zall, whose research into the topic will for sheer conscientiousness probably never be exceeded, has convincingly shown that a full sixty percent of the tales assigned to Lincoln during his lifetime (and the numbers have grown considerably in the post-Lincoln years) can be linked to previously printed sources.[14]

On the other hand, the sixteenth president never claimed otherwise. As he asserted to a member of the press corps, "You speak of Lincoln stories. I don't think that is the correct phrase. I don't make the stories mine by telling them." To another acquaintance he said, "I remember a good story when I hear it, but I am only a retail dealer."

Indeed, he liberally gave credit where credit was due. He loved in particular the comical stories of Petroleum V. Nasby (David Ross Locke in private life) and once said of them, "For the genius to write these things I would gladly give up my office," and memorized long excerpts from Nasby's works. (Nasby reciprocated, declaring that Lincoln's "flow of humor was a sparkling spring gushing out of a rock—the flashing water had a somber background which made it all the brighter.")

Another humorist, Orpheus C. Kerr, was also a favorite, and Lincoln told his rather grim quartermaster general that anyone "who has not read [Kerr's writings] must be a heathen." (But Kerr at times turned his humor on the president himself, and Lincoln, employing a double standard, in these instances was not so lavish in his praise. He once said good-naturedly to his secretary of the Navy, "Now the hits that are given to you, Mr. Welles, I can enjoy, but ... vice versa as regards myself.") A third witty storyteller of his day, Artemus Ward, also frequently received special presidential praise.

Lincoln additionally got many of his tales from bona fide joke books, especially *Joe Miller's Jest-Book* and *James Quin's Jests*, and from such other joke-providing publications which he regularly perused as *Harper's Weekly* and the Springfield (Illinois) *Sangamo-Journal*.

Three other printed sources, none of them particularly noted for humor, likewise had a significant influence on Lincoln's storytelling abilities. He was especially fond of Shakespeare's tragedies (although he equally admired some of the Bard of Avon's comedies) and once boasted that he had read several of the more serious Shakespearean offerings—*King Lear*, *Macbeth*, *Hamlet*, and *Henry VIII* among them—"perhaps as frequently as any unprofessional reader." He wryly remarked that he had only a single criticism to make of the heroes in these plays, that they made long speeches when they were killed.

Aesop's Fables, which Lincoln spent countless hours reading as a boy, generated in particular many of the animal metaphors that were liberally included in the Lincoln narratives. On one occasion, when his cousin and closest childhood companion, Dennis Hanks, offered the not particularly provocative observation regarding Aesop that "them yarns is all lies," Lincoln—who even in his early years recognized that animals did not speak and act like human beings—responded, "Mighty darn good lies, Denny."

The King James version of the Bible, with which Lincoln was also conversant starting in his childhood, had a further impact. "God," said the sixteenth president, "tells truth in parables." Lincoln did, too, although he could rarely resist embellishing the truth with humor.

Lincoln found many of his contemporaries to be fruitful sources of humorous material as well. As a lawyer travelling the circuit in Illinois, he heard and mentally saved for future reference literally hundreds of amusing anecdotes. His tenure as a legislator—he served four consecutive terms in Illinois and two years as a U.S. congressman—added many more to his inventory.

He especially prized the comedic facility of men like Ohio's Senator Ben Wade, who once commented (in words that a delighted Lincoln frequently repeated) that in praying for the prolongation of the dying chief justice Roger Taney's life (so that then–President James Buchanan could not appoint a successor), he may have "overdone the matter."

Another senator from Ohio, Tom Corwin, also frequently tickled the Lincoln funny bone. Despite his celebrated dictum, Corwin had a highly developed sense of humor that he rarely hesitated to use. He told, for example, about a Frenchman who complained to him that the United States had been sending ill-chosen diplomats abroad. America, the Frenchman contended, should send "good-looking men who speak some language." Corwin countered by asking, "Don't they all speak *some* language?" And the Frenchman rejoined, "No. I met a gentleman at Copenhagen who speaks no language at all. He speaks some patois which they call Ohio." As president, Lincoln appointed Corwin his ambassador to Mexico.

Even political opponents could provide grist for Lincoln's anecdotal mill. One was Lincoln's old Whig rival from Illinois, Justin Butterfield, who had bought himself a permanent spot in Lincoln's fund of stories by announcing, when asked if he would join the heavy majority of Whigs in opposing the Mexican War, "No, indeed! I opposed one war, and it ruined me. From now on, I am for war, pestilence, *and* famine."

What Lincoln did do as he constantly drew from his huge treasure house of cherished anecdotes to entertain and amuse his audiences and, above all, to make his points, was to endow the stories with an entirely new and generally quite imaginative dimension through his great gifts of mimicry, impersonation, and verbal inflection. He was, as Zall has aptly described him, "a performer rather than a playwright," freely passing on stories that he had enjoyed when he had read them or heard them.[15]

Lincoln played his tales like an accomplished musician. He once told his minister, "There are two ways of relating a story. If you have an auditor who has the time and is inclined to listen, lengthen it out, pour it out slowly as if from a jug. If you have a poor listener, hasten it, shorten it, shoot it out of a popgun."

And he was his own best audience. A student in his Springfield law office during the last years of Lincoln's practice his reported that he had heard the future president tell the same humorous story three times within as many hours to people who came in at different times to the office. Each time, the student added, Lincoln "laughed as heartily and enjoyed it as if it were a new story." The student himself "had to laugh," he said, "because I thought it funny that Mr. Lincoln enjoyed a story so repeatedly told."[16] Some years later a visiting German scholar said much the same thing after meeting Lincoln: "He seemed to enjoy his own jests in a childlike way, for his unusually sad-looking eyes would kindle with a merry twinkle, and he himself led in the laughter; and his laugh was so genuine, hearty, and contagious that nobody could fail to join in it."[17]

At times, Lincoln physically went even further in his enjoyment of his stories. A congressman who knew him well reminisced, "He would sometimes throw his left foot across his right knee, and clenching his foot with both hands and bending forward, his whole frame seemed to be convulsed with the effort to give expression to his sensations."[18] Another friend said that, when Lincoln told a story, mirth "seemed to diffuse itself all over him, like a spontaneous tickle."[19]

In an 1860 speech, Lincoln described laughter as "the joyous, beautiful, universal evergreen of life," and no one who saw him at these moments could doubt the sincerity of this sentiment.

His use of humor also served the Civil War president well in two other ways. Although Lincoln generally ignored his critics, saying that if he were ever "to try to read, much less answer, all the attacks made upon me, this shop might just as well be closed for any other business," he did at times introduce an appropriate story to take the wind out of the sails of his detractors. He once said of a critic:

> He's the biggest liar in Washington. He reminds me of an old fisherman who had the reputation for stretching the truth. He got a pair of scales and insisted on weighing every fish he caught in front of witnesses. One day a doctor borrowed his scales to weigh a new baby. The baby weighed forty-seven pounds.[20]

In 1864, he was reminded by a series of rather generalized but quite harsh newspaper attacks on his administration of a frontier traveller who

> found himself out of his reckoning one night in a most inhospitable region. A terrific thunderstorm came up to add to his trouble. He floundered along until his horse at length gave out. The lightning afforded him the only clue to his way, but the peals of thunder were frightful. One bolt, which seemed to crash the earth beneath him, brought him to his knees. By no means a praying man, his petition was

short and to the point,—"O Lord, if it is all the same to you, give us a little more light and a little less noise!"[21]

When the wife of a notorious antiwar politician from Ohio, whom Lincoln had banished to Confederate territory for his conspicuous absence of loyalty, left to join her spouse and loudly announced that she would not return to her home state until she did so as the wife of Ohio's governor, Lincoln was reminded of yet another story:

> A gentleman was nominated for Supervisor. On leaving home on the morning of election, he said—"Wife, to-night you shall sleep with the Supervisor of this town."
>
> The election passed, and the confident gentleman was defeated. The wife heard the news before her defeated spouse returned home. She immediately dressed for going out, and waited her husband's return, when she met him at the door. "Wife, where are you going at this time of night?" he exclaimed.
>
> "Going?" she replied, "why, you told me this morning that I should tonight sleep with the Supervisor of this town, and as Mr. L. is elected instead of yourself, I was going to his house."[22]

The Great Emancipator sometimes introduced his sense of humor to sidetrack issues that were especially sensitive or difficult or simply to get rid of unwanted visitors (including many job-seekers).

In the wake of Lincoln's removal from his cabinet of his venal first secretary of war, Simon Cameron (Lincoln once said that Cameron was so corrupt that the only thing he wouldn't steal was a red-hot stove), several leading Republican senators visited the president to lobby for the replacement of the six other cabinet officers as well. They argued that most of the six had originally been competitors of Lincoln for the presidency, had generally retained their political ambitions, and were not in any event particularly competent administrators. Lincoln patiently heard them out and then, according to a ranking official who was there, said:

> Gentlemen, your request for a change of the whole Cabinet because I have made one change reminds me of a story I once heard in Illinois of a farmer who was much troubled by skunks. They annoyed his household at night, and his wife insisted that he should take measures to be rid of them. One moonlit night he loaded his old shotgun, and stationed himself in the yard to watch for the intruders, his wife remaining in the house anxiously awaiting the result.

After some time she heard the shotgun go off, and in a few minutes, the farmer entered the house. "What luck had you?" said she. "I hid myself behind the wood-pile," said the old man, "with the shot-gun pointed towards the hen-roost, and before long there appeared not one skunk, but *seven*. I took aim, blazed away, killed one, and he raised such a fearful smell that I concluded it was best to let the other six go."[23]

The ranking official reported that the senators laughed heartily, took their leave of the chief executive, and never brought up the matter again.

For one especially boring visitor from Philadelphia, who frequently and insensitively tried to take as much of the president's limited time as he possibly could, Lincoln had a novel solution in the form of a different kind of story. On one of the unwanted gentleman's visits, Lincoln went to a shelf in his office, removed a bottle from it, and said to the visitor, who was bald, "Did you ever try this stuff for your hair?" "No, sir," responded the bore, "I never did." "Well," the president remarked, "I advise you to try it and I will give you this bottle. If at first you don't succeed, try, try again. Keep it up. They say it will make hair grow on a pumpkin. Now take it and come back in eight or ten months and tell me how it works." The visitor took the bottle and left the White House. When another visitor was admitted to the Executive Office a few minutes later, the president was laughing hysterically.

Aside from his storytelling abilities, Lincoln was also a genuinely witty man. He has been reliably credited with saying of a soldier, who was accused of spying on a young woman by peeping at her through a transom while she was undressing, "He should be elevated to the peerage, with the title of Count Peeper" (Count Piper was the Swedish minister in Washington at the time). When a Catholic priest asked Lincoln to suspend the sentence of a man imminently scheduled for capital punishment, the president replied, "If I don't suspend it tonight, the man will surely be suspended tomorrow." Of a contagious illness that he had while president, Lincoln quipped, "I've got something now that I can give to everybody," and when asked why he shined his own boots, he replied, "Whose boots do you think I should shine?"

Once he looked out a window, saw a matronly woman with a multiplumed hat slip and fall on the muddy street below, and commented, "Reminds me of a duck. Feathers on her head and down on her behind." When told by visitors to the White House that there

was a body of water in Nebraska that bore an Indian name meaning "weeping water," Lincoln retorted, "As 'laughing water,' according to [the poet Henry Wadsworth] Longfellow is 'Minnehaha,' this
evidently should be 'Minneboohoo.'" Informed by an angry Senator that "this country is headed straight for hell," the president sur-
veyed the extension of Pennsylvania Avenue from the White House
to the Capitol and responded, "Yes, sir, Senator, and it's not more
than a mile from there right now." On one occasion, he noted to a
visitor, who was a bit taller than his own six feet four inches, "You
actually stand higher today than your president."

During the Civil War, a young female visitor to a military hospital asked a wounded soldier, within Lincoln's hearing, where his
wound was, the injured man was embarrassed and could think of
no acceptable way to frame an accurate answer, but Lincoln without hesitation informed the young lady, "Ma'am, the bullet that
wounded him would not have wounded you."

His quips were typically rendered quite good-naturedly, consistent with this dominant personality trait of his. But every now and
then a remark had a bite to it. When someone asserted of a personage who was well known to Lincoln, "It may be doubted whether
any man of our generation has plunged more deeply into the sacred
fount of learning," Lincoln rejoined, "Yes, or come up drier." Old
Abe also noted, in a memorandum concerning a man who claimed
descent from the effete and impotent John Randolph of Virginia,
that the claimant was a "direct descendant of one who was never a
father." When financier Jay Cooke observed that Lincoln's attorney
general, Edward Bates, had white whiskers but dark hair, Lincoln
ventured the opinion that this was due to the fact that Bates "uses
his jaws more than he uses his brain."

Hundreds of other such Lincoln bons mots have come through
history—some of them undoubtedly apocryphal, but many of them
apparently authentic.

Abraham Lincoln's sense of humor was not something that
became visible only in his White House years. It was a personality
trait that stood out throughout his entire life.

As a late teenager in the 1820s, as he gravitated after his farm work
to the country store in the tiny Indiana settlement that was a mile and
a half from his father's cabin, his ability to amuse was well established.
"He was so ... original and humorous and witty," Dennis Hanks
reported, "that all the People in town would gather around him. He
would keep them there until midnight or longer telling Stories and

cracking jokes."[24] Subsequently, as a young riverboat ferryman and then (starting in 1831, when he was 22) as a general store clerk in New Salem, Illinois, he was similarly in demand among the paying customers for his anecdotes, witticisms, and tales.

Lincoln liked to tell in his adolescence, for example, about the midwestern backwoods preacher who was delivering a sermon:

> The preacher was wearing old-fashioned baggy pantaloons fastened with one button and no suspenders. His shirt was fastened at the neck with one button. In a loud voice the preacher announced his text for the day. "I am the Christ whom I shall represent this day." About that time a little blue lizard ran up one leg of the pantaloons. The preacher went ahead with his sermon, slapping at his legs. After awhile the lizard came so high the preacher got desperate, and going on with his sermon, unbuttoned his pants, let them fall down and kicked them off. By this time the lizard had changed his route and was circling around under his shirt. The preacher, repeating his text, "I am the Christ whom I shall represent today," loosened his shirt button and off came the shirt. The congregation sat in the pews dazed and dazzled. Everything was still for a minute, then a dignified elderly lady stood up, pointed a finger at the pulpit and called out at the top of her voice: "I just want to say, sir, that if you represent Jesus Christ, then I'm done with the Bible."[25]

Sometimes the young Lincoln included himself in these stories, as in his account of his father's calf, which drowned in a swamp. Thomas Lincoln instructed Abraham to take the skin down to a nearby tannery and have it appropriately treated, which the future president dutifully did by informing the tannery manager that "his father wanted his hide tanned."

At times in this early period, Lincoln succumbed to an urge to tell bawdy anecdotes (although he never did so in mixed company). Included in this genre is a possibly woven-out-of-whole-cloth tale of Colonel Ethan Allen's visit to England immediately after the Revolutionary War. In the toilet of one of his hosts, Allen found a picture of George Washington and was informed that the latter had been placed there not by accident but quite logically because "there is nothing that will Make an Englishman Shit so quick as the sight of Genl. Washington."

Even in these early days, the self-deprecating wit that would be a hallmark of the full-grown Lincoln was present. More than thirteen decades before Groucho Marx announced that he would never join a country club that would admit anyone like himself, Lincoln on more than one occasion declared that he did not plan to marry because he could never be satisfied with anyone who would be "blockhead enough" to have him.

In 1832, responding to a call by the governor of Illinois to repel the aggressive actions of Indian Chief Black Hawk and some five hundred of his braves, Lincoln volunteered for military service. His army company consisted primarily of his fellow New Salem townsmen, and he was promptly elected—as a consequence of the huge reservoir of good will that he had already established for himself—the company's captain. Even after he had been nominated for the presidency, he was to remember that tribute as the greatest honor of his life. And in the army, too, he contrived to exhibit his witty ways.

Like many tall men, Lincoln regularly walked with a stoop. His commanding officer, a Napoleonic autocrat of a colonel who was almost a full eighteen inches shorter than the future president, once ordered him to stand as tall and erect as he possibly could. "Am I always to remain so?" Lincoln asked. "Certainly, fellow," was the response from the superior. "Then goodbye, Colonel," Lincoln replied, "for I shall never see you again."

On another occasion, as Lincoln later reminisced, he was unable to remember the appropriate command for getting his company to pass through a gate and continue to march. He finally hit on a way around the dilemma: as his soldiers approached the gate he shouted, "This company is dismissed for two minutes, when it will fall in again on the other side of the gate."

Lincoln never made any subsequent claim that he had been a wartime hero, nor could he have, since in his three months of service in the Black Hawk War, he engaged in no fighting at all. But he was not above using the experience some years later to mock Democratic presidential nominee Lewis Cass's military career while at the same time good-naturedly making fun of his own:

> By the way ... did you know I am a military hero? Yes, sir, in the days of the Black Hawk war I fought, bled, and came away.... I was not at Stillman's defeat, but I was about as near it, as Cass was to Hull's surrender; and, like him, I saw the place very soon afterwards. It is quite certain that I did not break my sword, for I had none to break; but I bent a musket pretty badly on one occasion.... If Gen. Cass went in advance of me in picking huckleberries, I guess I surpassed him in charges upon the wild onions. If he saw any live, fighting Indians, it was more than I did; but I had a good many bloody

struggles with the mosquitoes; and although I never fainted from the loss of blood, I can truly say I was often very hungry.[26]

Ex-serviceman Lincoln never put patriotism per se on any unwarranted pedestal either. He liked to tell the story of the man who once said to him, "I feel patriotic" and who explained what he meant when Lincoln asked him to do so by declaring, "Why, I feel like I want to kill somebody or steal something!"

One of Honest Abe's single most effective public ripostes was registered not long after his military service, at the very beginning of his political career. As a candidate for the Illinois Legislature, Lincoln had the responsibility on behalf of his Whig party to reply in a public forum to the remarks of one George Forquer, a leading citizen of Springfield who in the recent past had drawn attention to himself in two ways: although for years a key Whig, he had rather abruptly become a Democrat in order to receive a well-paying political appointment; and he had placed a lightning rod, the first one ever owned in the entire country, on his expensive new house.

Forquer's speech, after proclaiming that "this young man [Lincoln] must be taken down and I am truly sorry that the task devolves upon me," quite patronizingly and sarcastically attacked Lincoln on several fronts including the ungainly and rough-hewn young man's physical appearance and style of dress. Lincoln calmly awaited his turn and, when it came, said:

> I am not so young in years, as I am in the tricks and trades of a politician, but, live long or die young, I would rather die now, than, like the gentleman, change my politics, and with the change receive an office worth three thousand dollars a year, and then feel obliged to erect a lightning rod over my house to protect a guilty conscience from an offended God.[27]

The effect of these words on the unsophisticated, God-fearing audience surpassed anything that could have been predicted. Forquer immediately started to be known far and wide as a man who needed an artificial aid to ward off God's righteous wrath. He would never again be a force in Illinois political life.

Lincoln served four successive two-year terms as a state legislator and distinguished himself in this arena, too, for his ready wit and powers of raconteurship. Indeed, these attractive qualities played no small part in his elevation to the position of Whig floor leader at the start of his second term.

Once, replying to a Democratic legislator's charge that an expanded system of railroads and canals (which Lincoln favored) could lead to severe financial problems for the state, Lincoln was reminded of the old Indiana bachelor who,

> like the gentleman from Montgomery [Lincoln's adversary in this debate], ... was very famous for seeing *big bugaboos* in every thing. He lived with an older brother, and one day he went out hunting. His brother heard him firing back of the field, and went out to see what was the matter. He found him loading and firing as fast as possible in the top of a tree.
>
> Not being able to discover any thing in the tree, he asked him what he was firing at. He replied a squirrel—and kept on firing. His brother, believing there was some humbug about the matter, examined his person, and found on one of his eye lashes a *big louse* crawling about. It is so with the gentleman from Montgomery. He imagined he could see squirrels every day, when they were nothing but lice.

The official record of this debate contains the notation that the "House was convulsed with laughter,"[28] but in achieving such a result Lincoln undoubtedly supplemented the relatively thin material that he had here with the considerable powers of mimicry and verbal inflection that rarely left him in his storytelling.

The mimicry in these legislative years, as would also be the case later, at times involved an ethnic dialect. In one speech, referring to Democrats who had stolen money from the public treasury, he related the tale of a "witty Irish soldier, who was always boasting of his bravery, when no danger was near, but who invariably retreated without orders at the first charge of an engagement...." Asked by his captain why he did so, the Irishman responded, "Captain, I have as brave a *heart* as Julius Caesar ever had; but somehow or other, whenever danger approaches, my *cowardly* legs will run away with it."

To illustrate the greater pull of instant gratification over distant punishment, Lincoln told of another Irishman, this one having been observed in an act of theft and warned, "Better lay down that spade you're stealing, Paddy—if you don't you'll pay for it at the day of judgment." Paddy answered, as relayed by the future president, "By the powers, if ye'll credit me so long, I'll take another." Lincoln was also known to tell jokes in which Germans and blacks had the featured parts.

The last six of Lincoln's eight years as a state lawmaker were appreciably strengthened for him financially by the fact that he was simultaneously a practicing lawyer. Having immersed himself in law books, which he had borrowed from a fellow legislator who was already an attorney, he was admitted to the bar in 1836. He thereafter travelled the circuit for several months each year, as he would for many years after he left the legislature. In the process, he added considerably to his trove of stories while at the same time he became a major provider of amusing tales as he and his circuit-riding colleagues exchanged humorous anecdotes to while away the often-empty evening hours at inns and taverns on the road.

On one cold winter night in such circumstances, Lincoln joined a group of fellow attorneys in front of a tavern's fireplace. "Pretty cold night," one lawyer observed to him. "Colder than hell," Lincoln responded. "You've been there, Mr. Lincoln?" asked a third representative of the legal profession, presumably playing for a cheap laugh. "Oh, yes," the future president replied "And the funny thing is that it's much like it is here—all the lawyers are nearest the fire."

Many of the stories that were swapped in these Eighth Circuit after-hours sessions related various witty comments that Lincoln made in the courtroom. In one of these occurrences, Lincoln sought to have several prospective jury members disqualified on the grounds that the opposing lawyer had unfairly become friendly with them. The judge in the case reacted to the attempt by stating, "Mr. Lincoln, the mere fact that a juror knows your opponent does not disqualify him." Lincoln replied, "No, Your Honor, but I am afraid some of the gentlemen may *not* know him, which would place me at a disadvantage."

In another, young lawyer Ward Hill Lamon (later President Lincoln's bodyguard) had been wrestling with a challenger near the Bloomington, Illinois, courthouse and emerged from the encounter with a large rip in the seat of his pants. Before he had time to change his attire, he was called into the court to address the jury and, because his rather short coat failed to conceal the damage, his bad luck was visible to all. As a joke, one of the members of the bar circulated a pledge paper, which was passed around from one lawyer in the room to the next to buy Lamon ("a poor but worthy young man") a new pair of trousers. Several of the attorneys signed it, pledging some ridiculous amount. When Lincoln's turn came, he simply wrote on the document, "I can contribute nothing to the end in view."

Another story, which is documented by court records, centered on a case involving a young army officer indicted for assaulting a man several decades his senior. Lincoln, the prosecutor here, began his presentation by telling the jury, "This is an indictment against a soldier for assaulting an old man." The defendant immediately interrupted him to say, "Sir, I am no soldier. I am an officer." And Lincoln rejoined, "I beg your pardon. Gentlemen of the jury, this is an indictment against an officer, who is no soldier, for assaulting an old man."

Yet another short story involved the tactic that Lincoln employed to counter a claim that his client had used unnecessary force to thwart an assault upon him. Lincoln told in this instance of a farmer who, having been attacked by his neighbor's dog, had killed the dog with a pitchfork. When queried by the neighbor as to why he hadn't hit the animal with the other end of the fork, the farmer asked, "Why didn't he come at me with his other end?"

The effect on attorney Lincoln's audiences of such efforts as these sometimes, undoubtedly, exceeded Honest Abe's highest expectations. A court clerk once reminisced that in his entire career he

> was never fined but once for contempt of court. [Judge David] Davis fined me five dollars. Mr. Lincoln had just come in, and leaning over my desk had told me a story so irresistibly funny that I broke out into a loud laugh. The Judge called me to order, saying, "This must be stopped. Mr. Lincoln, you are constantly disturbing this court with your stories." Then to me: "You may fine yourself five dollars." I apologized but told the Judge the story was worth the money. In a few minutes the Judge called me over to him. "What was that story Lincoln told you?" he asked. I told him, and he laughed aloud in spite of himself. "Remit your fine," he ordered.[29]

Lincoln's legal career was also marked by his observation to one client, when the latter asked him whether a certain individual was a man of means, that he reckoned that he ought to be, since he was about the meanest man in town. And fellow lawyers recalled his comment to them that the "strongest example of 'rigid government' and 'close construction' I ever knew, was that of [a certain judge]. It was once said of him that he would *hang* a man for blowing his nose in the street, but that he would *quash* the indictment if it failed to specify which *hand* he blew it with!"

At Mrs. Sprigg's boardinghouse where Lincoln lodged during his single two-year term in the U.S. House of Representatives, which began in 1847, he was no less the life of the party. The young Dr. Samuel C. Busey, who also stayed at Mrs. Sprigg's, remembered that, when set to draw from his seemingly endless supply of anecdotes at the dining table, the future president "would lay down his knife and fork, place his elbows upon the table, rest his face between his hands, and begin with the words, 'that reminds me,' and proceed. Everybody prepared for the explosions sure to follow."[30]

In Congress itself, the targets of his humor were understandably the Democrats. In one speech, referring to unfavorable allegations regarding the behavior of some members of that party in New York, he told his fellow congressmen about what the

> drunken fellow once said when he heard the reading of an indictment for hog-stealing. The clerk read on till he got to, and through, the words "did steal, take, and carry away, ten boars, ten sows, ten shoats, and ten pigs," at which he exclaimed, "Well, by golly, that is the most equally divided gang of hogs I ever did hear of."

"If there is any *other* gang of hogs more equally divided than the Democrats of New York are about this time," declared Lincoln, warming to his theme, "I have not heard of it."[31]

In another effort, he poked fun at Democratic claims that he considered outrageous by asserting, "A fellow once advertised that he had made a discovery by which he could make a new man out of an old one, and have enough of the stuff left to make a little yellow dog."

General Cass, whose campaign for president took place in 1848, came in for more ridicule in what was possibly Lincoln's single most publicized verbal attack while in Congress. Referring to expense accounts that the military figure had submitted to the government many years earlier, Lincoln asserted on the House floor:

> Mr. Speaker, I adopt the suggestion of a friend, that General Cass is a general of splendidly successful charges—charges, to be sure, not upon the public enemy, but upon the public treasury.
>
> I have introduced General Cass's accounts here chiefly to show the wonderful physical capacities of the man. They show that he not only did the labor of several men at the same time, but that he often did it at several places many hundred miles apart, at the same time.
>
> And at eating, too, his capacities are shown to be quite as wonderful. From October, 1821, to May, 1822, he ate ten rations a day in Michigan, ten rations a day here in Washington, and near five dollars' worth a day besides, partly on the road between the two places.
>
> And then there is an important discovery in his example—the art

of being paid for what one eats, instead of having to pay for it. Hereafter if any nice young man shall owe a bill which he cannot pay in
any other way, he can just board it out. Mr. Speaker, we have all heard
of the animal standing in doubt between two stacks of hay and starv-
ing to death; the like of that would never happen to General Cass.
Place the stacks a thousand miles apart, he would stand stock still midway between them, and eat them both at once; and the green grass
along the line would be apt to suffer some, too, at the same time.

By all means, make him President, gentlemen. He will feed you
bounteously—if—if there is any left after he shall have helped himself.[32]

Lincoln also said of Cass, whose undistinguished military record
compared unfavorably with that of the Whig presidential nominee,
Zachary Taylor, that he

invaded Canada without resistance, and he outvaded it without pursuit.... He was a volunteer aide to General Harrison on the day of the
battle of the Thames; and ... Harrison was picking huckleberries just
two miles off while the battle was fought. I suppose it is a just conclusion with you, to say Cass was aiding Harrison to pick huckleberries.[33]

Long before 1858, when he engaged in a series of seven debates
in towns across Illinois with his Democratic rival for the U.S. Senate, incumbent Senator Stephen A. Douglas, Lincoln's reputation as
an active user of humor was well established. But these debates,
which attracted widespread attention in newspapers and magazines
as well as much word-of-mouth publicity in that pre-radio, pre-television era and which vaulted Lincoln into the national consciousness, cemented that reputation. They also enhanced Lincoln's general
reputation as a man of potential presidential stature:

"No amount of argumentation," the distinguished historian
Norman A. Graebner has written,

could have dramatized the conflict between popular sovereignty [Doug-
las's solution to the problem of slavery in the territories] and the Dred
Scott decision [of the U.S. Supreme Court, which ruled that Negroes
could not be U. S. citizens] ... more effectively than Lincoln's humor.
Lincoln lived in a time of trouble ... his generation faced the awful
prospect of civil war. That age, like any age, needed its share of humor.
If Lincoln accepted the special obligation to find the political arguments that would meet the threat of slavery expansion without appearing to be unduly radical or sectional, he also accepted the challenge

to rise above the tensions and troubles of the times to create endless occasions for laughter. It was a laudable purpose, a remarkable feat, one worthy of scholarly attention.[34]

In one debate, after Douglas had revealed to the abstemious rural audience that the first time he had met Lincoln it was across a store counter where Lincoln sold whiskey, Lincoln affably responded:

What Mr. Douglas has said, gentlemen, is true enough; I did keep a grocery, and I did sell cotton, candles and cigars, and sometimes whiskey; but I remember in those days that Mr. Douglas was one of my best customers. Many a time have I stood on one side of the counter and sold whiskey to Mr. Douglas on the other side, but the difference between us was this: I have left my side of the counter, but Mr. Douglas still sticks to his as tenaciously as ever.[35]

When, on another occasion, Douglas painstakingly outlined his many differences with his fellow Democrat, the incumbent president James Buchanan, Lincoln in effect said that this was not persuasive to him. In fact, he asserted, he felt like the long-suffering woman in an old joke book who, when her husband was fighting with a bear, shouted, "Go it, husband! Go it, bear!"

In the debate at Quincy, Illinois, the future president informed the audience that, in his opinion, Douglas's popular sovereignty argument was "as thin as the homeopathic soup that was made by boiling the shadow of a pigeon that had starved to death." At Galesburg, claiming that Douglas and one of his supporters had used forged documents against him and that because this ploy had been so effective they had tried to use it again, Lincoln was reminded of the fisherman's wife, whose drowned spouse was brought home with his body covered with eels. When she was asked, "What was to be done with him?" the woman commanded, "Take the eels out and set him again."

At one point, Lincoln accused Douglas of using the "horse-chestnut style" of argument, which to the delight of his many supporters in the crowd he defined as meaning "a specious and fantastic arrangement of words, by which a man can prove a horse-chestnut to be a chestnut horse." When Douglas tried to negate a Lincoln argument by questioning the honesty of the senator whom Lincoln had quoted in support of it, Lincoln good-naturedly replied that the issue was one of argument and not of honesty. "By a course of reasoning," he asserted, "Euclid proves that all the angles in a triangle are equal to two right angles. Now, if you undertake to disprove that proposition, would you prove it to be false by calling Euclid a liar?"

Lincoln was not above the occasional use of ridicule. In the first debate, he announced:

> Judge Douglas has read from my speech in Springfield, in which I say that "a house divided against itself cannot stand." Does the Judge say it *can* stand? (Laughter) ... If he does, then there is a question of veracity, not between him and me, but between the Judge and an authority of a somewhat higher character. (Laughter and applause)[36]

But for every exercise of such relatively hard-edged language, the record is replete with examples of Lincoln's almost constitutional kindness. Far more typical was Old Abe's amiable response at Ottawa, Illinois, after the judge had given him some begrudging compliments. After thanking his opponent for them, Lincoln added, "I was not very much accustomed to flattery and it came sweeter to me. I was rather like the Hoosier with the gingerbread, when he said he reckoned he loved it better than any other man and got less of it."

Lincoln was not elected to the U.S. Senate. His Republican party actually got more votes than the Democrats in the statewide voting for the state legislature, which would select the man who would go to Washington. But newly gerrymandered districts allowed the Democrats to control the legislature, and they sent Douglas back to the Senate, leading a crestfallen Lincoln to tell some visitors at his Springfield law office, "I feel like the boy who stubbed his toe. I am too big to cry and too badly hurt to laugh."

Francis B. Carpenter, a portrait painter who spent six months at the White House in close proximity to Lincoln in 1864, once wrote that of all of the latter's humorous stories, he could not remember even one "which would have been out of place uttered in a ladies' drawing-room."[37] According to presidential secretary W. O. Stoddard, when a dirty joke was attributed to Lincoln, the president's face would "flush and darken," for he had "never so much as heard" most of these off-color stories.[38]

With both men, however, the Civil War commander in chief must have been on his best behavior, since he was well known to tell bawdy tales when not in the company of women. Leonard Swett, an old Illinois friend who remained in close contact with Lincoln to the end, was convinced that the latter's love of fun made him oblivious to everything except the point of the joke. If Lincoln told a good story that was "refined," in Swett's opinion, he did not like it any better for its cleanliness; similarly, if a tale was a vulgar one, he never really saw that aspect of it, either. "Nothing," Swett reported, "ever reached him but the wit," and he would pick the wit "up out of the mud or dirt just as readily as he would from a parlor table."[39] Thus, jokes about an old gentleman from Virginia who stropped his razor "on a certain *member* of a young negro's body" or about a young man who engaged in sexual intercourse with a female cat were fair game for the Great Emancipator, since he considered them not only funny but also worthy illustrations of points that he was trying to make.

Unlike other kinds of Lincoln stories, however, by and large the lewd tales were unprintable, and the specifics of most of these stories—perhaps fortunately—have been denied posterity. Zall has incisively pointed out that while a handful of them can today be found interred in various historical documents, no one can say how many others were suppressed.[40]

One story that has survived intact is a ribald contribution entitled "Bass-Ackwards," which Lincoln originally offered in his lawyer days and actually handed over in writing to a Springfield bailiff. While there is no convincing evidence that he ever retold it as president, many of its more earthy words were no strangers at all to his vocabulary even in the White House. "He said he was riding *bass-ackwards*," on a "*jass-ack*," went this tale:

> through a *patton-cotch*, on a pair of *baddle-sags*, stuffed full of *binger gold*, when the Animal *steered* at a *scump*, and the *lirrup-steather* broke, and throwed him in the *forner* of the *kence* and broke his *pishing-fole*. He said he would not have minded it much, but he fell right in a great *tow-curd*; in fact, he said it give him a right smart *sick* of *fitness*—he had the *moleracorbus* pretty bad. He said, about *bray dake* he came to himself, ran home, seized up a *stick* of *wood* and split the *axe* to make a light, rushed into the house, and found the *door* sick abed and his *wife* standing open. But thank goodness she is getting right *hat* and *farty* again.[41]

As every other chief executive of the United States, Lincoln as president quickly discovered that the number of people seeking positions in his administration vastly exceeded the number of patronage jobs at his disposal. He deemed this phenomenon "too many pigs for the teats," but he undoubtedly recognized that having to dash many job applicants' expectations came with the presidential territory. Indeed, he had indirectly registered his philosophy on this count some years earlier, when a Springfield neighbor saw him in the street outside of his home with two of his boys, both of whom were loudly crying, and asked what the problem was. Lincoln had responded, "Just what's the matter with the whole world. I've got three walnuts, and each wants two."

On the other hand, the frequency with which he had to resist applicant pressure may have surprised even him. "Every time I appoint someone to office I create ten enemies and one ingrate," he said, and the presumed exaggeration in this statement was not necessarily a large one. The exasperated president on at least one occasion told the following fable about a king and a jackass:

> Well, Sir, it seems like there was once an old king who was going hunting one day with all his courtiers. He soon met a farmer on the road. The farmer told the king it was going to rain. But the king's astrologer didn't think so. About an hour later there came a cloudburst that proved the farmer to be right; so the king cut off the astrologer's head, and sent for the farmer and offered him the vacant office.
> "It ain't me that knows when it's going to rain," he said. "It's my jackass. He lays his ears back."
> "Then your jackass is hereby appointed court astrologer," said the king. And afterwards he realized it was the biggest mistake of his life, because every jackass in the country wanted an office.[42]

But Lincoln at least softened his many unavoidable rejections with his gentle humor. When political allies sought a diplomatic post for Pennsylvania Governor Andrew G. Curtin, Lincoln agreed that the governor deserved such an appointment but told his visitors:

> I'm in the position of young [Richard Brinsley] Sheridan when old Sheridan called him to task for his rakish conduct and said to him that he must take a wife; to which young Sheridan replied: "Very well, father, but whose wife shall I take?" It's all very well to say that I will give Curtin a mission, but whose mission am I to take?[43]

In a related vein, he wrote back to two community leaders who had urged that one General Allen be appointed quartermaster general, "What nation do you desire Gen. Allen to be made quartermaster general of? This nation already has a quarter Master general."

The sixteenth president, who once called his office hours "the Beggar's Opera," could not easily be moved by hard-luck stories that lacked the ring of sincerity. After he had narrowed a list of applicants for the highly prized commissionership of the Sandwich Islands to a reasonably wieldy eight candidates, a delegation called on him for the purpose of advocating still another person. Lincoln patiently heard its members out until they argued that their candidate, in addition to being eminently qualified, was also ill, and that a tour of duty in the islands would do wonders for his health. "Gentlemen," the president interjected, "I am sorry to say that there are eight other candidates for that place, and they are all sicker than your man."

Nor did Lincoln see the appointment process as one that readily allowed compromises. He wryly told of "a fellow who ... came to see me to ask for an appointment as minister abroad. Finding he could not get that, he came down to some more modest position. Finally he asked to be made a tide-waiter. When he saw he could not get that he asked me for an old pair of trousers."

As for job seekers who had incurred the generally charitable Lincoln's displeasure, they might just as well forget the whole thing. A woman once asked the president to commission her son a colonel and somewhat haughtily attempted to buttress this request by informing Lincoln, "Sir, my grandfather fought at Lexington, my father fought at New Orleans, and my husband was killed at Monterey." Lincoln in response said, "I guess, madam, your family has done enough for the country. It's time to give somebody else a chance."

A politician whose support for Lincoln's war effort had been at best tepid until the North clearly was in the ascendancy some two years after the war began, met a similar fate when he visited the president in search of an appointed position for himself. The situation reminded Lincoln of the time he purchased a new suit and a new hat and went to his first dance in Springfield. He enjoyed the dance so much that he was among the last to leave, and when he went to get his hat he was handed an old and not very attractive one. "This is not mine, I had a new hat," he gently complained. "Mr. Lincoln," he was told, "the new ones were all gone two hours ago."

The Great Emancipator often met pressures that stemmed from requests other than for jobs in much the same way. He told the following not very subtle story to a rather morbid civilian who had asked him for a pass to visit the much-bloodied Bull Run battlefield after the first battle there:

> A man in Cortlandt ... once raised a porker of such unusual size that strangers went out of their way to see it. One of them the other day met the old gentleman and inquired about the animal. "Well,

yes," the old fellow said, "he'd got such a critter, might big un; but he guessed he would have to charge him about a shillin' for lookin' at him." The stranger looked at the old man for a minute or so, pulled out the desired coin, handed it to him and started to go off. "Hold on," said the other, "don't you want to see the hog?" "No," said the stranger, "I have seen as big a hog as I want to see!"[44]

An army officer who had been accused of embezzling forty dollars from the government had appealed to Lincoln, rather brassily telling the president that it "wa'n't but thirty dollars," similarly reminded Lincoln of a story. This one involved a man from Indiana who got into a violent argument with a neighbor. "One charged that the other's daughter had three illegitimate children. 'Now,' said the man whose family was so outrageously scandalized, 'that's a lie, and I can prove it, for she has only two.'"

"This case is no better," said Lincoln. "Whether the amount was thirty dollars or thirty thousand dollars, the culpability is the same.... I believe I will leave this case where it was left by the officers who tried it."

Old Abe had a relevant story, too, for the politician who urged him to surrender the federal military installations and other property in the South so as to bring the Civil War to a speedy close. In Aesop's tale of the "Lion and the Woodsman's Daughter," the former, Lincoln recounted, was much in love with the latter, and the lion consequently went to the woodsman and asked for his approval of the desired marriage. When the woodsman replied that he would not give such a blessing because the lion's teeth were too long, the lion went to a dentist and had the teeth extracted. He was then informed by the woodsman that he still couldn't have the daughter because his claws were too long, and he consequently returned to the dentist and had this objection removed. When he then went back to the parent to claim the girl, the woodsman, taking advantage of the fact that the lion was now disarmed, set upon him and beat his brains out.

Lincoln's flair for the funny also served him well when an irate governor visited the president's adjutant general to register a long list of grievances. The governor got no satisfaction from the underling and not much more from Secretary of War Edwin M. Stanton when, with the adjutant general, he went to Stanton shortly thereafter. Still mad as a hornet, he decided to take his problems to the top and went alone to see Lincoln. A few hours later, he returned to

the adjutant general and affably announced that he simply wanted
to bid the adjutant general goodbye, saying nothing whatsoever
about the problems that had sparked his rage when the adjutant general had last seen him.

The extremely curious adjutant general told the president when
he next saw him that he assumed that Lincoln had given the governor much, if not all, of what he had sought. "Oh, no," Lincoln
replied:

> I did not concede anything. You know how that Illinois farmer man-
> aged the big log that lay in the middle of his field? To the inquiries of
> his neighbors one Sunday he announced that he had got rid of the big
> log. "Got rid of it!" said they, "How did you do it? It was too big to
> haul out, too knotty to split, and too wet and soggy to burn. What
> did you do?" "Well, now, boys," replied the farmer, "if you won't
> divulge the secret, I'll tell you how I got rid of it. I plowed around
> it."

"Now," Lincoln told his subordinate, "don't tell anybody, but that
is the way I got rid of [the governor]: I plowed around him, but it
took me three mortal hours to do it, and I was afraid every minute
he would see what I was at."[45]

While there was nothing at all that Lincoln could do to termi-
nate the relentless pressure that senators Thaddeus Stevens, Charles
Sumner, and Henry Wilson were putting on him to issue an emancipation decree before he was ready to do so—all three of these legislators being highly influential leaders within his own Republican
party—he could insulate himself with humor, at least by analogy,
even in this situation. When he caught sight of the three men
approaching the White House for yet another attempt to get him to
see things their way, he told a visitor who was with him at the time
a story involving a small boy named Bud, whose reading skills left
much room for improvement. The members of Bud's class were asked
to read out loud from the Bible's third chapter of Daniel, and Bud's
assignment was verse 12, which contained the names of Shadrach,
Meshach, and Abednego, the Israelites who were thrown into the
fiery furnace. "Little Bud," said Lincoln, as he and his visitor
watched the three senators arrive,

> stumbled on Shadrach, floundered on Meshach, and went all to pieces
> on Abednego. Instantly the master dealt him a cuff on the side of the
> head and left him wailing and blubbering as the next boy in line took

up the reading. But before the girl at the end of the line had done reading he had subsided into sniffles and finally became quiet. His blun-
der and disgrace were forgotten by the others of the class until his
turn was approaching to read again. Then, like a thunderclap out of
a clear sky, he set up a wail which even alarmed the master, who with
rather unusual gentleness inquired, "What's the matter now?"

Pointing with a shaking finger at the verse which a few moments
later would fall to him to read, Bud managed to quaver out the answer:
"Look there marster," he cried, "there comes them same damn three
fellers again."[46]

Abraham Lincoln's ability to amuse did not, generally speaking, extend to the members of his own cabinet. The defective and
quickly replaced war secretary, Cameron, did have a strong appreciation of the ludicrous (he once defined an honest politician as "a
man who when he's bought stays bought"). And, as noted, Seward's
sense of humor took second place to no one, including Lincoln himself—one reason why the two men got along so well. The secretary
of state was given to such utterances as:

Did you ever hear Webster's recipe for cooking cod? "Denude your
cod of his scales, cut him open carefully, put him in a pot of cold
water, heat it until your fork can pass easily through the fish, spread
good fresh butter over him liberally, sprinkle salt on the butter, pepper on the salt and—send for George Ashmun [a Massachusetts politician and lawyer who was close to the administration] and me."[47]

But most of Lincoln's cabinet members were conspicuously devoid
of levity.

The highly regarded Lincoln biographer J. G. Randall has
asserted of Cameron's replacement, the puritanical Stanton, that "if
Lincoln would be telling a rich story and Stanton would enter, the
story and the laughter would die."[48] Secretary of the Treasury Salmon
P. Chase was so serious that Senator Thomas ("If you would succeed in life, you must be solemn") Corwin said that he was definitely
destined for distinction. And the president himself in describing yet
another of his cabinet officials quoted the British wit Sydney Smith's
remark regarding an earlier statesman, that "it required a surgical
operation to get a joke into his head."

Even in his dealings with these top officials, however, Lincoln was
not easily deterred in his efforts to elicit smiles. He frequently laced
his instructions to Stanton, with whom he maintained an especially

close relationship despite the latter's severity, with droll comments. One document from Lincoln to the war secretary said, "Please have the Adjutant General ascertain whether Second Lieutenant of Company D, 2nd infantry, Alexander E. Drake, is entitled to promotion. His wife thinks he is. Please have this looked into." Another missive informed Stanton, "I personally wish Jacob R. Freese, of New Jersey, to be appointed a Colonel of a colored regiment—and this regardless of whether he can tell the exact shade of Julius Caesar's hair."

In another instance, Lincoln overheard the short-tempered Stanton telling a visitor who was delivering what she thought were important war-related papers to him that they were not that important and could wait. The chief executive soon thereafter told his secretary about an Army colonel who disliked profanity and who consequently

> when he had enlisted a regiment ... informed the men that he would do all the swearing done in that organization. They agreed, as they had to, and for some time no one heard any profanity around that camp. Then, one day, John Todd, a teamster, encountered several miles of mudholes, each one worse than the one before. About midway along this road, Todd let go a flood of cussing that reached even [the colonel's] ears. The colonel called John into his tent and said: "Look here, John, didn't you agree to let me do all the cussing for this regiment?" "Yes, Colonel, I did," John answered, "but this job of cussing had to be done right there and then and I couldn't see you anywhere around to do it."

"The point of that story is, Stanton," Lincoln concluded, "that anything which comes up today in this war must be done today in order to finish this war."[49]

Lincoln often felt free to joke good-naturedly about the secretary of war in his absence, as well as in his presence. He asked on one occasion, "Did Stanton tell you I was a damned fool? Then I expect I must be one, for he is almost always right and generally says what he means." He was also referring to the strong-willed Stanton when he waggishly told a favor seeker who had gotten no satisfaction from the secretary, "I can do nothing; for you must know that I have very little influence with this administration."

But Chase and the other cabinet officers with whom the president was less intimate than with Stanton and Seward were also fair game for Lincoln's anecdotal treasury. Chase actually submitted his resignation a few times before it was finally accepted by Lincoln. The president recognized that the treasury secretary was not the most loyal of his cabinet members but valued the Ohioan's undeniable administrative efficiencies. He once told an associate that

> it is not so easy a thing to let Chase go. I am situated very much as the boy was who held the bear by the hind legs.... There was a very vicious bear which, after being some time chased by a couple of boys, turned upon his pursuers. The boldest of the two ran up and caught the bear by the hind legs, while the other climbed up into a little tree, and complacently witnessed the conflict going on beneath, between the bear and his companion. The tussle was a sharp one, and the boy, after becoming quite exhausted, cried out in alarm, "Bill, for God's sake come down and help me let this darned bear go!"[50]

Well before Chase had left the cabinet, Lincoln told the owner of the *New York Times* when the latter, a Lincoln supporter, had pointed out that Chase himself nurtured presidential ambitions for 1864 and therefore could be counted on to continue his not-very-subtle criticism of the president:

> My brother and I were once ploughing corn on a Kentucky farm, I driving the horse, and he holding the plough. The horse was lazy; but on one occasion rushed across the field so that I, with my long legs, could scarcely keep pace with him. On reaching the end of the furrow, I found an enormous *chin fly* fastened upon him, and knocked him off. My brother asked me what I did that for. I told him I didn't want the old horse bitten in that way. "Why," said my brother, "that's all that made him go!" Now if [Chase] has a presidential *chin fly* biting him, I'm not going to knock him off, if it will only make his department *go*.[51]

Whatever would motivate the secretary to do his best job in running the Department of the Treasury was quite acceptable to the personally secure Lincoln.

No one in the cabinet was immune from Lincoln's attempts at the jocular when the seven officials met together with their leader. Indeed, immediately before he read—in September 1862—the first draft of his Emancipation Proclamation to his cabinet, Lincoln read these top-level appointees a lengthy new story written by the humorist Artemus Ward. After he had revealed the contents of the intended proclamation itself, there was complete silence in the room, which Chase finally broke by announcing that he very much liked the document, but did have one small suggestion for improving its language. After each of the six other department heads had followed

Chase's lead by volunteering language modifications of their own, Lincoln cheerfully said, "Gentlemen, you remind me of the story about a man who had been away from home, and when he was coming back he was met by one of his farm hands, who greeted him after this fashion. 'Master, the little pigs are dead, and the old sow's dead, too, but I didn't like to tell you all at once.'"

In another meeting, when a course of action that he wanted to take was opposed by six of the seven, Lincoln related a tale of a drunk at a midwestern prayer meeting who, because he was asleep at the time, failed to rise when the preacher asked, "Who are on the Lord's side?" and everyone else in attendance stood up. After the preacher then asked, "Who are on the side of the Devil?" however, the drunk woke up and did rise, becoming of course the only person in the crowd to do so. Surveying the situation, he asserted, "I don't exactly understand the question but I'll stand by you, parson, to the last. But it seems to me that we're in a hopeless minority."

The major challenge that faced this greatest of all presidents was, of course, the winning of the hugely traumatic Civil War. In meeting this, Lincoln was significantly hampered by the fact that it was not until thirty-five months after the start of hostilities that he had an army commander in chief who was capable of leading the Union forces to victory. Several generals were given the chance to do so—one of them, George B. McClellan, twice—and all were found, in various degrees, wanting. Only when the assignment was placed in the hands of Ulysses S. Grant did Lincoln finally have his man.

McClellan, despite his undeniably good organizational skills, turned out to be both overly cautious and indecisive. He regularly complained about the consistently rainy weather in the spring of 1862, using it as one of many reasons why he had not moved his numerically superior troops forward in an attempt to take the Confederate capital of Richmond. Lincoln, whose patience with McClellan was considerable, observed that Robert E. Lee's Army of Northern Virginia went on the attack regardless of the weather and deadpanned that McClellan, the Scriptures notwithstanding, appeared to believe that heaven sent its rain exclusively on the just and not the unjust. Lincoln also asserted in regard to the Army of the Potomac's nonactivity in this same campaign that if McClellan did not want to use the army, he himself would like to borrow it.

Later that year, with McClellan continuing to make excuses for his conspicuous lack of success, the president wrote to his commander, "I have just read your dispatch about sore tongued and fatigued horses. Will you pardon me for asking what the horses of your Army have done since the battle of Antietam that fatigue anything?" On another occasion, commenting again on McClellan's consistent reluctance to let his soldiers go into battle, he said, "He's got the slows." On yet another, Lincoln observed that sending soldiers to McClellan was like shoveling fleas across a barnyard—so few of them ever got there.

Rejecting the request of a constituent to go to Richmond, the chief executive explained, "My dear sir, if I should give you one, it would do you no good. You may think it very strange, but there are a lot of fellows who either can't read or are prejudiced against every man who takes a pass from me. I have given McClellan, and more than 200,000 others, passes to Richmond, and not one of them has gotten there!"

McClellan's indecisiveness tended to annoy Lincoln every bit as much as did the little general's inactivity. The president once found some soldiers at McClellan's headquarters constructing something and inquired of them what it was. Informed that it was a new privy for their commanding officer, Lincoln asked if it was "a one-holer or a two-holer" and was told that it was the former. Waiting until he and his small entourage had walked out of earshot of the McClellan subordinates, Lincoln then whispered to an aide, "Thank God it's a one-holer, for if it were a two-holer, before McClellan could make up his mind which to use he would beshit himself."

As a form of protest against Lincoln's request that he send back more detailed reports from the front, McClellan for a time went out of his way to feed Lincoln trivia, and during this period he sent the president a dispatch which in its entirety read: "We have just captured six cows. What shall we do with them? George B. McClellan." Lincoln's answer was equally succinct and to the point: "As to the six cows captured—milk them. A. Lincoln."

McClellan's immediate successors fared little better in winning either decisive victories or the admiration of their president, who once estimated the size of the Confederate Army at "about 1,200,000 men" and explained that he had arrived at this figure because "whenever one of our Generals is licked he says he was outnumbered three or four to one, and we have 400,000 men." Regarding the notorious bragging of General Joseph "Fighting Joe" Hooker, Lincoln commented, "The hen is the wisest of all animal creation because she never cackles until the egg is laid." Lincoln also observed of Hooker, who frequently sent his dispatches from "Headquarters in the saddle," that the "trouble with Hooker is that he's got his headquarters where his hindquarters ought to be."

Another commander, who sent the president a not-very-credible report that his troops had killed hundreds of southern soldiers in battle while "our loss was twelve men killed, wounded and captured," reminded Lincoln of a man who gave lectures about his trips to interesting places around the world. Unfortunately, the lecturer had a tendency to exaggerate his statistics greatly. To his credit, he was well aware of this failing, and he ultimately asked a friend who always travelled with him and sat behind him on the lecture platform to pull his coattails whenever he significantly tampered with the truth. Soon thereafter, he told an audience about his visit to a tall building in Europe and remarked that this structure was "a mile and a half long; and really it must have been a mile high!" Immediately after this declaration, his friend pulled strenuously on his coattails, and a member of the audience simultaneously shouted, "And how *wide* was that building, please?" The lecturer, now quite shattered and desiring to offset his embarrassing hyperbole of a moment earlier as much as he possibly could, replied, "Oh, just about a foot!"

Once during the war, Lincoln told a friend about still another top commander who the friend knew had not ranked at all high in the president's opinion but who, Lincoln now said, "has proved himself a really great man." The military figure, Lincoln continued, "has grappled with and mastered that ancient and wise admonition, 'Know thyself'; he has formed an intimate acquaintance with himself, knows as well for what he is fitted and unfitted as any man living." Indeed, in Lincoln's opinion, the war "has not produced another like him." Quite surprised by the high praise now lavished on this person, the friend asked why Lincoln had changed his opinion so drastically. "Because," said the president, with a twinkle in his eye, "he has resigned."

Lincoln's enormous and well-justified high regard for General Grant stood, obviously, in stark contrast to all of these other opinions on the president's part regarding his army leaders. And it was concerning Grant that Honest Abe uttered what is undoubtedly the best known of his comments on his commanders. When, in 1864, a group of temperance advocates urged Lincoln to relieve Grant of his command because he drank too much whiskey, Lincoln asked if anyone knew what Grant's brand of whiskey was because, he said, "If I can find out, I will send every general in the field a barrel of it!" (While there is little doubt that the president really made this statement,

almost the same words were used much earlier by George III in rela-
tion to General Wolfe and his alleged inebriation. George's quip was
reported in *Joe Miller's Jest-Book*, and the "retail dealer" Lincoln, an
avid Joe Miller devotee, undoubtedly got it from that source.)

Not everyone, by any means, applauded Lincoln's use of humor.
The Dutch ambassador complained that Lincoln's conversation "con-
sists of vulgar anecdotes at which he himself laughs uproariously."[52]
The prominent author Richard Henry Dana said, "He likes to tell
stories to all sorts of persons ... rather than give his mind to the noble
and manly duties of his great post."[53] (Dana also asked, "Can this
man Lincoln *ever* be serious?") Judge David Wills, the person who
officially invited the president to Gettysburg and consequently triggered the immortal Gettysburg Address, seemed to have had some
concerns beforehand that the humorist and crude storyteller Lincoln
would not be sufficiently solemn on the occasion. He thus empha-
sized to the president the "sacred" nature of the event and added in
his correspondence that "these ceremonies ... will doubtless be very
imposing and solemnly impressive."[54] And it was as much for Lincoln's constant use of the jocular as for anything else that the noted
abolitionist Wendell Phillips deemed him to be "a first-rate second-
rate man."[55]

Nor were all newspapers and magazines favorably disposed. As
early as 1839, the well-meaning *Illinois State Register* warned Lincoln that his "assumed *clownishness*" did not wear well: "Mr. Lincoln will sometimes make his language correspond with this clownish
manner, and he can thus frequently raise a loud laugh among his
Whig hearers; but this entire game of buffoonery convinces the *mind*
of no man, and is utterly lost on the majority of his audience." The
newspaper's advice to the young state legislator was that he "correct this clownish fault before it grows upon him."[56] An editorial
cartoon in the respected *Harper's Weekly* of January 3, 1863,
depicted Columbia pointing an accusatory finger at President Lincoln and asking, "Where are my 15,000 sons—murdered at Freder-
icksburg?" Lincoln answers her in the drawing with the comment,
"This reminds me of a little joke," to which Columbia retorts, "Go
tell your joke at Springfield!!"

Even Lincoln himself at times seemed to be quite aware of the
downside of humor. He asserted in a lecture in Springfield that "it
was a common notion that those who laughed heartily and often
never amounted to much—never made great men." "If this be the
case," Lincoln added, "farewell to all my glory."

He fully comprehended, moreover, that those who kid around can at times expect to be misunderstood. In fact, he enjoyed, and often repeated, one story concerning his constant use of levity:

> Two Quakeresses were riding on the railroad and were heard discussing the probable outcome of the war. "I think," said the first, "that Jefferson [Davis] will succeed." "Why does thee think so?" asked the other. "Because he is a praying man." "And so is Abraham a praying man," the other objected. "Yes," replied the first, "but the Lord will think Abraham is joking."[57]

But, as his fondness not only for that last tale but also for many other anecdotes relayed on previous pages might indicate, Lincoln was sustained in his acceptance of the criticism heaped upon him—for his executive actions, of course, as well as for his humor—by the ample possession of an eminently sunny disposition.

He was quite unwilling to hold a grudge (he once told his young secretary John Hay that he was "in favor of short statutes of limitations in politics"), and he rarely took umbrage at remarks directed at him that might have antagonized a person with less aplomb.

When the general who had been selected to escort him from the White House to Gettysburg on the occasion of his address urged him to hurry, for there was not much time left in which to get to the train, Lincoln affably asserted:

> Well, I feel about that as the convict did in Illinois, when he was going to the gallows. Passing along the road in custody of the sheriff, and seeing the people who were eager for the execution crowding and jostling one another past him, he at last called out "Boys! you needn't be in such a hurry to get ahead, for there won't be any fun till I get there."[58]

In 1864, when John C. Frémont led a group of malcontented Republicans hostile to Lincoln's renomination out of the party and held his own Republican convention in Cleveland, Lincoln similarly seemed to be far more amused than irate. When the president learned that only about four hundred people had attended the rebel convention, he delighted in going to his Bible, locating the relevant portion of I Samuel, and reading, "And every one that was in distress, and every one that was in debt, and every one that was discontented, gathered themselves unto him; and he became a captain over them: and there were with him about four hundred men."

At the February 1865 Hampton Roads Peace Conference, one of the three Confederate participants announced that the recognition of the Confederacy by Lincoln was a prerequisite to any ending of the war, and in support of this ultimatum he cited Charles I of England and that leader's recognition of his rebel parliament. Lincoln, who could have been incensed by such a statement, given both the South's utter absence of bargaining leverage at the time and the many differences between the autocratic British monarch and himself, merely turned to the man who had made it and replied: "On the question of history I must refer you to Mr. Seward, who is posted in such matters. I don't pretend to be; but I have a tolerably distinct recollection, in the case you refer to, that Charles lost his head, and I have no head to spare." (At this same conference, Lincoln watched another southern delegate—his old friend, the tiny and sickly vice president of the Confederacy, Alexander H. Stephens—remove the several layers of outer garments which he had initially worn as protection against the chilly weather and cheerfully asked, "Was there ever such a nubbin after so much shucking?")

Lincoln was capable, too, of genially inquiring of a very tall soldier, whom he saw at a Washington military hospital, "Hello, comrade, do you know when your feet get cold?" Bringing his short, chubby wife, Mary, to stand beside him on the platform of a train, Lincoln told the assembled crowd that this "is the long and short of it." He also straight-facedly announced, in recognition of his general willingness to dispense with rigid doctrines and instead to do what at the time seemed to offer the greatest prospects of success, "My policy is to have no policy."

Lincoln's humor also had in it a marked strain of wry self-deprecation. He said that his own absentmindedness reminded him of the story of an old Englishman who was so absentminded that when he went to bed, he put his clothes carefully into the bed and threw himself over the back of the chair. He wrote in 1843, after his Whig party had failed to nominate him for Congress, "It would astonish, if not amuse the older citizens, to learn that I have been put down here as the candidate of pride, wealth and aristocratic family distinction." When as a young lawyer he returned to Springfield after months of travelling the circuit to find that the modest residence that he had left behind had been transformed by his wife into an imposing two-story Greek Revival house, he feigned ignorance, walked up to a neighbor, and inquired, "Stranger, do you know where Lincoln lives? He used to live here." When asked whether the members of his wife's socially prominent family spelled their name with one or two *d*s, he replied, "One *d* is enough for God. But the Todds need two."

He had no exaggerated view of his own professional importance, either. As president-elect, when a zealously pro–Lincoln partisan told him that he would if necessary give up his life to ensure that Lincoln's inauguration would proceed without disruption, Lincoln replied that the situation reminded him of the youth setting out for the battlefront whose sisters were making him a magnificent belt highlighted by the motto "Victory or death." The soldier said to his siblings, "No, no, don't put it quite that strong. Put it 'Victory or get hurt pretty bad.'" Asked, some years later, how he liked being president, he responded, "You have heard the story, haven't you, about the man who was tarred and feathered and carried out of town on a rail? A man in the crowd asked him how he liked it. His reply was that if it was not for the honor of the thing, he would much rather walk."

Above all, he could poke fun at something that his enemies aggressively mocked to a degree that seems almost incomprehensible today: his own physical appearance. To be sure, Lincoln—at six feet four inches, our tallest president—was a gawky, long-limbed, big-eared man. His eyebrows, his law partner William Herndon once noted, "cropped out like a huge rock on the brow of a hill."[59] And his long, sad face, even from young adulthood, was prematurely wrinkled. But to say of Lincoln that

> His cheekbones were high and his visage was rough,
> Like a middling of bacon, all wrinkled and tough,
> His nose was as long, and as ugly and big
> As the snout of a half-starved Illinois pig

—as a well-circulated Confederate poem did—and to frequently employ words like "ape" and "gorilla" in describing him, as many of his adversaries did (even Lincoln's own General McClellan, in a private letter to his wife, referred to the president as "the original gorilla") was to take extreme liberties with fact. He was, as more than one of his biographers has said, a man of many faces, with his innate kindness and constant good nature often doing much to improve any first impressions concerning his appearance. Many would agree with Herndon that "he was not a pretty man ... nor was he an ugly one: he was a homely man, careless of his looks, plain looking and plain acting."[60]

Nonetheless, perhaps guided by the hypothesis that the best defense is a good offense, Lincoln frequently took the initiative in mocking his outer features. Making a speech in Pinesville, Ohio, five weeks before he became president, he told the crowd, "I have stepped out upon this platform that I may see you and that you may see me, and in the arrangement I have the best of the bargain." He told, often, the story of the man who once said to him, "They say you're a self-made man," and who, when Lincoln conceded that this was the case, retorted, "Well, all I've got to say is that it was a damned bad job." He announced to a conference of editors in Bloomington, Illinois, that he was not a journalist and consequently felt somewhat out of place at the event. "I feel like I once did," he amplified, "when I met a woman riding on horseback in the wood. As I stopped to let her pass, she also stopped and looked at me intently, and said, 'I do believe you are the ugliest man I ever saw.' Said I, 'Madam, you are probably right, but I can't help it.' 'No,' said she, 'you can't help it, but you might stay at home.'"

In the same vein, he enjoyed telling audiences about the time that he was splitting rails and looked up to find a stranger pointing a gun, presumably loaded, at him. Lincoln asked, "What do you mean?" The stranger answered that he had promised to shoot the first man he met who was uglier than he was. Lincoln took a good look at the stranger and then said, "If I am uglier than you, then blaze away."

Even in his one-on-one conversations, he often introduced this theme. When a newspaper reporter asked him why no artist had ever done him justice, he genially quipped, "It is impossible to get my graceful motions in—that's the reason why none of the pictures are like me." He once told Hay of a dream that he had had the previous night, in which he was in what he called "a party of plain people." As its members realized who he was, they started to comment on his appearance. One of them declared, "He is a very common-looking man." Lincoln replied, "Common-looking people are the best in the world; that is the reason the Lord makes so many of them."

The amused tolerance with which Lincoln treated his own appearance was the same attitude that he displayed toward another favored topic, organized religion. The latter also fell, in his view, far short of perfection—with its preachers who were too lazy to write short sermons or not dignified enough to deal appropriately with little blue lizards—but there wasn't much that it or they could do about these shortcomings. These servants of God, consequently, warranted being the subject of irreverent, gentle humor. It was hard, however, to be really upset with them.

An example of his many efforts in this direction was a story that the president told to a visiting delegation of three clergymen, all of whom were relentlessly pressing him for a change in the wartime system of chaplain appointments (about which Lincoln could actually do nothing):

> Once, in Springfield ... a little ... boy, whom I knew, named "Dick," [was] busily digging with his toe in a mud-puddle. As I came up, I said, "'Dick,' what are you about?" "Making a '*church*,'" said he. "A church?" said I. "What do you mean?" "Why, yes," said "Dick," pointing with his toe, "don't you see? ... there's the 'steps' and 'front-door'—here the 'pews' where the folks set—and there's the 'pulpit.'" "Yes, I see," said I, "but why don't you make a 'minister'?" "Laws," answered "Dick," with a grin, "I hain't got *mud* enough!"[61]

To a White House visitor who was rather negative in his evaluation of a veteran Washington minister, Lincoln said:

> I think you are rather hard upon [the clergyman]. He reminds me of a man in Illinois who was tried for passing a counterfeit bill. It was in evidence that before passing it he had taken it to the cashier of a bank and asked his opinion of the bill, and he received a very prompt reply that it was a counterfeit. His lawyer, who had heard of the evidence to be brought against his client, asked him, just before going into court, "Did you take the bill to the cashier of the bank and ask him if it was good?" "I did," was the reply. "Well, what was the reply of the cashier?" The rascal was in a corner, but he got out of it in this fashion: "He said it was a pretty tolerable, respectable sort of a bill."

The president added that the clergyman was "a pretty tolerable, respectable sort" of a clergyman.[62]

A ranking federal official brought a minister to see Lincoln one day, saying, "Mr. President, allow me to present to you my friend, the Rev. Mr. F. ... Mr. F. has expressed a desire to see you and have some conversation with you, and I am happy to be the means of introducing him." Lincoln invited his visitor to sit down, sat down himself, and said, "I am now ready to hear what you have to say." "Oh, bless you, sir," the man of the cloth responded, "I have nothing special to say; I merely called to pay my respects to you, and ... to assure you of my hearty sympathy and support." "My dear sir," said Lincoln, his countenance now suddenly relaxed and vigorously shaking the clergyman's hand, "I am very glad to see you, indeed. I thought you had come to preach to me!"

In the closing days of the war, General William T. Sherman asked Lincoln if the president wanted him to capture the fleeing Confederate president, Jefferson Davis. Lincoln made his desires clear by telling a story of which he was particularly fond (and often recounted in other situations as well). He was reminded, he said, of the old temperance preacher who, on a particularly hot summer day while travelling in rural Illinois, stopped at a house for refreshment and was offered a glass of lemonade but was also asked by his host if he might not perhaps prefer something stronger. The preacher, mindful of his chosen vocation, quickly said, "No, no." But, thinking the matter over, after a few seconds' pause, he added, "If you could manage to put in a drop unbeknownst to me, I guess it wouldn't hurt too much."

"Now, General," Lincoln told Sherman, "I'm bound to oppose the escape of Jeff Davis, but if you could manage to let him slip out unbeknownst like, I guess it wouldn't hurt too much."

The minister was not always the fall guy in Old Abe's substantial arsenal of religious stories. Sometimes, laypeople played that role, as in a tale that Lincoln loved to tell about the itinerant preacher who sternly reproached one family that he visited for their apparent lack of regard for the Bible, there being no such publication visible in their small home. The mother insisted that the family did in fact own one and sent her children to locate it. They finally did return but with only a few torn pages from what had at one time been a full-fledged Bible. "I had no idea," said the parent, "that we were so nearly out."

Sometimes a whole community was the object of Lincoln's irreverence, as in a story that the president related about an "itinerant quack preacher" who requested from Lincoln's friend, Illinois State Auditor Jesse Dubois, permission to use a hall within the Illinois State House in Springfield to deliver a religious lecture. Dubois asked the cleric, "What's it about?" When he received the answer, "The Second Coming of Christ," he nipped the man's unwelcome effort in the bud by saying, "Nonsense. If Christ had been to Springfield once, and got away, he'd [stay] damned clear of coming again."

John Hay wrote that while Lincoln "continued always the same kindly, genial, and cordial spirit he had been at first," in the White House, "the boisterous laughter became less frequent year by year.... He aged with great rapidity."[63] A Union Army Officer reported that he visited the White House and was enjoying a good laugh with Lincoln's secretaries when the president looked into the room and said, "I thought you were laughing pretty loud in here and that I should like to come in and laugh too."[64] This story was from early in Lincoln's first term; it probably could not have happened much later. Certainly, in his speeches, Lincoln used humor far less often as chief executive than he had prior to assuming the enormous burdens of his wartime office, quite possibly because he agreed with his critics that much levity was indeed inappropriate in such circumstances.

But the droll ways and dry jokes that Stephen Douglas had so admired in Lincoln before he became president were as much a part of Old Abe's personality as gravity was a part of Douglas's, and the first authentic humorist to occupy the Executive Mansion continued to make listeners smile to the end. Even in his last days Lincoln didn't deviate from his long practice of spending the bulk of his free evenings in his office, trading funny stories with old friends. Hay observed that at these times he was at his best, for when "his wit and rich humor had free play, he was once more the Lincoln of the Eighth Circuit, the cheeriest of talkers, the riskiest of story tellers."[65]

Only a few days before Lincoln died, Attorney General James Speed apologized for disturbing the exhausted president for a minor matter. Lincoln amiably told the cabinet member, "Speed, you remind me of a story of Henry Ward Beecher. One day as he was going to preach, he saw some boys playing marbles in the street. He stopped and looked at them very hard. 'Boys,' he said presently, 'boys, I am scared at what I see.' 'Then,' replied one of the boys, 'why the hell don't you run away?'"

In that same second week of April 1865, he informed a large crowd that had converged on the White House to celebrate Lee's surrender to Grant at Appomattox that he was asking the brass band that had accompanied the crowd to play "Dixie." With mock seriousness, he said that the attorney general had just told him that the song was "a lawful prize" since "we fairly captured it."

Just hours before his assassination, Lincoln related to a congressman, who wanted one of his friends appointed to an army staff position, the story of a lady who lived in his neighborhood when he was a young man. She made shirts for a living, and one day an Irishman asked her to make one for him. She proceeded to do so and gave it to him, but when he put the shirt on he found that it had been starched throughout instead of just in its collar. He thereupon returned it, saying that he didn't want a shirt that was all collar. "The trouble with you," Lincoln informed the congressman, "is that you want the army all staff and no army."

There is a sad appropriateness that the last sound that Lincoln ever heard was that of laughter, by the audience at the theatrical comedy *Our American Cousin*, in response to a humorous line uttered by an actor.

Very likely, the Great Emancipator—whose irrepressible sense of humor served him so well in whistling down sadness, augmenting his popularity, making his points, cutting his detractors down to size, and sidetracking both difficult issues and unwanted visitors— would have wanted it that way.

CHAPTER 2

CALVIN COOLIDGE

In Calvin Coolidge's first week as president, following Warren G. Harding's unexpected death in August 1923, the foreman of a gang of laborers working in the street in front of the federal government's executive offices observed Coolidge and the chief of his Secret Service staff taking a walk. He said to another member of the staff, who was standing near him, "What a fine looking man our new president is! So tall and straight! Who's the little fellow with him?" Informed that the little fellow was Coolidge, he exclaimed, "Glory be to God! Now ain't it a grand country when a wee man like that can get to be the grandest of them all!"[1]

When the unprepossessing man who would be known as "Silent Cal" first went to Boston to take his seat in the Massachusetts House of Representatives as a Republican state legislator, a Democratic leader observed of him, "This fellow is either a schoolteacher or an undertaker from the country. I don't know which." In Coolidge's vice presidential years, the tart-tongued Alice Roosevelt Longworth commented that his dour visage made him look as though he had been "weaned on a pickle." His taciturnity was so marked that it was once said that a moth flew out whenever he opened his mouth. So deep was his Vermont nasal drawl that he reputedly could pronounce the word "cow" in four syllables. And he was so phlegmatic that, upon receiving the news that he had died, Algonquin Roundtable wit Dorothy Parker asked, "How could they tell?" (Parker, never one to let go of a good thing, also is believed to have asserted that Coolidge ran the whole gamut of emotions, from A to B.)

But few chief executives have ever been as popular while in office or left the White House with this popularity as intact as Coolidge. Indeed, he was enormously popular throughout his political career, facing the voters twenty times and losing only once (in 1905, for a seat on the school board in his adopted community of Northampton, Massachusetts).

In 1924 he won the presidency with the largest Republican plurality in history to that date, and he could unquestionably have been nominated in both 1928 and 1932 had he only indicated an interest. He had never really enjoyed his presidential years, however, and he consistently turned down overtures. When one of his 1932 supporters told him that if he were back as chief executive, "it would be the end of this terrible depression," Coolidge replied, "It would be the beginning of mine." As one of his most respected biographers wrote long after he had passed from the scene, "In the course of reaction against his political philosophy people have forgotten how popular Calvin Coolidge was up to the very moment of his death."[2] And it is generally agreed by historians that an incalculable but undoubtedly significant portion of the explanation for this popularity was Coolidge's possession of an extremely wry sense of humor.

He invariably delivered his witticisms with a straight face, and some of his drollest remarks were consequently missed. Vaudevillian Will Rogers, the foremost professional humorist of his time and a great admirer of Coolidge's attainments in this department (he said of the man from Vermont that he "had more subtle humor than almost any public man I ever met"[3]), thought that the thirtieth president wasted "more humor on folks than anybody."[4] But Rogers also recognized that Coolidge tossed off his lines primarily for his own entertainment and diversion. "You see," the man who never met a man he didn't like once pointed out, "most fellows notify you that they are about to pull one.... Mr. Coolidge never did that, his were pulled with not even a change of inflection, you got it or you didn't, and it didn't make any difference to him."[5]Millions of Americans did, however, get it, at least much of the time, and they ran a large gamut.

A White House maid asserted that Coolidge was the funniest of all six presidents she'd known in her thirty White House years.[6] The legendary comedy director Mack Sennett deemed Silent Cal to be an "expert practitioner" of "deadpan" humor, which called, he pointed out, for not only a true comic gift but also a highly developed sense of timing.[7] Edmund W. Starling, Coolidge's closest aide during his presidential years, later wrote:

> The average person's serious and humorous aspects are separate. In President Coolidge they were mixed, so that the one interpenetrated the other. To me it seemed a step forward in evolution, for the serious side of life needs to be looked at with the tolerance and understanding which

a sense of humor provides, and our laughter should be grounded in an understanding of the spiritual purpose of our existence.[8]

Even Coolidge's secretary of commerce, the essentially humorless Herbert Hoover, collected and savored Coolidge stories, while longtime U.S. Congressman Morris K. Udall—the possessor of an excellent sense of humor—wrote in his 1988 book, *Too Funny to Be President*, that of the twelve presidents in his lifetime to that point, Coolidge had the driest wit.[9] In the opinion of a major scholar of the art of prose, Coolidge was "not only the master of the understatement but commander of the punch line." (The president's comment regarding the necessity for nations to repay their World War I debts—"they hired the money, didn't they?"—was, this scholar thought, "like a glass of dry, sharp, Yankee wine."[10])

The "greatest man ever to come out of Plymouth, Vermont," as H. L. Mencken once deemed him, Calvin Coolidge was an absolute master of the dry, whimsical remark. He told the White House messenger who brought him his first chief executive's salary check, "Call again." He took long, deep naps in his presidential office almost every afternoon, and once, when a staff member awakened him, he grinned and asked, "Is the country still here?" One day, his walking companion, Senator Selden P. Spencer of Missouri, looked over at the White House and jocularly asked him, "I wonder who lives there?" Coolidge responded, "Nobody. They just come and go." At his first cabinet meeting, one member quietly called for a cheer for the new president but others—on the premise that such an action would be in dubious taste with the newly widowed Mrs. Warren G. Harding still a resident of the Executive Mansion—rejected this proposal. Coolidge (who had overheard this whispered discussion) quietly observed, "Seems to be opposition to my administration already."

Coolidge was capable of telling a prominent architect who was visiting him at the White House and extolling the architectural beauty of the place at some length, "Suits me." When General Edward L. Logan called on him in Washington to pay his respects, was invited to lunch, and responded, "As a matter of fact, I'm going to be here only today and tomorrow," Coolidge deadpanned, "We lunch on both days." Silent Cal commented, as he was being driven in his presidential limousine through Washington's Rock Creek Park and saw U.S. Senator William E. Borah of Idaho, a man who prided himself on his fierce independence, on horseback, "Must bother the senator to be going in the same direction as the horse." Taken on a special dignitary's tour of Emily Dickinson's cottage, he stared at one of the great poet's manuscripts and nonchalantly declared, "She writes with her hands. I dictate."

When a "revisionistic" biography of George Washington, which was quite critical of the first President, achieved unexpectedly large sales, Coolidge looked out of his White House office window and observed to a group of visitors, "I see his monument is still there."

Inevitably, as Coolidge came into national prominence, there was much circulation of his bons mots and, as in the case of Lincoln, many remarks were attributed to him that he never made. An informed chronicler of the Coolidge presidency wrote that "any man so celebrated for silence, so redolent of the northern New England flavor, must give rise to many humorous stories,"[11] and as spontaneously puckish and droll as the phlegmatic politician genuinely was, he was made far more so in his public imagery by the Calvin Coolidge legend. His wife, Grace, when asked after his death if the stories told about him were true, said only "the best of them are."[12] Regarding any of a number of specific quips attributed to him, she frequently replied, "I don't know whether or not he said it, but it's certainly the kind of thing that he could have said." But, whether in myth or reality, the only chief executive of the United States who was born on the Fourth of July had a rare ability to make the public smile, and much of his considerable appeal rested on this circumstance. As a leading national magazine of his day said of him and his drolleries, "Mr. Coolidge is a character; he has a pungency and flavor that most public men lack. Even if one does not admire, one cannot help having a certain liking for him."[13]

Still and all, Will Rogers was hardly alone in appreciating the fact that Coolidge used humor more for self-amusement than for any other purpose. Many who knew the Vermonter far better than Rogers fully shared this opinion. Grace Coolidge definitely did, and she more than once illustrated this point by telling of a Smith College professor who had been a missionary in what was then Palestine for nine years before he came to Smith and who subsequently lived across the street from the home of her parents. With the Coolidges temporarily in residence, the professor came to visit the future president's mother-in-law one afternoon and talked rather continuously on the porch until twilight. The future president, not particularly enthralled by the visitor, quietly withdrew into the house not long after the latter arrived. "After supper," Grace reported, "when the family was seated around the evening lamp, Mother had much to say of Professor Grant and his talk about Palestine. From behind his paper I heard my husband mumble, 'He's used to talking to the heathen.'"[14] His witticisms were most often intended for an audience of one: himself.

His use of humor served Coolidge well as self-entertainment and also had, as it did for Lincoln, the enormous if unintended further consequence of greatly increasing his popularity. But these were not the only dividends that it produced.

At the many press conferences that he held as president—Coolidge tended to offer two of these weekly, on Tuesdays and Fridays, setting a precedent for both volume and regularity in the process—the humor at least partially made up for the occasional unwillingness of the closemouthed chief executive to give his attendees information that they wanted to hear. Only a man with Coolidge's well-recognized sense of the incongruous could, for example, straight-facedly conclude a session in which he had allowed most of the presubmitted written questions to fall through his hands to the floor unanswered with the announcement, "I have no questions today" and generate entirely friendly laughter in so doing. These meetings, which a veteran newsman who attended virtually all of them described as "a forum for sly, wry humor,"[15] were marked by mutual good will between president and reporters—something which only increased the favorable treatment that Coolidge was generally accorded in print, and which, of course, pushed his popularity even higher.

The humor also more fully cemented the Coolidge marriage. Grace too had a strongly developed sense of humor, but one which was very different than her husband's. Hers was, as her biographer Ishbel Ross pointed out, "open, friendly and joyous, like herself,"[16] in definite contrast to his dry, insouciant, and often poker-faced variety, with many of its witticisms coming as a complete surprise to his listeners because of both his deadpan delivery and his general taciturnity. (Indeed, when he met her, she was a teacher at Northampton's Clarke Institute for the Deaf, and he expressed the hope, subsequently widely publicized, that having taught the deaf to hear she might now perhaps cause the mute to speak.) He smiled so infrequently that she once declared, "I have to smile for two." But she unfailingly appreciated his funny remarks, as he did hers. It was, in Ross's informed opinion, "one of the bonds that sweetened their life together."[17]

A final benefit to the thirtieth president of his use of humor—

although this one must remain strictly conjectural—was possibly that it helped Coolidge acquire a reputation for wisdom. This was probably warranted in any event: historians have generally conceded that he was one of the more intelligent of America's chief executives. But his constant ability to offer up his bone-dry aphorisms ("If you don't say anything, you won't be called on to repeat it"; "The worst thing about the presidency is that there's no chance for advancement") did nothing to lose him points on this score. George H. Mayer is one of many Coolidge scholars who have contended that the dry wit was a definite contributor to the widespread Coolidge-as-wise-man public concept.[18]

Not unlike Abraham Lincoln, whom Coolidge greatly admired (a portrait of Lincoln was the only decoration on Coolidge's presidential office wall, and he copiously quoted from his Republican predecessor in his own speeches), Coolidge long before he became a national figure established a reputation as a man who could amuse.

His fellow members of the Class of 1895 at Amherst College recognized him as a deadpan humorist and despite his equally visible shyness increasingly sought out his company in the hopes of hearing something funny. One story that circulated widely involved a breakfast at the inexpensive boardinghouse where Coolidge regularly ate all of his meals. The main item on the menu on that occasion was hash, and when he was served his allotment of it he suddenly appeared to be quite uneasy, called the waitress in from the kitchen and asked her, "Where is the dog?" Informed that the animal was in the kitchen, he straight-facedly requested that it be brought in. The waitress whistled to the dog, who immediately made his appearance, tail wagging. Coolidge murmured, "Thank you" to the waitress and began eating the hash.

He could be witty in Latin, too, as when the red-headed Vermonter converted the Amherst motto—"Terras irradient," translated as "They shall enlighten the earth"—into a personal quip, "I am enlightening the earth."

None of these Coolidge offerings were particularly sophisticated by the standards of mature adulthood. But in combination they were funny enough to get Coolidge elected by his classmates as the wittiest member of the class and, as such, the man to deliver a humorous address, the Grove Oration, on the day before graduation.

The address, which Coolidge characteristically read in a restrained, expressionless manner, was a huge success. Replete with sly references, ironies, and whimsy, it was a forerunner of what would become the full-blown Coolidge style. The words seem quite dated now, but observations by the Grove Orator that the college experience "begins with a cane rush where the undergraduates use Anglo-Saxon and ends with a diploma where the faculty use Latin— if it does not end before by a communication from the president in just plain English" and that it "may not be such a misfortune to be out of college. It is not positive proof that a diploma is a wolf because it comes to you in sheep's clothing" received much laughter and applause.

In 1897, Coolidge was admitted to the bar in Massachusetts, where he decided to remain because of its greater career opportunities, despite his abiding love for Vermont, and he quickly became active in local Republican affairs in Northampton, a stone's throw from Amherst in the picturesque Pioneer Valley.

As the young chairman of the Northampton City Council, he once presided at a Republican rally at which the governor of Massachusetts was the main speaker, and he offered the crowd the following words in introducing his party leader:

> Years ago, when I thought what I saw in the magazines was true, I read an article on "Campaigning with [Theodore] Roosevelt." It told how to preside at a rally. The rule was that when a speaker was already known to waste no time in introducing him. I now propose to try that rule on the author of that article. Watch me. His Excellency, Curtis Guild, Governor of the Commonwealth.[19]

The Coolidge irreverence continued on display as Silent Cal moved up the political ladder to the Massachusetts House of Representatives and then, following a one-year stint in 1910-11 as Northampton's mayor, to the state Senate.

After a long-winded fellow legislator in the House had prefaced each of the many arguments that he advanced in favor of a bill with the affirmative wording "It is," Coolidge rose in opposition to the same legislation, said merely, "Mr. Speaker: It isn't," and sat down to considerable appreciative laughter. The bill failed to pass.

As president of the Senate in 1914-15, he had to handle many heated sessions, but he did so calmly and diplomatically. On one occasion, an emotional senator informed a member of the other party that he could "go to hell." No less emotionally, the recipient of this insult demanded of presiding officer Coolidge, "Did you hear what he said?" "Yes," responded the future president of the nation, "I heard what he said. But I've looked up the law and you don't have to do it."

A year later, at a dinner party in Boston, a woman asked, "Oh, Mr. Coolidge, what do you do?" When Coolidge responded, "I'm the lieutenant governor," she then fawned, "How interesting. You must tell me all about it." Coolidge's rejoinder was "I just did."

He was governor when he addressed the members of Massachusetts's august Middlesex Club and began by saying, according to that organization's minutes:

> Mr. President, fellow members of the Middlesex Club, the only apology I have for again trespassing upon your hospitality is the fact that the president of this Club and myself know more about the life of General Grant than any two other men in Massachusetts. (laughter) But in order to demonstrate that it is necessary for both of us to speak. (laughter)[20]

During gubernatorial years, a newspaperman friend and fellow Republican told Coolidge the following tale from his childhood:

> When I was a boy in Springfield, another youngster met me on the street one day and asked me whether I was a Republican or a Democrat. I said I didn't know and asked what difference it made. "Well," said the other boy, "if you are a Democrat you can march in our torchlight parade and come up to my father's flag-raising and have some ice cream." I replied, "All right, I'm a Democrat."

"So you see," the journalist said to Coolidge, "I sold my first vote to the Democratic party for a dish of ice cream." Coolidge mulled the story over and then matter-of-factly replied, "Well, you got more than some of the Democrats get."[21]

Coolidge observed, well into his term as governor, "So far as I am aware, I have signed every bill which had the backing of the workers, with the exception of the bill to increase the salaries of members of the legislature."

Also as the first citizen of Massachusetts, Coolidge was asked if he had ever participated in athletic events at Amherst, to which he replied, "Some." When the questioner pressed for an elaboration, he was informed by Coolidge, "I held the stakes, mostly."

Some time after he was elected vice president, in 1920, Coolidge spoke at the Plymouth, Massachusetts, tercentenary, with the formidable and quite arrogant Senator Henry Cabot Lodge also on the program. Lodge, speaking first, informed the audience that while he had addressed them on a previous occasion and at some length, he did not think that he had "fully covered the subject, so I am coming back to discuss the further historical significance of Plymouth." When Coolidge had his turn, he announced, "I likewise was present on the occasion the senior senator so eloquently refers to and I also spoke on that occasion, but unlike him, I exhausted the subject." The crowd, a man who was there later reported, erupted at this in "a tumult of laughter and applause."[22] (The two Republicans had never really warmed to each other prior to this: Lodge had not long before been quoted as saying, "I have known Calvin Coolidge only as long as it has been necessary to know him." And that same year, just before the Republicans had assembled at their quadrennial convention, the Bay State blue blood and powerhouse of the Massachusetts delegation had airily dismissed Coolidge's prospects for receiving the presidential nomination with the words, "Nominate a man who lives in a two-family house? Never! Massachusetts is not for him.")

Also as vice president, when asked why he accepted so many invitations to luncheons and dinners, Coolidge replied, "Got to eat somewhere!"

On one occasion after Coolidge became president, a large group of visitors arrived to be photographed with him on the South grounds of the White House. Although its members had clearly been informed beforehand that Coolidge would not give a speech to them, the head of the organization, just before it was time for the party to line up, cheerfully declared to Coolidge's secretary, Everett Sanders, "I am delighted to learn that the president is to make us a little speech." Sanders replied emphatically that the man had been misinformed: Coolidge was to join them for a photograph but would not say anything. "I went in," the secretary wrote, "and explained to the president how many times I had told them he could not make a speech, so that if they called on him he would understand."

"As he started to join them," Sanders related, "the president said to me, with a smile, 'If they have not understood, I will elaborate on what you have said by saying nothing.'"[23]

Possibly no ingredient in Calvin Coolidge's personality impressed itself on the public consciousness after he emerged from the relative obscurity of the vice presidency to a position where his every move got national attention more than did his taciturnity. There was some mythology here: he actually could be quite chatty at times, particularly with family and close friends or if he were especially interested in the topic. But the native Vermonter's aversion to verbiage never really left him. What was asked about him on the night before his wedding—when a woman who had not arrived at the wedding rehearsal in time for introductions but who knew that Grace taught at the Institute for the Deaf late in the evening inquired of Coolidge's future mother-in-law, "That young man standing by himself in the corner, is he one of Grace's pupils?"—could in its essence have been asked about him in his retirement years.

Coolidge was quite aware that silence had many advantages. In addition to his "If you don't say anything, you won't be called on to repeat it" statement, he believed that "nine-tenths" of his White House visitors "want something they ought not to have. If you keep dead still, they will run down in three or four minutes. If you cough or smile they will start up all over again." Throwing in another fraction, he once observed, "Four-fifths of all our troubles in this life would disappear if we would only sit down and keep still."

In a similar vein, he had a simple explanation for a puzzle that his successor as Massachusetts governor, Channing Cox, posed to him when Cox was in Washington: how was it, Cox asked him, that Coolidge had been able, when he had that job, to see throngs of visitors each day but always wind up the day by 5:00 P.M.? He himself, Cox said, found that he was frequently still in the office even at 9:00 in the evening. To Coolidge, there was no mystery at all about the large difference: "You," he told Cox, "talk back."

Certainly, Silent Cal did nothing to discourage his reputation for closemouthedness, and at times he seemed to actively encourage it, invariably with his sly wit and possibly in a Jack Bennyesque recognition that exaggerating one or two dominant personality traits could only add to his mystique.

William Allen White, in his prize-winning biography of Coolidge, *A Puritan in Babylon*, wrote that his first experience with the president was on the wharf from which the presidential yacht, *Mayflower*, was set to embark. A cameraman was filming a silent newsreel of the Coolidge party assembled there, and, attempting to get a bit more action out of his subjects, he rather irreverently cried, "Look pleasant, and for heaven's sake say something—anything; good morning or howdy do!" Displaying a good nature worthy of Lincoln, the thirtieth chief executive dryly commented to White, "That man gets more conversation out of me than all of Congress."[24]

On another occasion, the conduit for self-parody was a physician. When Coolidge was getting a haircut while on vacation in his small Vermont hometown, the town doctor entered the barber shop, sat down to wait his turn, and asked, "Cal, did you take the pills I gave you?" Coolidge was silent for well over a minute and then responded, "Nope!" A bit later, the medical man inquired, "Are you truly feeling any better?" After another lengthy interval, Coolidge answered, "Yup!" When the barber was finished with him, Coolidge started to leave. With as much tact as he could muster, the barber asked, "Aren't you forgetting something, Mr. Coolidge?" Coolidge apologetically stammered, "I'm sorry. I forgot to pay you. I was so busy gossiping with the doctor it just slipped my mind."

Another time, the channel was none other than the stern-visaged political figure who followed Coolidge into the presidency, Herbert Hoover. En route to the 1928 Republican convention which would nominate him, Hoover stopped in Wisconsin to pay his respects to the incumbent chief executive, who was vacationing at a fishing camp. The accompanying photographers arranged for the two men to sit down together, and one of them also suggested, "Do a little talking; it will make the picture better." Acquiescing, Coolidge turned to Hoover and said something, but Hoover made no audible response. "I'm sorry," declared Coolidge, "but I cannot make him talk."

In a story that has all the appearances of apocrypha but nonetheless was authenticated by Grace Coolidge (who talked to the woman involved), a prominent society matron told Coolidge as she sat next to him at a dinner party, "Oh, Mr. Coolidge, you are so silent. But you must talk to me. I made a bet today that I could get more than two words out of you." Responding to this plea, Coolidge said, "You lose."

A similarly true, if seemingly contrived, happening took place when Coolidge was on vacation in the Black Hills. His fishing guide, to the president's infinite satisfaction, succeeded in eluding the ubiquitous Secret Service contingent, and the two men sat quietly alone at a pool not far below a small rapid. A few minutes later, they heard both shouts and splashings upstream. A canoe paddle drifted by them, followed shortly by a pillow. Not long thereafter, the hat of a Secret Service agent joined the passing parade in the water, and Coolidge, who had been casting in silence, finally had something to say: "Been expecting that."

Interviewed on the radio in California as he departed to return to Washington and asked if he had any message for his West Coast listening audience, Coolidge was silent for a moment and then said,

"Goodbye." Asked by an important U.S. senator if he thought that
the seemingly endless rain in the District of Columbia would ever
stop, he replied, "Well, it always has!" On August 2, 1927, he
stunned the nation with a statement that read in its entirety, "I do
not choose to run for president in 1928."

In March 1929, requested to say something by a radio interviewer who approached him at Washington's Union Station as he
and his wife—no longer the first family of the land—were set to board
the train that would take them back to Northampton, he said a bit
more than he had in California, but not by much: "Goodbye. I have
had a very enjoyable time in Washington." In the fall of 1932, he
made a speech in New York City in support of Hoover's second presidential term, and afterward a woman came up to him and gushed,
"Oh, Mr. Coolidge, what a wonderful address! I stood up all through
it." Coolidge in response merely shrugged his shoulders and lacon-
ically replied, "So did I."

He could be taciturn in his writing, too. The full content of a
letter that, shortly after he became president, he wrote to a
Northampton politician was: "Dear George: I know you will be
thinking about me. I am all right." An Amherst classmate, E. S. New-
ton, received the following missive: "Dear Newt: I am glad you liked
what I did. I knew you would. Cal." The daughter-in-law of a close
Coolidge friend opened her mail to find as an appreciation of her
recent hospitality a letter that read in its entirety: "My Dear Mrs.
Stearns: Thank you. Cordially, Calvin Coolidge."

Coolidge's fellow Amherst alumni, who were convening in
Madrid, Spain, and had asked him to cable a message to be read at
their dinner, got one that took no time at all to read: "Greetings.
Calvin Coolidge." (But in these and many similar cases, Coolidge
had a rival for brevity in his own father. By all accounts, Colonel
John C. Coolidge was a man of as few words as his son. He once
decided not to attend one of the many fund-raising dinners in
Calvin's honor to which he had been invited, and the members of
the dinner committee received the following reply from him: "Gentlemen: Can't come. Thank you. John Coolidge." The apple here
didn't fall very far from the tree.)

A myriad of stories about Coolidge's legendary frugality also
made the nation smile. One of them involved the former treasurer of
the Republican National Committee, who after he had become vice
president of a Washington bank paid Coolidge a visit and in the course
of it said, "Mr. President, you know the success I had in securing funds

for the Republican party. I did not ask for any recognition or thanks at the time and I do not ask for any now. But it would do me an enormous amount of good and be a feather in my cap if you would become a depositor in my bank. Will you do it?" The president thought the matter over in silence for literally several minutes and then responded, "Couldn't you make me an honorary depositor?"

Coolidge did, however, make a real deposit in the bank. Subsequently, he and a friend were walking by the bank building and heard a loud noise emanating from inside. "What in hell is that noise?" the friend asked. Coolidge calmly answered, "That deposit of mine drawing interest."

New Jersey Senator Joseph Frelinghuysen enjoyed telling about the time he informed the tightfisted president that he had had some high-quality Havana cigars made especially for him in Cuba, but that it would take a while longer to produce the lithographed bands bearing the initials C.C., which were to go around the cigars. Coolidge mulled over this information for a moment and then said, "Well, Joe, you know I don't smoke the bands."

Coolidge was no spendthrift when it came to governmental money, either. He hated twenty-one–gun salutes—not only because they made his white collie howl but because, he announced, "It costs money to fire so many guns. So I have the band play the 'Star Spangled Banner'." Urged to spend more on military aviation, he asked his cabinet, "Why can't we just buy one airplane and have all the pilots take turns?"

He also saw no reason to part with the financial resources at his disposal if even the remotest justification dictated otherwise. Alfred E. Smith, the presidential candidate of the Democrats in 1928, once related that when he was governor of New York he told Coolidge that he'd like to sell the Erie Canal to the federal government. "It was costing New York state a lot of money," Smith said,

> but it would be a good buy for the Federal Government as part of a ship canal from the Great Lakes to tidewater. Mr. Coolidge said he had heard some talk about the project.
>
> After a while our conversation got around to the measures we had been taking in the state to assure an adequate water supply to the vast, growing population of New York City. I pointed out that some day the state would be faced by a serious problem in supplying water to the people of New York.
>
> The President looked at me with a twinkle in his eye and said, "Why don't you sell *them* the Erie Canal?"[25]

Coolidge was on the side of U.S. taxpayers when it came to a major renovation of the White House during his presidency. Inspecting the mansion's attic with the chief architect and the contractor one day, he was informed by the former that the rafter and girder timbers, which had been badly charred from the fire that the British set during the War of 1812 had, because of safety considerations, to be replaced. The architect wanted to know whether the replacement should be with wood or with more costly steel beams. Coolidge took a careful look at the burned wood and then said, "All right. Put in the steel beams and send the bill to the king of England."

Nor did even the smallest of expenses escape his notice. After he and his aide Starling returned from their regular afternoon walks, he generally took the subordinate to the White House butler's pantry and made two sandwiches of strong Vermont cheese, one for himself and one for Starling. He cut the cheese with great care and, if the two sandwiches did not appear to be equal, he would carefully remove enough cheese from the bigger one to make them balance. One day he declared to Starling, "I'll bet no other president of the United States ever made cheese sandwiches for you." "No," the aide agreed. "It is a great honor." Coolidge added a bit gloomily, "I have to furnish the cheese too."

On the eve of his retirement from public life, Coolidge was amused by a suggestion that he be sent to Scotland to give a course on thrift at the University of Aberdeen.

With his propensity for silence, Coolidge was hardly a Lincoln, telling anecdotes at the drop of a hat. But he did on occasion offer a humorous tale.

He liked to tell a story that involved himself and a small fire that took place at Washington's New Willard Hotel when, as vice president, he resided there with his family. The management, on the theory that it was better to be safe than sorry, ordered all of the guests to leave their rooms. After it was clear that the fire had been extinguished, Coolidge started to go up the stairs to return to his suite and was confronted by a stern fire marshal, who asked him, "Who are you?" The nation's second-in-command replied, "I'm the vice president" and was told, "All right, go ahead." But before Coolidge could proceed much further, the fire officer apparently had second thoughts and asked, "What are you vice president of?" When the future president responded, "I am vice president of the United States," the marshal snapped at him, "Come right down. I thought you were the vice president of the hotel."

As president, he announced that a rumor then making the rounds concerning the imminent retirement of the head of the Veterans Bureau was perhaps a mistake—Coolidge's Prohibition enforcer at the time had a similar name—and that this situation reminded him of the time that the governor of Pennsylvania asked a man on a street in a Pennsylvania town the whereabouts of the local spaghetti factory. The man said that he didn't know, but he then followed the governor up the street and said, "Perhaps you mean the noodle factory." The governor said, well perhaps it was the noodle factory. And the man said, "Well, I don't know where that is either."

Another story, which Coolidge was originally reminded of after the Boston police strike, when he as governor was informed that the new members of the police force in that city were particularly competent, but which he retold several times thereafter, involved a mouse which "happened to find in the cellar a liquor barrel with a leak in it. The mouse began lapping, and lapping, and pretty soon he sat up, looked around and squeaked fiercely, 'Where in hell's that cat?'"

Asked his opinion of a new book, he was reminded, he said, of a purportedly true story of a British reviewer of books, by reputation a great authority, who said he never read a book before he reviewed it because it might prejudice him.

Generally speaking, news reporters were fond of Coolidge despite his tendency to be as stingy with news as he was with money. At times, as when he was undecided as to whom to appoint as his secretary of the navy, he asked reporters for advice. On one occasion he even suggested to them that they put on rubbers to insulate their feet against the considerable early morning dew. And, of no small significance, he joked with them—despite his reserve, easily and often. If his press conferences sometimes lacked genuine newsworthiness, they were invariably fun to attend.

The White House press conference was originated by Theodore Roosevelt in the early years of the twentieth century, and every American chief executive since then has exposed himself to its challenges. Historian Arthur Schlesinger, Jr., has pointed out that it is the "great test of spontaneity for Presidents"[26] since presidential utterances in almost any other context can be scripted in advance (with or without, of course, the help of speechwriters). Some chief executives, not surprisingly, have met this test far better than others. (Lincoln, who met newsmen only in small private sessions and was never quoted directly by them, would quite likely have fared extremely well with his ready wit and huge supply of anecdotes, but we shall never know.)

Coolidge excelled at these conferences. His subtle wit was in evidence, for that matter, even when there was no news at all. During his 1924 presidential campaign, which he waged as the White House incumbent, Coolidge was asked by one reporter, "Have you any statement on the campaign?" He replied, "No." At the same news conference, another journalist queried, "Can you tell us something about the world situation?" The response from the interviewee was another "No." When a third member of the Fourth Estate asked, "Any information about Prohibition?" he received the same one-word answer. As the frustrated newsmen started to walk away, Coolidge looked at them and said with great seriousness, "Now remember—don't quote me."

Similarly, in answer to a question at another meeting with reporters about his prospects in that same presidential election, he said, "I haven't any specific reports about any states. My reports indicate that I shall probably carry Northampton. That is about as far as I can go into details."

When there was even a scintilla of new information to be given out at these press conferences, it was frequently conveyed with even more of a sly flair.

Regarding his delayed appointments of two commissioners for the District of Columbia, Coolidge announced that he had two men in mind but was taking extra time to investigate some protests that had been lodged against each person's nomination once their names had surfaced. He added, however, that he didn't think the protests had much validity. The men had been officeholders before, he pointed out, and it

> would be very unusual that [public servants] would be in office ... without there being two opinions as to whether they functioned properly. I know that, because I was Mayor of Northampton, and after I had given a very excellent administration for a year there was a division of opinion as to whether I ought to be re-elected.[27]

He didn't think that he would be able to go to the dedication of a new park near Hammond, Indiana, he declared on another occasion.

> A very large delegation [from Hammond] came down this morning in a special train to invite me, ... so large that I suggested to them that I might make them a speech here and save myself the trouble of going out there, but they seemed to want to make speeches themselves

down here, which they did, leaving me to make a proper response at some future occasion.[28]

Asked about his plans while he was on vacation in Superior, Wisconsin, he replied, "I am expecting to go over to Duluth some day.... I don't know just when I shall go. I have been so busy at the lodge catching fish—there are 45,000 out there—I haven't caught them all yet, but I have them all pretty well intimidated." Queried about rumors circulating that he might also go hunting in Kentucky, he said, "I think the idea that I might go hunting in Kentucky arose from the fact that the bird dog that was given me in Superior I had Colonel Starling send down to a friend of his in Kentucky, who is a very fine trainer of dogs. I presume that all the hunting I will do in Kentucky will be done by proxy through this dog." As for his working plans on a Vermont holiday, "I don't know whether I will take the report of the Tariff Commission on the sugar schedule to Vermont with me or not. It is quite a voluminous document, I find. I shall take it with me mentally."

After the press was informed at another conference that Coolidge was having several departments undertake assessments of the Alien Property Bill, the verbatim stenographic transcript reported:

> PRESIDENT: The Treasury Department reports to me that it isn't so good a bill as the one that they prepared, but I have not yet received their final report on it. There is one thing in the bill that hasn't been overlooked. Three salaries have been raised.
> PRESS: Could you say what they were, Mr. President?
> PRESIDENT: I think they are two drafting clerks of the House and the Senate that have been put on the same salary as the Solicitor General of the United States, and some person in the Treasury Department. Those are all people that have access to the Ways and Means Committee of the House and whenever any bill goes through the Ways and Means Committee of any particular importance it usually has a way of raising somebody's salary. So you can see that the Alien Property bill has some merit in it. [Stenographer's note: laughter.]
> PRESS: Was there any other feature?
> PRESIDENT: I think that is the outstanding feature. [Stenographer's note: laughter.][29]

Some of Coolidge's quips on religion received wide publicity in the print media, over the nascent radio waves, and by word of mouth, and served only to increase his reputation for drollery.

When a Baptist preacher dined at the Coolidge home in Massachusetts prior to holding a revival meeting and declined almost everything that was offered to him at the table on the grounds that not eating improved his preaching, Coolidge informed his wife after attending the meeting that the preacher "might as well have et."

Coolidge once told the Reverend Jason N. Pierce, the pastor of the Congregational church in Washington at which he regularly worshiped while vice president and president, "I attended the dedication of All Souls Church last week and heard your namesake preach." "I know you must have heard a fine sermon," Pierce graciously responded. As the cleric then directed his conversational attention to Mrs. Coolidge, the president reached out, touched Pierce's arm, and said, "It was two sermons!"

The deeply religious man from Vermont (Coolidge said in a 1924 address to the National Republican Club, "It is hard to see how a great man can be an atheist" and another time asserted that the "classic of all classics is the Bible") told a newspaperman friend about a speech that he had heard given by a rabble-rousing Missouri politician, in which the speaker concluded, "And now, my friends, you have heard my story, and you can vote for me or go to hell!" "It was," deadpanned Silent Cal, "a difficult alternative."

One famous story is not based on fact. It centered on a morning worship service at which the president had supposedly been present. He reported back to his wife when he returned home that the minister's sermon had been on the subject of sin. Mrs. Coolidge questioned to her husband as to what the clergyman had had to say on the topic, and Coolidge responded that "he was against it." The first lady wrote about this tale, "I happened to be present the first time the president heard it. He laughed mildly and remarked that it would be funnier if it were true."[30]

By all accounts, the Coolidges were devoted to each other (in 1929, he wrote about Grace in his autobiography, "For almost a quarter of a century she has borne with my infirmities and I have rejoiced in her graces"), but this hardly precluded them from engaging in much good-natured mutual teasing.

At one weekend dinner party on the presidential yacht, *Mayflower*, overnight guests Mrs. Dwight W. Morrow and Mrs. Frank Kellogg flanked the president, who in the course of the long meal said little to either of them. At breakfast the next morning, Coolidge asked his spouse, "And where are my two fair ladies?" Her answer was, "Exhausted by your conversation of last evening!"

She could imitate his mannerisms to perfection and often, to the considerable amusement of various audiences, did. She once asked him as he blew a whistle to summon the racoon that he kept as a White House pet and sometimes wrapped around his neck as he walked around the residence, "What's the matter, Poppa, don't your teeth fit tonight?"

On his part, he had a much-in-character response for her when, as a young bride, she was talked by a glib salesman into paying the then-enormous price of eight dollars for a book on medical information for laypersons, *Our Family Physician*. Somewhat embarrassed by her absence of sales resistance, she didn't say a word to her husband about the purchase but simply left the publication on the parlor table. One day, she looked inside and discovered that someone had written on the inside cover, anonymously but in handwriting that she immediately recognized as that of the other member of the household, "This work suggests no cure for a sucker."

Grace enjoyed telling the story about the first time that she tried to bake an apple pie. The finished product turned out to be quite hard, and neither she nor her husband consumed much of it at dinner. Later that same evening, two friends paid them a visit, and the same pie was served to them. After they had eaten their servings, Coolidge straight-facedly asked them, "Don't you think the road commissioner would be willing to pay my wife something for her recipe for pie crust?"

Coolidge also had a wry suggestion years later when First Lady Grace's portrait was being painted by the distinguished artist Howard Chandler Christy with the Coolidges' white collie in the foreground. Christy had asked her to wear a red dress so that there would be some beneficial color contrast, and Grace asked the president for his opinion on the matter. He, preferring one of her white dresses, declared, "If it's contrast you want, why not wear white and paint the dog red?"

Again in the White House, she was not happy about the inadequate notice that she was often given about events that she was expected to attend and sometimes even preside over, and another memorable Calvin Coolidge comment was rendered. She chose one morning at the breakfast table, while her husband had his head buried in a newspaper, as the occasion to register her complaint and said to him, "Calvin, look at me. I find myself facing every day a large number of engagements about which I know nothing, and I wish you'd have your Secret Service prepare for me each day a list

of the engagements for the coming week so that I can follow it."
The nation's chief executive peered at his wife from behind a corner
of his paper and responded, "Grace, we don't give out that information promiscuously."

If historians awarded a prize for Best Practical Joker among U.S.
presidents, Coolidge would probably be a hands-down winner.
Examples of his impishness along these lines abound.

Early one morning, with the prominently bearded and rather
self-important Judge Charles Evans Hughes an overnight guest at the
White House, Coolidge rang for the presidential valet and barber,
John Mays, and told him to knock at Hughes's door and "see if the
judge was ready for a shave and a haircut." According to the valet,
the president "did not move a muscle of his face," and Mays immediately submitted the matter to close Coolidge friend and key advisor Frank Stearns, along with the opinion that "the Hughes chin had
always been sacred from the touch of steel." Stearns responded that
an executive order was an executive order, not to be tampered with.
Mays thereupon, he later confided to a Republican National Committee member, "knocked at the door of Judge Hughes, but ...
knocked very softly" and was relieved when he was not admitted to
the room.[31]

Nor was this the only time that the humorless Mays was the
victim of a presidential prank. On another occasion, Coolidge
instructed his underling to fill a bucket half full of water, put yellow
wax beans in it, and then get a rag and rub the brown spots off the
beans. Mays dutifully commenced doing this and after wrestling with
the project for some time dolefully told a colleague, "Not a single
spot has come off." The colleague—recognizing the mischievous
Coolidge hand at work—instructed him correctly to use a knife.

Herbert Hoover was particularly fond of recalling a dinner that
he had with Coolidge in the state dining room. Throughout the meal,
the man whom Hoover was to follow as president was visibly dis-
tracted, and near its end Coolidge revealed the cause of the diversion by asking his guest, "Mr. Hoover, don't you think the light has
been a little too shiny on Mr. John Quincy Adams's head?" Without waiting for an answer, Coolidge ordered a servant to get a
stepladder and rubbed a rag in some fireplace ashes. He then
mounted the ladder, reached over to the nearby Adams statue, and
with the rag blackened out the large bald area on the top of the
Adams head. (Some years later, with the blackness still fully visible,
Hoover felt obliged to apologize to his secretary of the navy, Charles

Francis Adams, for this act of disrespect that had been accorded his forebear.)

At one of his presidential breakfasts for the members of Congress, the thirtieth chief executive poured coffee and cream into his saucer. Some of his guests, although surprised, concluded that their host was indicating to them his preferred way of serving a small café au lait and did exactly the same thing. Coolidge then leaned down and placed the saucer on the floor for his dog, leaving the legislators highly embarrassed and with now-unusable saucers sitting in front of them.

Another White House breakfast was also memorable in this regard. In late 1924, with major army and navy appropriation bills pending in Congress, Coolidge invited a group of high-ranking generals and admirals over for the meal. Logically assuming that their commander in chief wanted to confer with them because of the upcoming legislation, each of the military and naval luminaries did a considerable amount of advance preparation, and all arrived at the presidential mansion with reams of written documents to back up their intended oral comments. At the breakfast itself, the president ate his grapefruit, sausage, buckwheat cakes, and fried potatoes and drank his coffee in almost total silence, with not a mention of the impending bill. Only after much time had elapsed in this fashion did the guests—who inevitably had to trigger themselves whatever conversation was to take place—start to realize that an idiosyncratic joke was being played on them. When they were back on the White House steps, according to a general who attended the event, they "burst into gales of laughter."[32]

Some practical jokes were regularly repeated, presumably on the theory that if they were good for self-amusement once they were good for self-amusement more than once. The Secret Service man assigned as Coolidge's bodyguard reported that when the president was in his office, if "the mood suited him he would press the buzzer which notified everyone that he was on his way to the White House. Then, while ushers, policemen, doormen, and elevator operators were rushing about getting things ready and snapping to attention, we would stroll out West Executive Avenue and leave them."[33] At other times, Coolidge would ring all of the bells on his desk for the sole purpose of seeing his entire staff race into the presidential office. Sometimes the man from Vermont would ring for the White House elevator, then quickly walk down the stairs. Sometimes, he would elude his bodyguard by hiding in the police box at the East entrance of the White House (the Secret Service man once turned the tables on his boss, secure in the knowledge that Coolidge would not take umbrage at his action, by hiding in the same box himself).

Once, at a meeting of the Thomas Jefferson Centennial Commission, which was attended by congressional leaders and others, Coolidge read a telegram that he had received from financier Felix Warburg, a Jew, offering to contribute $100,000 to the Monticello fund if the same amount would be subscribed by a Catholic and a Protestant. He then, without a trace of a smile, announced, "I will authorize Senator [Joseph T.] Robinson to notify Vice President [Charles G.] Dawes that it is the sense of this meeting that he donate a like amount."

As many of the remarks attributed to him have already indicated, a pronounced strain of droll self-irreverence was as much a part of Calvin Coolidge's makeup as it was of Abraham Lincoln's. Silent Cal took his career seriously and was invariably quite conscious of the dignity of each elected position that he filled. But for all of his professional successes, he never overestimated his personal assets, and he was entirely capable of laughing at himself—with the deadpan expression that rarely left him.

Shortly after he had been inaugurated as vice president, he received a dinner invitation from a Washingtonian whose name rang no bell whatsoever with him. He thereupon asked his secretary if the name was familiar to *him*. The secretary said that it was not and added that the name was not listed in the *Social Register*, either. "No conclusion can be drawn from that," countered the new second citizen of the land, "I've been in it myself only half an hour."

As president, he argued that his long, deep afternoon naps in the White House were definitely in the national interest because he was unable to initiate anything while he was asleep.

When a portrait artist was painting him in a light suit (after convincing Coolidge that the black suit that he had worn for his initial sitting made him look "like a parson") and remarked to the president that he looked quite distinguished in it, Coolidge said, "This is a very distinguished suit."

In 1924, when a visiting congressman asked Coolidge for a photograph and explained, "I have one, but it was taken when you were lieutenant governor," the visitor was informed, "I don't see what you want another for. I'm using the same face."

As for his ability to produce results that other men couldn't, he viewed himself in perspective here also. On one occasion, he visited a tribe of Native Americans on a reservation where there had been a complete absence of rain for months. Nothing that either professional rainmakers or the Indian medicine men had attempted had done a thing to alleviate the devastating conditions, and the crops that had not already been destroyed now stood themselves on the brink of disaster. Coolidge got up to assure his gloomy audience, "Do not think that I in Washington have not been worrying about your lack of rain, and wondering what I could do to help you." At almost that exact moment, the skies—so uncharitable for all of those months—suddenly darkened, and a huge deluge thoroughly soaked everyone present, including Coolidge. Looking over the unexpected torrent, the president quipped, "Gosh, I didn't know I had it in me."

In his autobiography, which he wrote after leaving Washington and returning to Northampton, Coolidge rather characteristically noted:

> Nearly every young man who happens to be elected a member of his state legislature is pointed to by his friends and his local newspaper as on his way to the White House.
>
> My own experience in this respect did not differ from that of others. But I never took such suggestions seriously, as I was convinced in my own mind that I was not qualified to fill the exalted office of President....
>
> When I began to be seriously mentioned by some of my friends [in late 1919, after he had been chosen governor of Massachusetts for the second time by the second largest gubernatorial landslide in Massachusetts history] as the Republican candidate for President, it became apparent that there were many others who shared the same opinion as to my fitness which I had so long entertained.[34]

The man who succeeded Warren Harding also wrote in this volume that in the earliest days of his ascension to the presidency—a mere ten months before his party was scheduled to meet in convention to nominate a candidate for 1924—he received a good deal of praise from many people and that most of the praise was in his opinion quite sincere. "But," he went on,

> there were some quarters in the opposing party where it was thought it would be good strategy to encourage my party to nominate me, thinking that it would be easy to accomplish my defeat. I do not know whether their judgment was wrong or whether they overdid the operation, so that when they stopped speaking in my praise they found they could not change the opinion of the people which they had helped to create.

In March 1929, with Hoover all set to be inaugurated as president, the Coolidges had to move out of the White House, logistically no easy task. In addition to all of the possessions that they had brought into the Executive Mansion following Harding's death, more than 150 large boxes of gifts had been received by the presidential couple in the interval. "I am having," Coolidge commented, "rather more trouble in getting out of the White House than I had getting in."

But he professed, probably with total sincerity, to greatly prefer his new status as ex-president to his old position of president. Not long after his return to Massachusetts, he had occasion to fill out a card to be dispatched with the payment of his annual dues to the National Press Club. He furnished his name and address and then, in the space asking for "occupation," accurately wrote, "retired." The form solicited one more point of information, presumably voluntary, but Coolidge tried to accommodate it as well. On the line calling for "remarks," he wrote, "Glad of it."

In the less than four years remaining to him, this last president never to fly in an airplane was relatively inactive, but in addition to writing his autobiography he did serve on a few company boards and charitable committees. On one of the latter, a fellow committee member was former New York Governor Alfred E. Smith, and Smith later recounted a story that possibly captured the sly and insouciant Coolidge humor as much as did any other:

> In the course of our deliberations, a Jewish home for children was proposed as one of the beneficiaries. The man who was representing it, appearing before our committee, said to me, "By the way, Governor, you know So-and-So—he's deeply interested in the home. You know him well—you play poker with him." Without smiling or even looking up, Coolidge asked, "Is that why he needs the money?"[36]

The years have not been kind to the quiet man from Vermont. Historians have regularly placed him in the lowest third of all presidents, usually in an undistinguished just-above-bottom neighborhood inhabited by the likes of John Tyler, Zachary Taylor, Millard Fillmore, Andrew Johnson, and Gerald Ford. If he left office with one of the highest approval ratings of any U.S. chief executive and was successful by most yardsticks in his own time of peace and prosperity, he stands as a definite failure when viewed from our vantage point. If he had stood for office in 1928, in an election that he could easily have won, he would today presumably bear the stigma of having caused the Great Depression which is, instead, the property of Herbert Hoover.

Amid these circumstances, it is easy to forget how appealing the Coolidge persona, which was so solidly anchored to humor, really was to his nation. Millions of Americans, indeed people the world over, loved the Coolidge anecdotes and gleefully passed them on, often with their best imitations of the president's flat northern New England accent. That some of the stories were not based on actuality—although most of the most widely circulated ones seem to have been quite genuine—is absolutely irrelevant here. All of them added to the legend of an unforgettable personage who could amuse the electorate, the media, his wife, and—above all, in Coolidge's scheme of things—himself as few leaders have ever been able to do.

Coolidge once said, "Whenever I do indulge my sense of humor, it always gets me into trouble." But there is no evidence at all either that this observation was valid or that he really believed it. On the contrary, the thirtieth president derived immense benefit from the indulgence, a fact that he appears to have recognized as he quite consciously and steadily added to the trove of Coolidge anecdotes. There was no visible downside for Silent Cal as he displayed what was by far the most understated wit ever seen in a president.

CHAPTER 3

FRANKLIN D. ROOSEVELT

In pronounced contrast to that of Calvin Coolidge, Franklin D. Roosevelt's light touch was, much of the time, not at all subtle. Copiously displayed in most of his public appearances—speeches, press conferences, and radio "Fireside Chats" (a Roosevelt innovation)—FDR's humor tended to the rather ponderous use of sarcasm and ridicule when it was not being just plain corny. Much of it, when perused on the printed page today, seems both stilted and remarkably unfunny. It is hard to believe that lines such as the following brought the house down when they were delivered:

> You have heard for six years that I was about to plunge the Nation into war; ... that I was driving the Nation into bankruptcy; and that I breakfasted every morning on a dish of "grilled millionaire."... Actually I am an exceedingly mild mannered person—a practitioner of peace—a believer in the capitalistic system, and for my breakfast a devotee of scrambled eggs.[1]

Or that "this character Roosevelt was a villain. He combined the worst features of Ivan the Terrible, Machiavelli, Judas Iscariot, Henry VIII, Charlotte Corday and Jesse James.... I began to believe it myself. Didn't I read it in the columns of our great papers?"[2] did likewise, as did a myriad of comparable Rooseveltian efforts.

Although the two words in parentheses at the end of the following official excerpt from a typical Roosevelt press conference might cause a reader of today to question whether or not the assembled journalists were smoking something, they presumably represent an accurate portrayal of what did happen at the time:

> Q: Mr. President, does the ban on the highways [as part of the national defense program] include the parking shoulders?

FDR: Parking *shoulders*?

Q: Yes, widening out on the edge, supposedly to let the civilians park as the military goes by.

FDR: You don't mean necking places? [*Prolonged laughter*][3]

The same could be said for the "burst of laughter" that Roosevelt biographer James MacGregor Burns reports followed FDR's press conference statement that he was "trying to get across the idea that, if we have the right kind of people, the party label does not mean so very much," but that concept, of course, had "to be kept off the record."[4] We are also puzzled by the mirth that Roosevelt elicited in another media audience when, having been asked during his final White House campaign if he were going to wear his "navy cape" during the following day's predicted rain, he replied, "I suppose so" and then—dodging a sensitive question from another reporter—declared, "I'm tough this morning."

You had, to be there. But for those who were there, Roosevelt's warm personality and enormous self-confidence combined with a superb sense of timing, a dazzling smile, an infectious laugh, and a sunny disposition to generate a maximum appreciation of his ventures into humor (which came to be expected of him in each appearance).

The propensities to smile and laugh were as much a part of Roosevelt's personality as the urge to tell amusing stories was of Lincoln's or wry straight-facedness was of Coolidge's. His smile, a student of FDR's administration has asserted, "could tame a grizzly bear. It was a formidable asset and he employed it on all he came into contact with." Ira R. T. Smith, supervisor of the White House mail room under several presidents, said of Roosevelt, "He could turn on his ... smile as if somebody had pressed a button and sent a brilliant beam from a lighthouse out across the sea—shining on whatever ship happened to be there." FDR's laugh was no less a trademark: when one visitor to the executive residence in 1933 asked First Lady Eleanor Roosevelt, "Where is the president?" she responded, "Wherever you hear the laugh." "So," the visitor subsequently wrote, "I went in there, and there he was."[5]

Roosevelt also had excellent powers of mimicry and could convincingly parody the voices of such disparate individuals as a supposedly inebriated Supreme Court justice, Felix Frankfurter; his Scandinavian-accented War Production Board chief, William Knudsen; and his Indiana-born 1940 Republican opponent, Wendell

Willkie, among many others. He could tell jokes in French as well as in English. At least one authority in the field thinks that of all American presidents only Lincoln was a superior raconteur and storyteller.[6] Despite his tendency toward corniness and bad puns, FDR was at times capable of displaying impressive quick-wittedness. He was an accomplished tease and an inveterate prankster.

Much of Roosevelt's humor involved, as indicated by the first two samples offered above, negative remarks about himself—perhaps manifesting his pride in the fact that he was important enough to *be* reviled (as well as, in other quarters, revered).

He often referred to his favorite cartoon, which he had hung just outside his bedroom door at his Catoctin Hills, Maryland, weekend retreat. Appearing in the November 1938 issue of *Esquire* magazine, it shows a little girl running to tell her mother, who is standing in the doorway of an expensive-looking house, "Look, Mama. Wilfred wrote a bad word!" The bad word that Wilfred had written on the sidewalk in front of the house was "Roosevelt."

The architect of the New Deal also enjoyed alluding to a *New Yorker* magazine cartoon by Peter Arno, which subsequently became quite famous. It depicted a group of excited patricians yelling to a fellow aristocrat through the windows of what was obviously a highly selective gentlemen's club, "Come along. We're going to the Trans-Lux [a popular movie theater of the day, noted for newsreels] to hiss Roosevelt." When FDR was originally shown this by his press secretary, he scribbled on it one of his favorite words of approval, "Grand."

According to one close advisor, Roosevelt's favorite story involved a commuter in an affluent Republican suburb who each morning bought a paper from a newsboy, glanced at the front page, then gave it back to the newsboy, and boarded his train. Finally, the boy asked him why he only glanced at the front page and he was told, "I'm interested in the obituary notices." When the boy objected, "But they're way over on page twenty-four, and you never look at them," the customer responded, "Boy, the son of a bitch I'm interested in will be on page one."[7]

Another story that the nation's thirty-second chief executive loved and often retold was relayed to him by the governor of Pennsylvania. It concerned four wealthy members of Philadelphia's plush and very conservative Rittenhouse Club: the vice president of the Pennsylvania Railroad, the head of a major oil company, a retired millionaire art collector, and the president of a trust company. They were sitting in the club's opulent library one evening in 1935 drinking cocktails and cursing the liberal Roosevelt and his New Deal. At some point in these festivities, one of them turned on the elaborate, mahogany-mounted radio in the room, and the voice of FDR himself came on. He was making a speech at a stadium in Atlanta and, in it, mocking the criticisms of his administration by "my rich friends in their overstuffed armchairs in their well-stocked clubs." "My God," exclaimed one of the four, "do you suppose that blankety blank could have overheard us?"

Other FDR ventures into humor, invariably also offered with the winning Roosevelt smile and geniality, pivoted on pro–Roosevelt feelings.

Roosevelt asserted, during the 1936 presidential campaign, that he knew what he would do if he were the Republican nominee running against him: "I would say: 'I am for social security, work relief, etc., etc. But the Democrats cannot be entrusted with the administration of these fine ideals.' I would cite chapter and verse on ... inefficiency—and there's plenty of it—as there is bound to be in such a vast, emergency program." He concluded that "the more I think about it, the more I think I could lick myself." He explained that he had chosen the occasion of a Teamsters Union banquet to announce that he would run for an unprecedented fourth term because "Teamsters have such big hands," and he could consequently count on receiving the maximum amount of applause there. Speaking about his budget message to a group of White House correspondents, he said that he was somewhat like the professor who told his class, "I know very little about this but you know less." Expanding on this theme, he announced, "From personal experience I know that seventy percent of you, at the maximum, know the difference between a dollar and a dime, so I might as well go through with [his explanation of the actually quite complicated budget]."

As the tenor of those informal last remarks as well as the press conference comments quoted earlier might imply, FDR's talent to amuse (although the quips and anecdotes were rarely original, having been written or at least collected by his staff) helped him—like Coolidge—develop a particularly positive relationship with the media, and consequently, he garnered favorable reporting. In Roosevelt's case this generated an additional dividend: as is well known now, but was not nearly as fully appreciated in FDR's pre-television era, he was a paraplegic who because of a polio attack in 1921 had to use a wheelchair for the remaining twenty-four years of his life.

The pro–Roosevelt reporting fraternity was only too pleased to coop-
erate with him in concealing his handicap ("No movies of me getting out of the automobile, please, boys!"), and when he fell
full-length in front of thousands on the rostrum at the 1936 Democratic National Convention at Philadelphia's Franklin Field, no public reference to the mishap appeared anywhere. So well-concealed
from publicity was Roosevelt's disability that even the otherwise
well-informed Joseph Stalin apparently had no idea that his American counterpart was unable to walk until he met him at a conference in Teheran, Iran, in late 1943.

People who dealt with FDR at close range, of course, were aware
of his shriveled legs and confinement to a wheelchair. But his use of
humor helped immeasurably in this regard, too. His constant intro-
duction of the jocular into conversation tended to divert the attention
of his visitors from his physical condition to his extraordinarily ebul-
lient and happy personality. "It was almost," Peter Collier has pointed
out, "an exercise in the magician's act of misdirection—creating an illu-
sion ... that altered perceptions and affected his social reality itself."[8]

For Roosevelt, as for Lincoln, humor additionally—as has
already been indicated above—constituted an avenue for sidestepping
sensitive or tough issues. This was especially true of FDR's many
press conferences. (He held a staggering total of 337 of these in his
first term alone, 374 in his second, and he uttered an estimated five
million press conference words in the course of his twelve years in
office.) Frequently, as one media expert summarized the situation:

> He could avoid a difficult question with a quip that threw the whole
> room into laughter—often being abetted by several reporters whose
> main purpose, in the words of one of their more serious colleagues,
> "seems to be to say something so cute that the President doubles up
> with laughter." In either event, before the author of the embarrassing
> question might be tempted to follow it up, the conference was likely
> to have moved off in a different direction.[9]

Another person familiar with these FDR diversionary techniques
once admiringly declared, "I never met anyone who showed greater
capacity for avoiding a direct answer while giving the questioner a
feeling he *had* been answered."[10]

On occasion, Roosevelt even went further in his detouring by
not really listening to the question in the first place. In Eleanor Roosevelt's opinion, "Franklin had a way, when he did not want to hear

what somebody had to say, of telling stories and talking about something quite different."[11]

Sometimes the former governor of New York would tell a long and often quite irrelevant humorous anecdote simply to buy time when he didn't know what course of action to follow. While he spun his tale, the decision itself would often evolve. As journalist John Gunther later phrased it, on many such occasions "the external monologue and the inward processes of thought proceeded concurrently and concluded at exactly the same time."[12]

Often, the man whose presidency began during the greatest depression that the country has ever known and was ended by his death during the most costly foreign war in U.S. history told a joke or essayed an amusing anecdote simply as a tension reducer. "At a time when Americans wanted good cheer," biographer Burns has noted, Roosevelt "filled the White House with laughter."[13]

Such activity certainly gave him a personal outlet for stress alleviation: he was, his national emergencies notwithstanding, among the most unruffled and serene chief executives of all time. The humor also tended to be contagious: as Roosevelt's primary speech writer, Samuel I. Rosenman, later reported, "Those working with him were never afraid to interrupt or tell him a joke or a funny story, even during a serious discussion. He knew the benefits of that kind of brief relaxation [for all concerned]—how it relieved the strain and tension of hard, concentrated work." FDR's levity, Rosenman added admiringly, made these serious sessions "pleasant, light and enjoyable experiences."[14]

Above all, perhaps, Roosevelt recognized that humor brought perspective. As he told the assemblage of journalists at one of Washington's avowedly jocular Gridiron Club dinners: "It is good for me to be here. It is good, I think, for the Chief Justice to be here. It is good for Governor [Alf] Landon [Roosevelt's 1936 Republican opponent in the contest for the presidency] to be here."

> It is good for Republicans and Democrats and Socialists and Communists to sit at these tables and laugh at themselves and at each other. The Gridiron Club offers twice a year the largest of mirrors for us all to look at ourselves in.... Who of us cannot feel a spirit of humble gratitude for Providence that our national destinies are emerging from the strains of recent times with our American tradition of tolerance and perspective unimpaired?

Unlike both Lincoln and Coolidge, Roosevelt seems to have developed no reputation at all for being an especially humorous person before he became president. Even if he had utilized levity only one-tenth as frequently as he did, he would nonetheless quite probably have quickly been perceived as an amusing man if only because his immediate predecessor, Herbert Hoover, so totally lacked anything that remotely approached lightheartedness.

Of Hoover, sculptor Gutzon Borglum said, "If you put a rose in Hoover's hand it would wilt," and Hoover's secretary of state remarked of the gloom that surrounded his boss, "It was like sitting in a bath of ink to sit in his room."[15] FDR's son James never forgot or forgave a comment that the Republican chief executive made to his father when the two Roosevelts paid a courtesy call on Hoover the day before Roosevelt was to be inaugurated. After the strained meeting ended, Roosevelt thoughtfully said, "Mr. President, as you know it is rather difficult for me to move in a hurry. It takes me a little while to get up and I know how busy you must be, sir, so please don't wait for me." Hoover got up, directed a severe look at the incoming chief executive, and announced dourly, "Mr. Roosevelt, after you have been president for a while, you will learn that the president of the United States waits for no one." Then he walked out of the room.

Roosevelt was the exact opposite. He on one occasion told reporters, "I have a cheerful disposition, that is the only thing that is left," rarely complained about anything (and never about his physical condition), and more than once when asked about the enormous economic and foreign relations challenges that faced his administration replied, "If you had spent two years in bed trying to wiggle your big toe, after that anything else would seem easy!" Perhaps no less should have been expected of a man who could roar with laughter upon noticing that on a sign outside of his Hyde Park, New York, hometown, which accurately proclaimed the St. James Church to be "The Church of the President," someone had appended the words "(Formerly God's)." Hoover could brighten up a room considerably merely by leaving it, but Roosevelt never took life too seriously.

FDR presumably was engaging in hyperbole when, in April 1937, he wrote to the U.S. ambassador to France that he hadn't "a care in the world, which is going some for a President who is said by the newspapers to be a remorseless dictator driving his government into hopeless bankruptcy." But he probably wasn't doing so by any appreciable amount.

When he met superconservative North Dakota Senator Gerald P. Nye for the first time, Nye informed him with apparent relish, "Mr.

President, I've got a hundred percent voting record against you—on banking, economy, and beer." Roosevelt affably replied, "No, Senator, you were only twenty five percent against me. There were some things in those bills that neither of us liked." (In tribute to Roosevelt's charm, Nye subsequently described himself as having been "highly elated" by the encounter.)

Britain's King George VI and his wife, Queen Elizabeth, were dining at FDR's Hyde Park estate, when a huge crash of china and glass was suddenly heard from behind the dining room screen. Roosevelt nonchalantly told his distinguished guests, "Oh, this is just an old family custom. Think nothing of it." Immediately after the same dinner, the butler dropped a tray loaded with decanters of whiskey, vintage liquors, soda, ice, and glasses the mortified servant—after picking up the wreckage—left the room in disgrace, and the president roared with laughter, turned to the king, and cheerfully observed, "Well, there's number two! What next? These things usually come in threes!" The next day, while propelling himself backward on his palms from the swimming pool where he and his royal guests had taken a dip, Roosevelt himself landed in the middle of a large tray of assorted delicacies and teas. He turned once again to George and with a broad grin said, "Didn't I tell you there would be a third? Well, now I can relax; the spell is broken."

Roosevelt's War Production Board administrator, General Knudsen, once gave his chief executive a list of major names from corporate America who were, in Knudsen's opinion, suitable for appointment to that all-important agency. Roosevelt genially informed the general, "There must be a mistake here, Bill. One of the men on this list is a Democrat." Knudsen, no slouch at repartee himself, rejoined, "It's all right, Mr. President—I have checked on this man and found out that last year he voted for Willkie."

Only a man of eminent good nature like Roosevelt, could put up for years with the below-par cooking of White House housekeeper Henrietta Nesbitt, never take the obvious step of terminating her services, and then confide to his daughter that a primary reason why he wanted to be elected to a fourth term was "so I can fire Mrs. Nesbitt" (but he never did).

Only someone with FDR's perspective could barge in on his house guest, Winston Churchill, as the great British leader was in his bathtub, to tell him some important news and later, "chuckling like a small boy," inform his secretary, Grace Tully, "You know, Grace, I just happened to think of it now. He's pink and white all over."

It is impossible to imagine many people reacting as Roosevelt did when he was confined to his bed with a severe cold and the *Washington Post*, with unusual sloppiness for that generally efficient journal, ran a headline regarding this circumstance that read, "FDR in Bed with Coed." No sooner had the paper's early edition been delivered to the White House than a *Post* staffer, picking up the telephone, was astounded to hear the best-known voice in the country announce, "This is Frank Roosevelt. I'd like 100 copies of that first edition.... I want to send it to all my friends." Roosevelt's wish was never granted, however; the newspaper had already recognized its error and had retrieved and destroyed all of the incorrectly headlined copies.

Hoover's successor may or may not have possessed, as the preeminent Supreme Court Justice Oliver Wendell Holmes said of him, "a second-class intellect," but he definitely had—as Holmes also declared of Roosevelt—"a first-class temperament."

FDR was a master of the art of ridicule, characteristically delivered with the winning Rooseveltian grin and magnificent sense of timing.

Perplexed and distressed by the ill feelings toward him from big business leaders, he sincerely believed that his anti-depression economic moves had helped rescue capitalism, and he regarded his detractors as a bunch of ingrates. "In the summer of 1933," he declared in a 1936 campaign speech,

> a nice old gentleman wearing a silk hat fell off the end of a pier. He was unable to swim. A friend ran down the pier, dived overboard and pulled him out; but the silk hat floated off with the tide. After the old gentleman had been revived, he was effusive in his thanks. He praised his friend for saving his life. Today, three years later, the old gentleman is berating his friend because the silk hat was lost.[16]

In another speech that same year, he asserted,

> Some of these people really forget how sick they were. But I know how sick they were. I have their fever charts. I know how the knees of all of our rugged individualists were trembling ... and how their hearts fluttered. They came to Washington in great numbers. Washington did not look like a dangerous bureaucracy to them then.... It looked like an emergency hospital. All of the distinguished patients wanted two things—a quick hypodermic to end the pain and a course of treatment to cure the disease. They wanted them in a hurry; we gave them both. And now most of the patients seem to be doing very

nicely. Some of them are even well enough to throw their crutches at the doctor.[17]

Those who criticized him but had no constructive suggestions reminded him of the doctor who was called into consultation regarding a man who was about to die of an extremely large malignancy. The doctor, pointed out FDR, simply said, "What an amazing and wonderful tumor! I must write a paper about it."

In some informal remarks at Hyde Park in 1938, he told about a recent fishing trip that he had taken:

> This year I took a full-fledged scientist with me from the Smithsonian Institution in Washington, Dr. Waldo Schmitt, who was such a success that we decided to change the Smithsonian to "Schmittsonian."
>
> When we started from San Diego out on the West Coast, we ran down the Coast to Lower California.... In talking to Dr. Schmitt that first day, I said: "Is there any particular thing or animal that you would like to find?" He said: "Oh, yes, I am writing a monograph. I have been on it two years, and the one thing I am searching for in these waters of Mexico and the islands of the Pacific—I want to find a burrowing shrimp."
>
> "Well," I said, "Dr. Schmitt, why leave Washington? Washington is overrun with them. I know that after five years."[18]

The great diversity within the Republican party in 1940 (the GOP candidate, Willkie, had been endorsed not only by the American Communist party and by powerful labor leader John L. Lewis but also by a host of extreme reactionaries) also generated some highly effective Roosevelt ridicule:

> We all know the story of the unfortunate chameleon which turned brown when placed on a brown rug, and turned red when placed on a red rug, but who died a tragic death when they put him on a Scotch plaid. We all know what would happen to Government if it tried to fulfill all the secret understandings and promises made between the conflicting groups which are now backing the Republican party.[19]

Roosevelt also underlined what he saw as the incongruity of progressive Republican Senator Charles McNary running as the GOP vice presidential candidate that year by working into at least one campaign speech a tale about a schoolteacher who

after describing Heaven in alluring and golden terms, asked her class
of small boys how many of them wanted to go to Heaven. With eyes
that sparkled at the thought every small boy in the class held up his
hand—except one. Teacher said, "Why, Charlie, Charlie McNary."
[*Laughter*] "Charlie, you don't want to go to Heaven? Why not?"
"Teacher," he said, "sure I want to go to Heaven, but"—pointing to
the rest of the boys in the room—"not with that bunch." [*Laughter*][20]

Regarding U.S. military strategy in World War II, FDR said:

> One thing about these plans of ours: they are not being decided by
> the typewriter strategists who expound their views in the press or on
> the radio. One of the greatest American soldiers, Robert E. Lee, once
> remarked on the tragic fact that in the war of his day all the best gen-
> erals were apparently working on newspapers instead of in the Army.
> And that seems to be true in all wars.[21]

Even worse, he thought, were the doom criers. There were some
people, he declared in yet another 1940 speech, "who always look
on the dark side of life. There are some who complain that things
are not as they were once, and who firmly believe that everybody
who disagrees with them is a moron or a crook. They belong, it
seems to me, to the type of unfortunate individual ... of whom it is
said 'he is enjoying bad health.'"

"Sometimes," FDR went on, as he prepared to move into a convincing rural Yankee accent:

> when I listen and listen to people like that I can better understand old
> Uncle Jed. "Uncle Jed," said Ezra, one day, "ben't you gittin' a leetle
> hard of hearin'?" "Yes," said Uncle Jed, "I'm afraid I'm gittin' a mite
> deef." Whereupon Ezra made Uncle Jed go down to Boston, to see an
> ear doctor. Uncle Jed came back. And Ezra asked what happened.
> "Well," said Uncle Jed, "that doctor asked me if I had been drinkin'
> any. And I said, 'Yes, I been drinkin' a mite.' And then that doctor
> said, 'Well, Jed, I might just as well tell you now that if you don't
> want to lose your hearin' you've got to give up drinkin'.'" "Well,"
> said Uncle Jed, "I thought it over; and then I said, 'Doc, I like what
> I've been drinkin' so much better than what I've been a-hearin', that
> I reckon I'll jist keep on gittin' deef!'" [*Laughter*][22]

In his last political campaign, in 1944, Roosevelt responded to
the farfetched charge from the right that the Great Depression had

been caused by the Democrats. "We have been told," he said in the same speech to the Teamsters Union at which he announced his candidacy in this election

> that it was not a Republican depression but a Democratic depression from which this nation was saved in 1933—that this Administration ... is responsible for all the suffering and misery that the history books and the American people have always thought had been brought about during the twelve ill-fated years when the Republican party was in power.
>
> Now, there is an old and somewhat lugubrious adage that says, "Never speak of rope in the house of a man who has been hanged." In the same way, if I were a Republican leader speaking to a mixed audience, the last word in the whole dictionary that I think I would use is that word "depression"!

In this speech, FDR at least temporarily dispelled a growing and indeed accurate belief that he was in failing health. He was at his energetic best, in fact, in his use of ridicule. Lambasting those Republicans who were consistently anti-labor until they needed votes in elections, he declared that, at the latter point, "they suddenly discover that they really love labor and that they are anxious to protect labor from its old friends.... We have seen many marvellous stunts in the circus but no performing elephant could turn a handspring without falling flat on its back."

Much laughter from those in attendance ensued, and Roosevelt, sticking to his theme of alleged Republican misdoings, with mock earnestness went on, now with reference to GOP–encouraged rumors that millions of taxpayer dollars had been spent to bring his dog home from Alaska's Aleutian Islands: "These Republican leaders have not been content with attacks on me, or my wife, or on my sons. No, not content with that, they now include my little dog, Fala. Well, of course, I don't resent attacks, and my family doesn't resent attacks, but Fala *does* resent them. You know, Fala is Scotch ...—his Scotch soul was furious. He has not been the same dog since."[23]

What quickly became known as the Fala speech received favorable notices even in such generally pro–Republican publications as *Time*. Democratic publications tended to be ecstatic: the *New Republic* reflected a widely held sentiment in saying that "there have been few politicians in America who have been sure enough of themselves to use laughter and keep their dignity, and Mr. Roosevelt is one of them; and here he used humor against a humorless opponent [Thomas E. Dewey, the GOP's nominee], which made the contrast all the more striking."[24]

Although some of his stories—the sagas of Charlie McNary and Uncle Jed, for example—were used to ridicule opponents, Roosevelt told many others that were completely irrelevant, to achieve one or more of his purposes. Once he hit upon what he saw as a winner, he tended to repeat a tale over and over, seemingly quite indifferent as to whether or not he had told it previously to the same audience. But such were his skills at raconteurship that even Rosenman, who heard some stories at least five times, could not recall "being bored even the fifth time. He usually invented ... some new detail, and with each telling the anecdote seemed to become livelier.... He had ... a sure instinct for the dramatic ... and [could keep] the suspense alive even for those who had heard the story before and knew what the end was going to be."[25]

A special favorite was the story of a wealthy Chicago widow of advanced years who, her age notwithstanding, was intent on seeing the world on almost a continuous basis. She finally succumbed to the Grim Reaper while in Moscow, and her family, informed of the event, cabled Russia and asked that her body be shipped back to Chicago for an appropriate burial. When the casket arrived, the family members opened it to take one final look at the lady and to their extreme consternation found instead of their loved one a white-bearded Russian general in full military regalia. They immediately and excitedly transmitted a new cable to Moscow pointing out the error and received the following response: "Suggest you close the casket and proceed with the funeral. Your grandmother was buried in the Kremlin with full military honors."

Another frequently told anecdote involved a sailor who participated in the bidding on a parrot at an auction. The sailor began by bidding five dollars, was raised, bid ten dollars this time, was again raised, and finally won ownership of the parrot with a thirty-five-dollar bid. "Thirty-five dollars is a lot to pay for a bird," complained the sailor as he cleaned out his pockets. "Can the bird talk?" "Can the bird talk!" responded the auctioneer. "As it happens, that parrot was bidding against you!"

Still another story that seemed to tickle FDR's funny bone on a consistent basis dealt with a new U.S. World War I destroyer that left the United States for the coast of France in the summer of 1918:

About two hundred miles off the Irish Channel the commanding officer ... told one of the young lieutenants who had come into the Navy from [civilian] life to "shoot the sun" at noon; in other words, to determine the position of the ship. The young man "shot the sun," took his figures over to the chart board and after about ten minutes the commanding officer noticed he was still scratching his head. He went over and said, "Lieutenant, I will take your figures and work out our position," and the lieutenant moved off. About five minutes later the commanding officer, after doing a little figuring, summoned the lieutenant to come back and said, "Young man, take off your hat. This is a solemn moment." The lieutenant said, "Why, sir?" The commanding officer said, "My boy, I find from your figures that we are now in the middle of Westminster Abbey."[26]

Roosevelt liked to tell also about the indigent in his hometown who took four dollars from the Republicans and two dollars from the Democrats and almost voted for the Democratic ticket on the ground that it was the more honest but decided to abstain from voting altogether after he was given a pint of liquor by the Prohibitionists.

And, as always, he could easily laugh at himself in his tales:

An American Marine, ordered home from Guadalcanal, was disconsolate and downhearted because he hadn't killed even one Jap. He stated his case to his superior officer, who said, "Go up that hill over there and shout, 'To hell with Emperor Hirohito.' That will bring the Japs out of hiding." The Marine did as he was bidden. Immediately a Jap soldier came out of the jungle, shouting, "To hell with Roosevelt." "And of course," said the Marine, "I could not kill a Republican."[27]

If an indeterminate but presumably significant percentage of his material was not his own (FDR was the first president to regularly use the contributions of other people in his speeches), and if in his anecdotes he was every bit as much the retail dealer as was Lincoln, Roosevelt still exhibited a personal spontaneous wit on many other occasions.

He asked famed novelist Fanny Hurst to slowly turn around so that he could view her from all angles, when she visited him in his office and informed him that she had lost considerable weight through dieting. He then declared, "The Hurst may have changed, but it's the same old fanny." After dispatching an urgent plea for peace to Japan's Emperor Hirohito just hours before Pearl Harbor, he told a dinner guest that "this son of man has just sent his final message to the son of God." When Eleanor forwarded a rather steep physician's bill to his secretary for the latter to pay together with the notation, "I know [the president] will have a fit," he appended a further instruction to the secretary, "Pay it. Have had the fit. FDR." On election night 1944, he told his Hyde Park neighbors from his front porch that "we just have partial returns—but they seem partial to Hyde Park."

Edward Flynn, one of Roosevelt's closest political allies and a man possessed of an excellent sense of humor himself, constantly urged FDR to say something nice about mothers in his speeches. ("Everybody has them, Mr. President," he frequently pointed out, "and you ought to be for them.") On one occasion, when Flynn was showing a special interest in a forthcoming Roosevelt address, FDR sent him the following telegram right after the speech had been approved by the president, and it was judged by him to be ready for delivery. "Speech finished. All is well. Mother is in. Regards."

Roosevelt's quick-wittedness, almost always accompanied by his good cheer, frequently extended to those who opposed him politically, as well. When he first ran for the presidency, in 1932, he received an insulting letter from a distant cousin, Mary Willis Roosevelt. She, a staunch Republican, addressed him in it as "My dear Franklyn," a probably intentional mistake which added salt to the wounds that the letter itself generated. The contents of the missive read in part:

> I shall not sail under any false colors, but tell you that, because of your running mate, and your silly attitude about that "forgotten man" and all the rest, that you have said about [Hoover] ... I am unreservedly against you. James [her late husband], who saw hundreds of men a week in his work, said there were no "forgotten men" but plenty who thought they were owed something for *nothing*, [and] was dead set against such ideas of socialistic patting them on the back.... You have only belittled yourself by talking like this, and I know many people who, because of it, have decided they will *not* vote for you.

In his reply, FDR wrote "Dear Marye" and then a few but potent words: "Thank you very much for writing to me. It is good to hear from you. I am sorry that you feel as you do, but I must tell you quite frankly that it really never occurred to me that you would vote for me."[28]

At the Emporia, Kansas, railroad station, while campaigning in

1936, he scanned the crowd for a look at the distinguished *Emporia Gazette* editor, William Allen White, who was supporting the Republican nominee, Landon. "I wish he were here," Roosevelt remarked pleasantly. "He is a very good friend of mine for three and a half out of every four years." Suddenly, White appeared and went to the rear platform of the train to shake hands with the president. "Now that I see him," Roosevelt announced to his audience as the train pulled out of the station. "I shall not say anything about the other six months."

While FDR both liked and respected his 1940 GOP opponent, Willkie, he felt that the latter's relatively conservative tenets would be rejected by the electorate once Willkie's message was widely appreciated. When Willkie in the course of that campaign developed a husky voice that threatened the Republican with complete laryngitis, Roosevelt with a twinkle in his eye informed his own personal physician, "I think it would be a grand gesture on your part if you would get in touch with his doctors and offer them your own favorite prescription for treating such trouble. We've got to keep him talking."

He had been equally quick months before Willkie was actually nominated, when a White House aide told him that the Republican business executive had his eye on the president's chair. FDR had responded, "Ah, but look what I've got on it."

But the same man who could create these pearls of humor could also be extremely trite. The New Deal chief executive, whose matchbooks at one time had printed on them the message "Stolen from Franklin D. Roosevelt," once began a press conference by asking a newsman what was happening in the nation's capital. The reporter answered, "Only surmise," and FDR countered, "Sir who?"

Informed at another press conference that isolationist senator William E. Borah of Idaho, a dedicated anti–Rooseveltian, was ill and had gone to Poland Springs, Maine, for medical attention, FDR said, "Oh, I thought you said Poland. That would have been news!" When White House mail room administrator Smith was inundated by a blizzard of dimes, which contributors to the Roosevelt-sponsored March of Dimes infantile paralysis drive had sent in, the thirty-second president sent him a note, "I hope you are having a good dime."

At its lowest level, FDR's humor could also descend to asking his treasury secretary, Henry Morgenthau, Jr., on the telephone, "Hello, Henry. Who do you think I am in bed with?" and informing

Morgenthau, when the latter replied that he didn't know, "Well, I am in bed with a sore throat." There was nothing remotely subtle, either, about Roosevelt's response to an American journalist who—referring to the practice of many European statesmen of the day to spend some of their vacation time grouse shooting—suggested to FDR, "I think we ought to get some grouse over here." The president replied, "We have enough grousing in this country."

Only one notch above these were some of Roosevelt's less-sophisticated practical jokes. If Eleanor told him that a particularly attractive woman was coming to the White House for dinner, he liked to recoil in feigned fright, "Don't let me alone with that female!" Sometimes, while at his Warm Springs, Georgia, farm, he would summon reporters to what he called an "important" conference, then have his tenant farmer bring out some livestock and proceed to give a long talk to the media people on the need to have sound "stud bulls" and "good mules" on a farm.

At Warm Springs, too, Roosevelt loved to play a prank on his intense and extremely long-haired physical therapist, Helen Lauer. She administered, among the exercises that she prescribed for him, one in which he would stretch out on a treatment table in the swimming pool with his legs dangling in the water. She would pull on his legs, and he would pull in the opposite direction. At times, he would give a wink to family members or others who were in the know and, without any warning to the therapist, would then relax the pressure that he was exerting on his legs so that the conscientious Lauer would be thrown off balance and plunge under water. "Pa's laugh," his son James later wrote about this frequently displayed phenomenon, "could be heard all through the pool area as poor Miss Lauer came up spluttering, her hair streaming in wet strings down her neck and her [eyeglasses] hanging off one ear."[29]

Nor was it beyond FDR, on one occasion at Hyde Park, to get a member of his Secret Service detail on a pretext to climb a ladder to the roof of a farm building. Roosevelt then had a hired man remove the ladder, waved affably to the agent, and drove away in his automobile, leaving the Secret Service man stranded.

In both the theater and the movies, Roosevelt loved a heavy dose of slapstick comedy—he was, as his secretary wrote, "not a bit squeamish about the number of custard pies thrown"[30]—and situations such as these were, for him, classic cases of life imitating art.

On the other hand, some of Roosevelt's practical jokes were of a higher standard.

Shortly after Pearl Harbor, referring to his attorney general, Francis Biddle, he told a group of five key aides he had invited into the cabinet room for lunch, "You know, Francis is terribly worried about civil liberties—especially now. He has been on my neck asking me to say that the war will not curtail them too much. Now don't laugh and give me away, but I'm going to hand him a little line." After Biddle came into the room, Roosevelt with a grim expression said:

> Francis, I'm glad you came. All of us have just been discussing here the question of civil liberties in the war, and I have finally come to a decision to issue a proclamation—which I am going to ask you to draft—abrogating so far as possible all freedom of discussion and information during the war. It's a tough thing to do, but I'm convinced that it's absolutely necessary and I want to announce it in this speech we are working on now.

Biddle looked at all of his luncheon companions in amazement. Then, pacing up and down for fully five minutes, he argued passionately against the idea and concluded only when FDR and all five aides burst out laughing.[31]

Also well above the pie-in-the-face category was a note that Roosevelt had a treasury official hand his literal-minded secretary of the treasury, Morgenthau, when the latter was all set to make a war bond drive speech in Washington, together with an oral instruction that "the president wants you to work this into your speech." Morgenthau started to read the contents of the note to his audience, realized that FDR's communication contained something very off-color, and—although with far from total poise—stopped just in time.

It took a little imagination, too, for Roosevelt to telephone the main studio of the National Broadcasting Company, after several White House correspondents had sung "Home on the Range" on that network, and disguise his world-famous voice. He announced to the NBC official on the other end that he was "the advertising manager for Cascaret" (a well-known laxative of the day) and offered the reporters a contract. He was so pleased with this prank that at his next press conference he announced that the correspondents would resign because "they had a very handsome offer to sing on the Cascaret Hour."

A joke that the only U.S. chief executive to serve more than two terms particularly enjoyed planning and executing pivoted on the rumors that circulated widely as early as 1937 that he was seriously pondering an unprecedented third-term candidacy in 1940. At a March 1937 Democratic banquet, he straight-facedly informed his supporters that "a distinguished member of the Congress" had come to see him a few days earlier and that after their business had been transacted he had said to his visitor, "John, I want to tell you something that is very personal to me—something that you have a right to hear from my own lips. I have a great ambition in life." The friend, FDR reported, had "pricked up his ears" and "I went on: 'I am by no means satisfied with having twice been elected president of the United States by very large majorities. I have an even greater ambition.'" "By this time," Roosevelt said to his enthralled audience,

> my friend was sitting on the edge of his chair.... I continued, "John, my ambition relates to January 20, 1941." I could feel what horrid thoughts my friend was thinking. So in order to relieve his anxiety, I went on to say: "My great ambition on January 20, 1941, is to turn over this desk and chair in the White House to my successor, whoever he may be, with the assurance that I am at the same time turning over to him as President, a nation intact, a nation at peace, a nation prosperous, a nation clear in its knowledge of what powers it has to serve its own citizens ... [and] a nation which has thus proved that the democratic form and methods of a national government can and will succeed."[32]

Yet another practical joke, this one played by FDR in early 1943, was triggered by Roosevelt's discovery that a surprise sixty-first birthday party was being planned for Speaker of the House Sam Rayburn. He told his secretary to summon Rayburn and some of the latter's closest House friends (who had been let in on the escapade) to an urgent meeting at the White House, details of which would be furnished at the mansion itself. When they all arrived, FDR, looking directly at the speaker, grimly announced that he had heard some "very serious reports" related to the House of Representatives and that "I am sorry to inform you, Sam, that these reports involve you." "Therefore," the president continued as Rayburn squirmed uncomfortably, "I thought it best to invite you, and your friends on both sides of the aisle, to come down here so I could lay my cards on the table!" Before the entirely mystified Rayburn could utter a word in response, Roosevelt grinned, "My report is, Sam, that you're just getting too old!"

A toast was then proposed by the president for the "birthday child" (who was, in fact, exactly the same age as Roosevelt), and Rayburn was presented by FDR with a new Stetson hat, a suggestion that he try it on for size, and the flattering comment from Roosevelt that he was quite sure that Rayburn wore the same size hat at the present time that he wore the day he came to Congress some three decades earlier.

In the opinion of historian Arthur M. Schlesinger, Jr., Roosevelt's humor was "slapdash, lacking wit and consisting mostly of corny remarks."[33] George Allen, an FDR advisor and friend, believed that the thirty-second president was "most charming when he was most serious and least so when his mind turned playful."[34] Roosevelt's fellow Groton Academy alumnus Dean Acheson thought FDR's humor to be undignified. And these were all deep admirers.

Roosevelt's political enemies went much further. Some were known to spread the rumor that his loud laugh showed emotional instability and, indeed, that he had "a particular form of insanity which led him to laugh on the slightest occasion."[35] A typical negative reaction to his generally well-received Fala speech was contained in a telegram to him from a Los Angeles Republican: "Invective, billingsgate, high-school-kid wisecracking constitute a poor substitute for statesmanship." Columnist Westbrook Pegler, an inveterate Roosevelt hater, called the part about Fala a "corny aside ... Fountleroy humor of a man ... whose mama held him so precious that he never went to public schools with the uncouth sons of the common man."[36] The GOP's Dewey frequently asserted that he deplored Roosevelt's use of wisecracks and ridicule.

Some reporters, too, were critical of FDR's resort to humor, especially when he used it to avoid difficult questions at his press conferences.

And even family members were at times somewhat negative about his use of frivolity but for a different reason. Eleanor warned him that his "sardonic quips," which were not meant to be taken literally, might be so taken and consequently get him into embarrassing situations. His son James felt similarly and once gave as a specific example of grounds for his concern FDR's reply to a person who had asked his father after he returned from his Yalta meeting with Churchill and Stalin what he had thought of Stalin. Roosevelt breezily replied that he had "heard" that the Soviet leader had "poisoned his wife," and James worried that a private memorandum written by the person who had received this answer might someday not only become public but be taken seriously. (FDR, when warned by his intimates about his "careless levity," responded that it didn't matter a bit to him if some people couldn't tell when he was kidding.)

But the man who presided over the nation in what was one of the grimmest periods in its history clearly derived far more benefit from his use of humor than it cost him.

Much of his immense charm was based on that factor—his constant ability, as his biographer Geoffrey C. Ward once described it, to show that he could be both "amused and amusing"[37]—and he used this personality advantage to the maximum to get his way. For every journalist who lamented his evasiveness, there were undoubtedly many who were won over by his jocular informality, as well as by his accessibility to them, and were inclined as a result to accord him the benefit of any doubt. This admiration on the part of the working press extended, of course, to what was for Roosevelt the beneficial conspiracy of silence that surrounded his physical condition.

The favorable media coverage, in turn, did much to endear FDR to the electorate. It was, in fact, not easy to dislike him on a personal basis (as opposed to his politics and policies). Even in mid–1938, when the state of the economy had worsened so much that only half of all respondents in one nationwide survey said that they would vote for him again, eighty percent of the questioned citizenry answered "like" to the query "On the whole, do you like or dislike his personality?" Only ten percent answered "dislike," and the remaining ten percent appeared to be undecided about the matter. Even the occupational categories of "executives," "proprietors," and "professional people"—those far more inclined to be Republicans than Democrats—approved of his personality by at least, in all three cases, seventy-five percent.

If the humor was rarely subtle and if it generally lacked depth, these consequences alone would have amply justified Roosevelt's constant resort to it. Letting the New Deal leader distract those who dealt with him face-to-face from his massive disability and allowing him either to detour around ticklish issues or to buy time in which to decide how to deal with them were clearly additional dividends. So, too, his humor allowed him to reduce tensions, both for himself and for the people around him, and—of no small consequence given the times—to see matters in perspective.

As completely different as he was from both Lincoln and Coolidge, the Hyde Park aristocrat who smiled and joked his way through the longest presidency in the history of the nation was, as his secretary once said of him, "never boring nor bored,"[38] and his ability to perceive, enjoy, and communicate the comical was a powerful factor in his success.

CHAPTER 4

JOHN F. KENNEDY

John F. Kennedy greatly admired both Lincoln (he paid a special visit to Lincoln's tomb during the Cuban missile crisis) and FDR (he liked to pose in front of a White House portrait of Roosevelt). But his pronounced sense of humor had more in common with that of Coolidge, a man whom he resembled in almost no other way.

As his Yankee predecessor, Kennedy was not primarily a storyteller but rather a master of the wry, self-mocking understatement. His observation that "I have a nice home, the office is close by and the pay is good" could just as readily have been offered by Silent Cal, as could JFK's declaration that the "only thing that really surprised us when we got into office was that things were just as bad as we had been saying they were; otherwise we have been enjoying it very much."

Coolidge would have appreciated, too, Kennedy's announcement to a large audience at a Democratic fundraising meal in Denver: "I am grateful to all of you. I could say I am deeply touched, but not as deeply touched as you have been in coming to this luncheon." There were definite Coolidgean strains in Kennedy's statement to an enthusiastic crowd in Ohio's capital city that there "is no city in the United States in which I get a warmer welcome and less votes than Columbus, Ohio," and in his reply to a small boy who asked him, "Mr. President, how did you become a war hero?" that "It was absolutely involuntary. They sank my boat."

Indeed, one of the limited number of full-blown anecdotes that Kennedy did like to tell involved Coolidge's previously noted rejoinder to a walking companion when the latter looked in the direction of the White House and facetiously commented to Coolidge that he wondered who lived there ("Nobody. They just come and go"). It fit JFK's comedic values perfectly.

Kennedy was one of the most intellectual of all presidents—in a single public appearance he could toss off references from sources as diverse as Goethe, Peter the Great, Shakespeare, Faulkner, and Robert E. Lee—and in his speeches, interviews, and letters he displayed an enormous amount of knowledge. He was amused by and could readily cite Queen Victoria's description of the politician Lord John Russell: "He would be a better man if he knew a third subject—but he was interested in nothing but the Constitution of 1688 and himself." He was also taken with the explanation of French Liberal party leader Ledru-Rollin when the latter was seen some distance behind the pro–Liberal mobs who were storming the barricades in Paris during the 1848 revolution ("I've got to follow them. I am their leader") and the verbal exchange between Glendower and Hotspur in part 1 of Shakespeare's *Henry IV* in which Glendower boasts that he "can call spirits from the vasty deep," and Hotspur replies, "Why, so can I, or so can any man; But will they come when you do call for them?"

He appreciatively quoted the remarks of Will Rogers concerning an unsavory political candidate in Pennsylvania: "They told me that the better element were all against him. I knew that, but I also knew that there are very few of the better element in Pennsylvania. I warned them three months ago to procure more better element." And he included in a speech, "Some 2,500 years ago the Greek historian Herodotus described Africa south of the Sahara as a land of 'horned asses, dog-faced creatures, the creatures without heads, whom the Libyans declared to have eyes in their breasts and many other far less fabulous beasts.' Apparently when Herodotus found himself short on facts, he didn't hesitate to use imagination—which may be why he is called the first historian."

He once told the University of North Carolina student body that he did not propose to adopt "from the Belgian constitution a provision giving three votes instead of one to college graduates—at least not until more Democrats go to college." He several times referred in his speeches to the racketeer who "took the First, Fifth, Sixth and Sixteenth Amendments and deeply regretted the repeal of the Eighteenth." He quoted Archimedes, who—in explaining the principle of the lever—reportedly announced, "Give me a place where I can stand—and I shall move the world." After forcing the board chairman of a major corporation into an ignominious price retreat, he asserted, "I told him that his men could keep their horses for the spring plowing."

At the University of Maine, just five weeks before his death, he told the crowd:

In the year 1717, King George I of England donated a very valuable library to Cambridge University and, at very nearly the same time, had occasion to dispatch a regiment to Oxford. The king, remarked one famous wit, had judiciously observed the condition of both universities—one was a learned body in need of loyalty and the other was a loyal body in need of learning. I am deeply honored by the degree which you awarded me today ... at this university noted for both loyalty and learning.[1]

But the youngest man ever elected president (at forty-three) was no cerebral snob, and he disarmingly admitted to many gaps in his knowledge. He had great difficulty, for example, in remembering the difference between fiscal and monetary policy, finally handled the problem by associating his Federal Reserve Board chairman, William McChesney Martin, with the latter, and deadpanned, "If Martin ever quits his job, I'll have to get somebody else with the same last initial." Claiming a relative lack of expertise on what was during his presidential campaign a very sensitive issue, the Catholic Kennedy announced in a New York dinner speech that he had "asked Cardinal Spellman what I should say when people ask me whether I believe the Pope is infallible, and the Cardinal replied, 'I don't know, Senator—all I know is he keeps calling me Spillman.'" When he threw a switch in Salt Lake City to activate generators 150 miles away at the Green River, he informed his audience, "I never know when I press these whether I am going to blow up Massachusetts or start the project."

Nor did his intellectual proclivities prevent him at times from displaying a definite strain of earthiness. The man who once described himself as "an ivory-tower president" (to a Yale economist, when the latter initially demurred from accepting a major JFK appointment on the grounds that he was "just an ivory-tower economist") also remarked that "grace under pressure" was more than just an accurate definition of "courage": the phrase also reminded him, he said, of a female of that name with whom he was once acquainted. When his Interior secretary, Stewart Udall, told him that he feared that a fervently anti–Kennedy woman whom Udall knew might appear at a ceremony at which JFK would speak and try to disrupt it, "so if you see me in the crowd struggling with a woman and rolling on the ground, you will know what is going on," Kennedy responded, "In any case, Stewart, we will give you the benefit of the doubt."

The legacy of Camelot has been somewhat tarnished in recent

years, and Kennedy as viewed from today's vista seems—not unlike Coolidge in this regard, too—a lesser leader than he appeared to be both in his own time and for some period thereafter. But if he was not, as journalist Mary McGrory once described him, the "most attractive man of his generation,"[2] he did not in the eyes of millions fall short of this rarefied level by much.

He received consistently high scores in the Gallup polls taken during his presidency, attaining an impressive zenith of eighty three percent during the Cuban Bay of Pigs invasion fiasco (he once observed that the worse his performance, the greater his popularity) and invariably registering over sixty percent. In 1963, the respected *Public Opinion Quarterly* found that a staggering fifty percent of all U.S. adults believed him to be "one of the two or three best presidents the country ever had." In 1983, a full twenty years after his death, a *Newsweek* Gallup poll corroborated that he was, by some distance, the nation's most popular president, with two-thirds of the respondents believing that America would have been "much different" if he had lived. Dozens of presidential aspirants—Gary Hart, Joseph Biden, Albert Gore, Dan Quayle, and Charles Robb conspicuously among them— have seemingly given the Kennedy personality an endorsement by attempting to replicate some of it on the hustings.

What Kennedy possessed, as nationally syndicated columnist and television interviewer Christopher Matthews has written, "was an innate ability to be *liked*, to have people want him as a friend, lover, son, brother, leader.... Before his dazzling success in the Great Debate [with Richard M. Nixon, in 1960], we didn't know the Greek word *charisma*. After his early, ghastly departure, the name 'Jack Kennedy' evoked it. He had the gift."[3]

For all of this political capital, Kennedy owed much to the Fourth Estate, which was particularly enchanted by the Kennedy style and irreverent wit. Although his newsman friend Benjamin C. Bradlee's assertion that JFK "enjoyed better relations with the press than any president since Mergenthaler invented the linotype"[4] might be questioned on the grounds that both Coolidge and FDR had equally excellent rapports with the press, it is incontrovertible that the media—now including television, the rise of which certainly helped the photogenic and charismatic Kennedy—was taken with the creator of the New Frontier and greatly appreciative of his always-good-copy, gently sardonic sense of the absurd. That much of the public was also seduced by this irreverence, given the role of the media in molding public opinion, was not entirely coincidental.

Kennedy's televised press conferences, watched by millions, were tailor-made for JFK's amused tolerance and self-mockery. He viewed the rebroadcasts of all of them, tended to chortle at his own witticisms, and once said, "We couldn't survive without TV." He told a close aide that at these meetings with the press "he had to restrain himself. He was often tempted to make some humorous remark, but he was afraid that in cold print it wouldn't look very statesmanlike." On another occasion, in reference to the humorous answers that he and his staff often suggested might be offered if anticipated questions were actually asked by the journalists, he declared, "It is dangerous to have them in the back of my head." But these considerations clearly did not prevent him from using many of the quips. In charming the press he was aware that he was, as *New York Times* reporter James Reston put it, a "real master of the game" who could disarm "with a smile and a wisecrack."[5]

In his speeches, too, Kennedy adroitly used humor, primarily but hardly exclusively at the beginning of his remarks, to establish rapport with his audiences. His closest adviser, Theodore C. Sorensen, who often worked with him on such projects, later reported that he would strive "as diligently for the right opening witticism, or take as much pride the next day in some ... barb he had flung, as he would on the more substantive paragraphs in his text."[6]

An audience exposed to the rigors of the elements was greeted by the declaration, "I appreciate your welcome. As the cow said to the Maine farmer, 'Thank you for a warm hand on a cold morning.'"[7] A District of Columbia gathering learned in the speaker's salutation that Washington "is a city of southern efficiency and northern charm." Those in attendance at an Executive Mansion dinner honoring all of the living Western hemisphere winners of the Nobel Prize were informed in the opening remarks that their host thought that "this is the most extraordinary collection of talent, of human knowledge, that has ever been gathered together at the White House—with the possible exception of when Thomas Jefferson dined alone." The media was beguiled by this kind of thing, as were the various, quickly-won-over audiences at his speeches.

It can be argued that without his great asset of humor, Kennedy would never have entered the White House at all except as a guest, for in running for the presidency in 1960 he was faced with, and with humor successfully deflected, two major problems: his Catholicism and his father.

Although neither his opponents in the primaries nor the

subsequent Republican nominee, Nixon, could—understandably—talk about it, JFK's religion was the biggest single issue in his campaign, and dire warnings about a possible Kennedy victory were in ample supply. The eminent Protestant clergyman (and Nixon friend) Norman Vincent Peale, declared, "Our American culture is at stake. I don't say it won't survive [Kennedy's election], but it won't be what it was." (When later asked about this statement, Kennedy asserted, "I would like to think he was complimenting me, but I'm not sure he was.") In JFK's own words, it was widely feared that he wanted "to replace the gold at Fort Knox with a supply of holy water."

Even former President Harry Truman, who withheld his support from Kennedy until the latter was officially nominated, felt impelled to announce that it was not the candidate's Catholicism but his intense hostility toward Kennedy's controversial father, Joseph, that had made him so reluctant. As Truman put it, "I'm not against the Pope, I'm against the Pop." Kennedy himself was enough of a realist to know that his Catholicism would not, by any stretch of the imagination, help him. Asked by a reporter if he thought that he would lose any votes because of his religion, he responded, "I feel as a Catholic that I'll get my reward in my life hereafter, although I may not get it here."

Kennedy successfully defused the issue with droll remarks. In addition to his statement about Cardinal "Spillman," he said that he hoped that Protestant Bishop Bromley Oxnan would "be my personal envoy to the Vatican and he's been instructed to open negotiations for a transatlantic tunnel immediately." When a comment from the Vatican during the campaign indicated that Rome was uneasy about his views on the appropriate relationship between church and state, he mused, "Now I understand why Henry VIII set up his own church." When, in mid–October, the outspoken Truman—now a dedicated Kennedy backer—told the Republicans to "go to hell," JFK announced that he had sent Truman a telegram: "Dear Mr. President, I have noted with interest your suggestion as to where those who vote for my opponent should go. While I understand and sympathize with your deep motivation, I think it is important that our side try to refrain from raising the religious issue."

Nor, he wanted people to know, was he remotely intimidated by the church and its representatives. At one banquet, referring to an obese priest next to whom he had been seated, he declared, "It is an inspiration to be here with one of those lean, ascetic clerics who show the effect of constant fast and prayer, and bring the message to us in the flesh." When the consistently Republican *Wall Street Journal* surprised him at one point by criticizing some of Nixon's tactics, he said, "That is like the *Osservatore Romano* criticizing the Pope."

Kennedy's father, a self-made millionaire and former U.S. ambassador to Great Britain, was another campaign negative. Widely known as both ruthless and bigoted, he was also believed to have made much of his money illegally as a liquor smuggler during Prohibition and now to be single-mindedly dedicated to spending a significant percentage of his ill-gotten gains in buying the presidency for his offspring. In his eyes, his son could do no wrong. (After he telephoned Kennedy following the second Nixon-Kennedy debate and offered his usual unqualified praise, the future president said, "I still don't know how I did. If I had slipped and fallen on the floor, he would have said, 'The graceful way you picked yourself up was terrific.'") But JFK recognized that the converse was not true.

Thus, Joseph was treated with the same genial lack of reverence as was the church. Those attending a dinner for the party faithful were told, "I had announced earlier this year that if successful I would not consider campaign contributions as a substitute for experience in appointing ambassadors. Ever since I made that statement I have not received one single cent from my father." Another campaign audience was informed that the candidate had just received a telegram from his "generous Daddy" reading: "Dear Jack: Don't buy a single vote more than necessary. I'll be damned if I'm going to pay for a landslide." After a newspaper report on his sister Eunice's upcoming wedding said that one of Joseph Kennedy's business associates had "smilingly" stated that the cost of the event would be in six figures, JFK asserted, "Now I know that story is a phony—no one in my father's office smiles."

His humor also immeasurably helped the thirty-fifth president, who did not suffer fools gladly, in dealing with the numerous self-important or otherwise taxing people with whom he inevitably had to deal. After listening ad nauseam to his pompous under secretary of state Chester Bowles's drawn-out description of the state of the world, Kennedy said to his next visitor, "Chet tells me there are six revolutions going on in the world. One is the revolution of rising expectations. I lost track of the other five." Regarding the Republican leader of the House, he asked privately, "Have you ever tried to talk to Charlie Halleck? It's like trying to pick up a greased pig." He once told an interviewer that composing a birthday telegram to his egocentric and sensitive vice president, Lyndon Johnson, was like "drafting a state document." (On election night 1960, after conversing with LBJ on the telephone, he had informed his supporters, "Lyndon says he hears that *I'm* losing Ohio but *we're* doing fine in Pennsylvania.")

Lesser luminaries were also made more palatable by an injection of Kennedy irreverence. The conservative, segregationist white mayor of Jackson, Mississippi, was told by JFK that he had "full permission to denounce me in public as long as you don't in private." Even the valet-butler whom Kennedy inherited when he came to the White House and who seemed to be doing relatively little since he served only drinks and not meals, got the treatment, at least secondhand. The new president told a friend that the employee actually did something worthwhile beyond handing out the libations: "He leads in the guy who brings breakfast."

Finally, for Kennedy, as it had been most notably for Franklin D. Roosevelt among his predecessors, an ability to perceive and express the comedic was an effective means of releasing tension. When, during his ticklish and ultimately unsuccessful two-day Vienna meeting with Soviet leader Nikita Khrushchev in mid–1961, the Russian premier told JFK that he had made sure that Nixon had lost the 1960 presidential election by refusing to release the captured U-2 pilot Gary Powers before election day (something that would have helped the incumbent vice president, Nixon), Kennedy smilingly said to him, "Don't spread that story around. If you tell everybody that you like me better than Nixon, I'll be ruined at home." The Russian roared with laughter at this only-half-in-jest bon mot and did likewise when Kennedy told his Viennese translator after Khrushchev had stated that one of the medals he was wearing was the Lenin Peace Prize, "Tell him I hope they never take it away from him."

Subsequently, as the nation tensely stood for several days on the brink of war with the Soviets following Kennedy's October 1962 imposition of the Cuban missile blockade, the U.S. leader remarked, "Well, I guess this is the week I earn my salary." When that unprecedentedly frightening impending catastrophe was finally averted, JFK—implying that this success might actually constitute the zenith of his career—invoked a Lincolnesque image by commenting, "This is the night I should go to the theater."

Kennedy's style of humor was, in the eyes of many observers, rather aristocratic. It was based—as Aïda DiPace Donald has put it—

"not ... on the exaggerated language and gymnastics of the American [political arena] but on the gentler models of the House of Commons."[8] It was influenced by his several preparatory schools—especially Connecticut's Choate, where he spent his four high school years, was accused by the headmaster of being far more a prankster than a student and, at least partially because of his wry self-deprecation and facility for the insouciant comment, was voted by his senior year classmates "most likely to succeed."

Kennedy's humor was also molded by his four years at Harvard. He was intensely loyal to America's oldest university and often worked references to it into his speeches, as in "politics is an astonishing profession. It has enabled me to go from being an obscure member of the Junior Varsity at Harvard to being an honorary member of the Football Hall of Fame." When he received an honorary degree from Yale, he told those in attendance, "It might be said now that I have the best of both worlds: a Harvard education and a Yale degree." He included in a speech before the student body of George Washington University a tale about a man who came to Harvard one day decades earlier and "asked for President Lowell. They said, 'He's in Washington, seeing Mr. [William Howard] Taft.'" He added, "I know that some other day, when they are asking for the president of your university, they will say that he is over at the White House seeing Mr. Kennedy. They understood at Harvard, and you understand here, the relative importance of a university president and a president of the United States."

The Court of St. James (during his father's ambassadorship) and both Palm Beach and Park Avenue (where the Kennedy family had residences) undoubtedly further shaped the JFK brand of wit. JFK could be particularly appreciative of the drolleries of people such as British Prime Minister Harold Macmillan. After Kennedy had complained to MacMillan about the way in which the press in Vienna had written about his wife and asked him, "How would you react if somebody said, 'Lady Dorothy is a drunk?'" the prime minister claimed he would say, "You should have seen her mother." The U.S. president also relished and often retold Macmillan's witty account of how Eisenhower "wouldn't let Nixon on the property." Similarly, Kennedy was delighted by the patrician understatements of his deputy assistant secretary for inter–American affairs, Arturo Morales Carrión, who wrote in a memorandum, "No money-lender in history has ever evoked great enthusiasm. We have yet to see a charismatic banker"; and by the urbane mock seriousness of Republican

Senator Everett Dirksen (Kennedy laughed out loud when he learned that Dirksen had announced that one of his early economic actions would have "all the impact of a snowflake on the bosom of the Potomac").

Kennedy also admired the cultivated and subtle wit of his close friend and former Senate colleague George Smathers of Florida and often cited with approval a speech that Smathers made in 1950 when he entered the Florida primary against the then-senator, Claude Pepper. Pepper was thought by some to be overly friendly to the Soviet Union at the time and was under a cloud in some quarters for his friendship with the Soviet dictator, Joseph Stalin. Smathers said to a crowd of backwoods Florida residents, "Are you aware that Claude Pepper is known all over Washington as a shameless extrovert? Not only that, but this man is reliably reported to practice nepotism with his sister-in-law, and he has a sister who was once a thespian in Greenwich Village. Worst of all, it is an established fact that Mr. Pepper, before his marriage, practiced celibacy." Smathers won.

And the Choate-Harvard graduate moved easily among the likes of Mexico's sophisticated President Lopez Mateos, who once gave him an expensive and elaborately ornamented watch—in accordance with the custom of Mexico—after Kennedy had admired it. Shortly thereafter, First Lady Jacqueline appeared in a magnificent outfit, Lopez expressed his approval, and Kennedy said, "You had better take back your watch."

The upper-class British ambassador David Ormsby-Gore was a close friend with whom JFK enjoyed trading witticisms. So was McGeorge Bundy, the aristocratic former dean of Harvard College, who had originally known Kennedy at the elite private day school that both had attended and who served in an official capacity as JFK's special assistant for national security affairs. Kennedy often told of an experience that Bundy had as dean when Harvard Professor Charles R. Cherington called Bundy a "son of a bitch" in one of his lectures. The dean, learning of this lapse of good judgment on the part of a faculty member, summoned Cherington to his office; there, according to Cherington, he apologized to Bundy for calling him a son of a bitch, and Bundy apologized to Cherington for being one.

There was also a pronounced strain of robust Irish humor in the style of the Irish-American president, and he was often pleased by the amusing remarks and stories of the Boston Irish politicians (including his own maternal grandfather, a former mayor of Boston) he knew from childhood and, later, by Irish pols elsewhere, including Chicago's Richard Daley, Charlie Buckley of the Bronx, and Buffalo's Peter Crotty.

In particular, Kennedy enjoyed the witticisms of his fellow Irish-American and key assistant, Dave Powers, who was a close confidant from his earliest political days. JFK was known to break into a broad smile at the mere sight of Powers, who in escorting distinguished visitors from their limousines into the Oval Office, generally had something that was genuinely amusing to say to them. Powers told the shah of Iran, "I want you to know that you're my kind of shah," and asked Soviet First Deputy Premier Anastas Mikoyan, "Tell me. Are you the real Mikoyan?" He introduced Macmillan to Kennedy as "the greatest name in England" and regularly referred to the White House as "the greatest White House I ever was in." He was so taken by the beauty of Princess Grace (Kelly) of Monaco when she and Prince Rainier visited for lunch that he grabbed her hand and said, "Welcome to the White House, Princess," before he realized that she was not unaccompanied; undaunted, he stuck out his hand again in Rainier's direction and added, "and you too, Prince."

Powers, undoubtedly the funniest of the several jocular Irish Americans who reported directly to the president, actually functioned as a kind of court jester, and one of his major contributions to his boss's morale was the telling of numerous Irish stories, many of them related when the two men swam together in the Executive Mansion pool ("I had to learn to breast stroke," he later said, "because it's the only way to swim and talk"). An example of the genre, and a particular JFK favorite, involved the two Boston Irishmen who were reading the inscriptions on headstones in an old cemetery where British soldiers killed at the battle of Bunker Hill were buried. One headstone contained the epitaph, "Here lies an Englishman and a good man," and one of the Irishmen remarked to the other, "Now, Mike, sure that grave doesn't look as if it had room enough for two people, does it?"

Another Powers-conveyed story that amused Kennedy greatly and in this case was added to the modest number of tales that the New Frontier president himself frequently told, had as its centerpiece an Irishman who was newly arrived in the United States and bereft of both money and a job. He one day dropped in on the headquarters of Boston's powerful West End political boss Martin Lomasney, watched some of Lomasney's people working on voting lists, and picked up a broom and swept the floor. He then located a bed in the

Lomasney office and slept there not only that night but for several months thereafter. One day Lomasney asked his name, was informed that it was "Paddy Sullivan," and unaware that Paddy was sleeping in the offices, said, "You must be the hardest worker we've got. You're always the last one here at night and you're always here ahead of me in the morning. There's a vacancy in the House of Representatives at the state house. I'll put you into it."

After several years as a state representative, Paddy ran for a seat in the state senate and, backed by the influential Lomasney, easily won this position, too. A few years later, when as it happened Lomasney was not in a very good mood, Paddy drew him aside and said that he wanted a favor. "A favor?" Lomasney shouted, "I made you a state representative and then I made you a senator, and now you want a favor? What's the favor, for God's sake?" "Martin," Paddy replied, "I want you to make me an American citizen."

Another subordinate who especially tickled the Kennedy funny bone was a non–Irishman, presidential press secretary Pierre Salinger, who returned the compliment by asserting that his leader was responsible for the rebirth of humor in American politics following a long absence. Salinger once told the press, when queried on the escape of Caroline Kennedy's pet hamsters, "Our security is very tight but these were extremely intelligent hamsters." At another press conference, when reproached for sticking religiously to his prepared release announcement, he solemnly informed the journalists, "I am not a textual deviate."

The contemporary professional humorist whom JFK most admired was a good friend, the legendary Jack Benny, whose comic abilities so enthralled Kennedy that on many occasions he would stop whatever business of state in which he might be engaged just to watch Benny's television program. Benny felt sufficiently close to the president to crack at a 1962 gala, in recognition of both Kennedy's chronically bad back and Jacqueline's youth, that the "amazing thing to me is that a man in a rocking chair could have such a young wife." Kennedy and Benny left a Los Angeles fundraising dinner at the Beverly Hilton the following year to visit a high school prom being held elsewhere in the same hotel. He presented the sixty-nine-year-old Benny to the students as "my kid brother, Teddy."

The first president born in the twentieth century dropped hints of what was to come long before he ascended to the nation's top job. As a young naval officer serving in the Pacific during World War II, his PT-109 torpedo boat was sunk, and by all accounts he sustained the morale of the survivors with his humor. When he was finally rescued and told, "Hey, Jack! We've got some food for you," the famished Lieutenant Kennedy asserted, "No, thanks. I just had a coconut." In his first Massachusetts political contest, after each of his several rivals had been introduced individually as "a man who came up the hard way," he strode to the microphone and told the crowd, "I'm the one who didn't come up the hard way." As a junior U.S. congressman, parking his vehicle in front of a No Parking sign in downtown Washington, he genially noted, "This is what Hamlet means by the insolence of office."

In his years as a senator JFK consistently shook off suggestions that he try for his party's vice presidential nomination in 1956, sometimes quipping that he was "against vice in any form." After he did try for the second slot at the Democratic convention that year only to be denied it, he informed a Boston audience, "Socrates once said that it was the duty of a man of real principle to avoid high national office, and evidently the delegates at Chicago recognized my principles even before I did."

But the full-blown Kennedy irreverence and sense of the incongruous were really not widely recognized trademarks of the man from Massachusetts in those years. His intimates—at Choate his roommate considered him to be the funniest person he had ever known—were regularly treated to displays of the JFK humor, and it was rare for a Kennedy public appearance from the earliest days of his political career not to be marked by some witty remark. But even such a close professional associate and admirer as the late Senator Barry M. Goldwater told an interviewer years later that in his opinion Kennedy lacked a developed sense of humor until relatively late in his senatorial years, and the public flashes of JFK wit were memorable, if at all, for their quality and definitely not their quantity in this period.

A watershed came in the spring of 1958, in the form of an after-dinner speech that Kennedy delivered as a senator to the leaders of the Washington press corps at their purposefully lighthearted Gridiron Club banquet.

The future president was justifiably honored by the invitation. But he recognized that his appearance was politically far from risk free, since—as all club guest speakers—he was expected to be highly amusing. As Sorensen later reminisced, Kennedy "was hearing stories about Gridiron speakers who had fallen flat in their attempts to be funny. He was certain that if [his speech] were a success nobody would really care except to write him off as just another funny fellow. But if he were a *failure*, it would have an extremely adverse effect."[9]

He was also quite cognizant of a failed attempt at humor earlier in his senatorial career. At a meeting of Democrats, he had remarked, "I was almost late here today, but I had a very good taxi driver who brought me through the traffic jam. I was going to give him a very large tip and tell him to vote Democratic and then I remembered some advice Senator [Theodore F.] Green had given me, so I gave him no tip at all and told him to vote Republican." The Associated Press had publicized this fictitious anecdote as though it had actually happened, and JFK, who subsequently received a barrage of irate letters from taxi drivers, had been forced to arrange with the AP to print a denial that the incident had ever taken place. He did not want a repeat of this kind of thing at the Gridiron Club.

Accordingly, Kennedy agonized for weeks in advance, collected several hours' worth of potential material for the ten-minute speech, and tried out much of it on friends and associates. He gave the project possibly more attention than he did anything else in this period.

After being roasted by the club members, he was called on to talk, and he got up and said that he had been informed that the club file had been recently vandalized and that someone had stolen "your officers' election results for the next six years." Recognizing the many current senators in addition to himself who were seeking the 1960 Democratic presidential nomination, he asserted that there had been a recent poll in the upper chamber (then consisting of ninety-six elected legislators) regarding each member's preference for the presidency and that "ninety-six senators each received one vote." He acknowledged that the Democrats were once again beset by squabbling and indeed this time were "split right down the middle—and that gives us more unity than we've had in twenty years." Referring to the ongoing recession and incumbent President Eisenhower's attempts to put a bright face on what was by any standard a bleak situation, he declared, "As I interpret the president, we're now at the end of the beginning of the upturn of the downturn. Every bright spot the White House finds in the economy is like the policeman bending over the body in the alley who says cheerfully, 'Two of his wounds are fatal—but the other one's not so bad.'"

The speech was a resounding success, so much so that Kennedy, as Sorensen saw it, "tended more and more ... to use that kind of political, more subtle and self-belittling humor, for it was naturally consistent with his own personality and private wit."[10] The experience left him with such pleasant memories, indeed, that—unlike many other presidents—he was to speak at not only all of the Gridiron Club dinners held during his White House tenure but at most of the banquets of two similar journalist organizations, the White House Correspondents and the Alfalfa Club. Fond of paraphrasing Aristotle's definition of happiness—the full use of one's faculties along lines of excellence—he recognized that one area in which he excelled was in the use of drollery. Whatever misgivings he may have had prior to his 1958 Gridiron Club appearance, he was thenceforth not a bit reluctant to draw upon this talent in public as he always had in private.

As he ran against Nixon in the 1960 presidential contest, many of Kennedy's quips were clearly spontaneous, as in his interchange with host Lawrence Spivak when he appeared on NBC's widely watched "Meet the Press" television program. After Spivak had introduced him, he said, "I suppose, Mr. Spivak, that you have a long list of challenging questions for me." Spivak affably responded, "Knowing my high regard for you, Mr. Senator, I don't think you'd want me to pull my punches." Kennedy rejoined, "No. But I wouldn't mind if you lowered your regard a bit."

Similarly off-the-top-of-the-head was the Democratic candidate's answer to a reporter who asked him, "Senator, Governor [Edmund G.] Brown [of California] today issued a very optimistic statement about your chances. Yet the Field poll shows Nixon running ahead. Which of these two experts do you believe?" Kennedy said, "I believe Governor Brown."

In like vein, the following interchange between the candidate and another journalist took place in Anchorage, Alaska:

> REPORTER: "Senator, you were promised military intelligence briefing from the President. Have you received that?"
> KENNEDY: "Yes. I talked on Thursday morning to General Wheeler from the Defense Department."
> REPORTER: "What was his first name?"
> KENNEDY: "He didn't brief me on that."[11]

JFK's comment regarding Pennsylvania Senator Hugh Scott, made at another campaign stop, could not have been contrived: informed of a harsh attack on him that had just been made by Scott, Kennedy pointed out that the Pennsylvanian was a member of the self-described Republican "Truth Squad" and added that he "may well have lost his membership today." The same presumption of instinctive reaction goes for a Kennedy statement made at yet another stop, where an enthusiastic audience contained an unusually large percentage of children: "If we can lower the voting age to nine, we are going to sweep this state."

Other Kennedy utterances seemed a bit more scripted. A farm group was told, "I come from a nonagricultural state, Massachusetts, and, therefore, I am sure there are some farmers in Iowa and South Dakota and North Dakota who say, 'Why should we elect someone from New England?' Well, there is no farmer up for office this year. Whittier, California [Nixon's hometown], is not one of the greater agricultural sections of the United States." Several audiences one week heard the candidate say, "Last Thursday night Mr. Nixon dismissed me as 'another Truman.' I regard that as a great compliment, and I have no hesitation in returning the compliment. I consider him another Dewey." A Brooklyn group learned that its "district was the first district to endorse me as a candidate for president, nearly a year ago. My family had not even endorsed me when you endorsed me." And a Pikesville, Maryland, crowd was one of a number that heard an anecdote: "Mr. Khrushchev himself, it is said, told the story a few years ago about the Russian who began to run through the Kremlin, shouting, 'Khrushchev is a fool. Khrushchev is a fool.' He was sentenced, the premier said, to twenty-three years in prison, 'three for insulting the party secretary and twenty for revealing a state secret.'"

Incumbent Vice President Richard Milhous Nixon was more than just "another Dewey," as Kennedy saw him. Although the two nominees had at one time been friends—and Kennedy had gone so far in 1959 as to privately assert that if he weren't named as the Democratic standard-bearer in 1960 he would vote for Nixon for president[12]—relations had deteriorated to the point where at least JFK viewed his opponent as utterly lacking in class (although this sentiment appears not to have been reciprocated by Nixon). Kennedy reportedly winced when he viewed Nixon on television accepting the Republican nomination and told friends who were watching with him, "If I have to stand up before a crowd and wave my arms over my head like that in order to become the president of the United States, I'll never make it." He increasingly felt that Nixon was a man who was careless with the truth and would do almost anything to win. For all of this, most of Kennedy's campaign statements regarding the vice president were delivered good-naturedly.

On the only occasion during the presidential contest in which both nominees appeared on the same program, that of the Alfred Smith Memorial Dinner at New York's Waldorf-Astoria Hotel, the Democratic candidate used the host religious leader as the vehicle for his opening remarks. "Cardinal Spellman," he declared,

> is the only man so widely respected in American politics that he could bring together, amicably, at the same banquet table, for the first time in this campaign, two political leaders who are increasingly apprehensive about the November election, who have long eyed each other suspiciously, and who have disagreed so strongly, both publicly and privately—Vice President Nixon and Governor Rockefeller.

"One of the inspiring notes that was struck in the last [presidential] debate," he went on to say,

> was struck by the vice president in his very moving warning to the children of the nation and the candidates against the use of profanity by presidents and ex-presidents when they are on the stump. And I know after fourteen years in the Congress with the vice president that he was very sincere in his views about the use of profanity. But I am told that a prominent Republican said to him yesterday in Jacksonville, Florida, "Mr. President, that was a damn fine speech." And the vice president said, "I appreciate the compliment but not the language." And the Republican went on, "Yes, sir, I liked it so much that I contributed a thousand dollars to your campaign." And Mr. Nixon replied, "The hell you say."[13]

Delivered equally pleasantly in the course of the campaign were such lines as: (in reference to Nixon's constant emphasis on his experience) "Experience is what Mr. Nixon will have left after this campaign is over"; (regarding the vice president's vaunted "kitchen debate" with Khrushchev during Nixon's 1959 trip to the Soviet Union) "Mr. Nixon may be very experienced in his kitchen debates. So are a great many other married men I know"; and "Mr. Nixon, in the last seven days, has called me an ignoramus, a Pied Piper, and all the rest. I've just confined myself to calling him a Republican, but he says that is hitting below the belt."

Some displays of the Kennedy wit had more of an edge to them, however. When Nixon was forced to interrupt his campaigning because of an infected left knee that forced him to spend three weeks in a hospital, Kennedy told crowds, "Well, I said I would not mention him unless I could praise him, so I have not mentioned him." After the darkly stubbled Nixon had accused him of being a "barefaced liar," he countered, "Having seen him in close-up—and makeup—for our television debates, I would never accuse Mr. Nixon of being barefaced." When, during a widely publicized health scare involving cranberries, the two candidates found themselves in the same state, Kennedy informed his various crowds, "Actually ... the vice president and I are here on a mission for the secretary of Health, Education, and Welfare to test cranberries. Well, we have both eaten them, and I feel fine. But if we both pass away, I feel I shall have performed a great public service by taking the vice president with me." After his November victory, JFK told a Palm Beach friend, "If I've done nothing for this country, I've saved them from Dick Nixon."

Presidential Press Secretary Salinger often admiringly commented that his boss was so adept at public relations that he could have gotten along without any press secretary at all if only he had time to handle the everyday routine of the job.

No one, certainly, could accuse Kennedy of taking the media for granted. He fully appreciated and often quoted Oscar Wilde's dictum that in the United States "the president reigns for four years, but journalism governs forever," and he cultivated friendships among many members of the press corps by granting exclusive interviews and otherwise singling out journalists for special attention. He paid a social visit to the Georgetown townhouse of columnist Joseph Alsop in the small hours of the morning after he was inaugurated, played golf with the influential W. H. Lawrence of the *New York Times*, with Jackie spent dozens of evenings with the *Washington Post*'s Bradlee and the latter's wife, and invited countless editors and publishers to White House luncheons. He was accessible, relatively candid (at least in private), and invariably witty.

When columnist Leonard Lyons sent him a letter informing him that the current prices for autographed photographs of presidents, including the Kennedy ones, were at all-time highs, Kennedy wrote back: "Dear Leonard: I appreciate your letter.... It is hard to believe that the going price is so high now. In order not to depress the market any further, I will not sign this letter."

The *New York Times* board chairman, Arthur Hays Sulzberger, received a handwritten note after JFK learned that he, like the chronically sore-backed Kennedy, had purchased a rocking chair: "You will recall what has been said about the rocking chair—it gives you a sense of motion without any sense of danger."

After the publisher of the *Dallas Morning News* had rather rudely informed Kennedy at a White House luncheon that "we need a man on horseback to lead the nation, and many people in Texas and the Southwest think that you are riding Caroline's bicycle," and the publisher of the afternoon *Dallas Times Herald* had soon thereafter sent the president a note emphasizing that the *Morning News* magnate spoke only for himself, the note sender got a reply from Kennedy: "I'm sure the people of Dallas must be glad when afternoon comes."

His face-to-face encounters with representatives of the media were similarly marked by banter. Flying on Air Force One, he was asked by a reporter what would happen if the plane were to crash and, with a grin, he rejoined, "I'm sure of one thing: your name would be in the paper the next day, but in very small type." At a party that he gave for the White House press corps to celebrate his election victory, he introduced a United Press International newsman who had covered the presidency since 1941 to Jackie with the words, "I want you to meet Merriman Smith. We inherited him with the White House." A journalist who asked Kennedy how his staff had arrived at what seemed to be an unrealistically high crowd size figure for one JFK public appearance was informed, "[Salinger] counts the nuns, and then multiplies by 100." Addressing a group of Washington newspaper people during a time in which he was accused of managing the news with more slyness than any previous president, Kennedy began his speech with the words, "Fellow managing editors."

"Reporters," political satirist Gerald Gardner once pointed out, "tend to place a high valuation on humor. It is a quality that most good reporters possess and they value it in others."[14] In the thirty-fifth president, they had the quality in spades.

Nowhere, however, did the wry and derisive Kennedy style show to better advantage than in his sixty-four televised press conferences, which were always conducted before live audiences in the huge auditorium of the State Department.

In some ways, the scores of reporters present at these events were almost superfluous: George Herman of CBS News later remembered Kennedy looking "right over our heads, right into the camera.... This was a man who was extraordinarily professional," and a *Chicago Daily News* reporter thought that all of the journalists were merely "props in a show ... we should have joined Actors Equity."[15] But any latent Fourth Estate resentment that might have existed on these grounds was more than offset by JFK's disarming smiles and witticisms.

The trademark self-deprecation was rarely absent. Informed by a reporter that "the Republican National Committee recently adopted a resolution saying you were pretty much of a failure," Kennedy responded, "I am sure it was passed unanimously."

When the spirited May Craig shouted out, "Mr. President! Mr. President! What have you done lately for women?" he replied, "Obviously, Miss Craig, not enough." He was asked at the end of his first White House year, "If you had to do it over again would you work for the presidency and would you recommend the job to others?" JFK answered, "Well, the answer to the first is yes and the answer to the second is no. I don't recommend it to others, at least not for a while."

In response to the question, "Mr. President, you have said that you are in favor of the two-term limit to the office of the presidency. How do you feel about former President Eisenhower's suggestion that the terms of congressmen also be limited?" Kennedy answered, "It's the sort of proposal which I may advance in a postpresidential period, but not right now." After the stock market had registered a huge if temporary one-day plunge, an influential columnist wrote that the attitude of the business community toward Kennedy was "now we have you where we want you." The president—asked about the alleged attitude—asserted, "I can't believe I'm where business— big business, wants me." Asked whether he was annoyed by the best-selling record album parodying his voice by the talented JFK imitator Vaughn Meader, he said, "I listened to Mr. Meader's record, but I thought it sounded more like Teddy [Kennedy] than it did me—so *he's* annoyed."

But Kennedy in his press conference appreciations of life's incongruities was not always at center stage. Institutions, too, came in for their share of his irreverence. When queried as to whether he had narrowed his search for a new postmaster general and whether he sought a person with a business background or a political background, he responded, "The search is narrowing, but there are other fields that are still to be considered, including even a postal background." A reporter asked him, "Mr. President, back on the subject of presidential advisors, Congressman Baring of Nevada, a Democrat, said you would do much better if you got rid of some of yours— and he named Bowles, Ball, Bell, Bunche, and Sylvester." Kennedy rejoined:

Yes, he has a fondness for alliteration and for "Bs." And I would not add Congressman Baring to that list as I have a high regard for him and for the gentlemen that he named. But congressmen are always advising presidents to get rid of presidential advisers. That is one of the most constant threads that runs through American history and presidents ordinarily do not pay attention, nor do they in this case.[16]

Asked if he would comment on an announced series of Republican leadership seminars, he mused aloud as to who could be supplying the G.O.P. members with leadership and added, "But I'm sure they'll have a varied program."

Enamored as he knew that most working reporters were of him, Kennedy nonetheless was a realist. He recognized that the heavy majority of the nation's editors and publishers were Republicans and consequently that some large amount of negative editorials and commentary came with his Democratic territory (running for the presidency in Anderson, Indiana, and referring to one conservative publication, he had observed not entirely good-naturedly, "I understand that this town suffered a misfortune this morning when the bank was robbed. I am confident that the *Indianapolis Star* will say, 'Democrats Arrive and Bank Robbed'").

He was, accordingly, grateful for the considerable good will that he did enjoy with the media and essentially asked no more than this. To the end, his opinion as to how he was treated was no different from what he had expressed in answer to a question on this subject at a press conference held after he had been in office for about a year:

> Well, I am reading more and enjoying it less [Laughter] and so on, but I have not complained nor do I plan to make any general complaints. I read and talk to myself about it, but I don't plan to issue any general statement to the press. I think that they are doing their task, as a critical branch, the Fourth Estate. And I am attempting to do mine. And we are going to live together for a period, and then go our separate ways [Laughter].[17]

Able to see himself in perspective, JFK also viewed other people that way, and he was as quick to subject others to affable irreverence as he was to accord himself this treatment.

When Harvard professor and Kennedy ambassador to India John Kenneth Galbraith, complained to him that a *New York Times* article about Galbraith had referred to him as "arrogant," Kennedy rejoined, "I don't see why not. Everybody else does." (Galbraith, who received that presidential comment with his typical good grace and has often repeated it with relish in the many years since, yields to no one in his appreciation of the JFK humor. Kennedy, he says, was "one of the most perceptively amusing people I've ever known."[18])

Thomas P. "Tip" O'Neill, Jr., later to be speaker of the House, succeeded Kennedy as U.S. congressman from the Eleventh District of Massachusetts in 1958, but in winning the seat he received four fewer votes in one precinct than the future president had when he ran. The two men analyzed the voting and concluded that the difference stemmed from a French-Canadian family that disliked O'Neill. On January, 20, 1961—JFK's Inauguration day—Kennedy saw O'Neill in a ballroom and yelled over, "Hey, Tip, how many votes did you get in the North Cambridge precinct—and how many did I get?" When O'Neill shouted back the returns, Kennedy smiled broadly and responded, "That Lefebre family is still voting against you!"

Regarding Washington lawyer Clark Clifford, in charge of the transition in late 1960 from the Eisenhower White House to the Kennedy one, Kennedy had this to say: "Clark is a wonderful fellow. In a day when so many are seeking a reward [for] what they contributed to the return of the Democrats to the White House, you don't hear Clark clamoring. He was invaluable to us and all he asked in return was that we advertise his law firm on the backs of one dollar bills."

C. Douglas Dillon, the patrician Republican investment banker who served as Kennedy's secretary of the treasury, almost four decades later told an interviewer with great enjoyment one of his favorite tales of JFK irreverence:

> I used to come over to the White House from the Treasury Department through a special door into the Oval Office that was reserved for cabinet secretaries and the like to use if there was something important to discuss with the president. For some presumably pressing reason I came into the Kennedy office one day, sandwiched between two of the president's regular appointments and on a generally busy presidential day. Kennedy glanced at me, then just stared at me for what seemed like a very long period of time, and then deadpanned, "Stripes on stripes on stripes! That's a 'no-no'!" Apparently, I'd worn a striped suit with a striped shirt and a striped tie that day. As busy as he was, he thought about all kinds of ways to have fun.... We on the New Frontier worked very hard and didn't have time to be especially funny. Kennedy tried to lighten us up.[19]

The eminent historian Arthur M. Schlesinger, Jr., who served JFK as special assistant with an office in the White House, has another special memory: "From time to time, I did something that made the headlines in a way that certainly didn't help [Kennedy], and I'd go to him and tell him, 'I'm more of a hindrance than a help now. I think maybe I'll resign and go back to teaching.' He said, 'Don't be silly. If they're going to attack people around here, better you than me.'" ("Most people who worked for JFK in the White House were devoted to him," Schlesinger said, "And he earned this by giving a lot to his people."[20])

When the avid photographer Goldwater, during the entire Kennedy presidency the front runner for the 1964 Republican presidential nomination, which he would receive, took a picture of JFK and sent it to him for an autograph, it was returned to the senator with the inscription, "For Barry Goldwater, whom I urge to follow the career for which he has shown so much talent—photography. From his friend, John Kennedy."

Smathers of Florida, who had been an even closer friend of Kennedy's in the Senate than had Goldwater, received the following tribute at a Miami Beach fundraising banquet:

> I actually came down here tonight to pay a debt of obligation to an old friend and faithful adviser. He and I came to the Eightieth Congress together and have been associated for many years, and I regard him as one of my most valuable counselors in moments of great personal and public difficulty. In 1952, when I was thinking about running for the ... Senate, I went to the then Senator Smathers and said, "George, what do you think?" He said, "Don't do it. Can't win. Bad year." In 1956, I was at the Democratic convention, and ... I didn't know whether I would run for vice president or not, so I said, "George, what do you think?" "This is it. They need a young man. It's your chance." So I ran—and lost. And in 1960, I was wondering whether I ought to run in the West Virginia primary. "Don't do it. That state you can't possibly carry." And actually, the only time I really got nervous about the whole matter at the Democratic convention of 1960 was just before the balloting and George came up and he said, "I think it looks pretty good for you." It will encourage you to know that every Tuesday morning ... we have breakfast together and he advises with me—Cuba, anything else, Laos, Berlin, anything—George comes right out there and gives his views and I listen very carefully.[21]

But perhaps no one ever got the Kennedy treatment as fully as did the megalomaniacal then-senator from Texas, Lyndon Johnson, when Kennedy, Johnson, and Missouri Senator Stuart Symington were all campaigning in 1958 for the upcoming Democratic nomination. JFK often told audiences about a dream that he claimed to have recently had:

> Several nights ago, I dreamed that the good Lord touched me on the shoulder and said, "Don't worry, you'll be the Democratic presidential nominee in 1960. What's more, you'll be elected." I told Stu Symington about my dream. "Funny thing," said Stu, "I had exactly the same dream myself." We both told our dreams to Lyndon Johnson, and Johnson said, "That's funny. For the life of me, I can't remember tapping either of you two boys for the job."[22]

In general, the business community took to Kennedy about as well as a hay fever sufferer takes to ragweed, and this was obvious even from the 1960 election returns. "I do not think it wholly inaccurate to say," JFK commented not long after his victory, "that I was the second choice of a majority of businessmen for the office of president.... Their first choice was anyone else."

Elaborating on these remarks in a subsequent speech to the National Association of Manufacturers, he opined that the only managers who voted for him over Nixon were "a very few who were under the impression that I was my father's son." In this same speech, he added that he understood that William McKinley and he were the only two U.S. presidents ever to address an NAM convention and that he supposed that McKinley and he were "the only two that are regarded as fiscally sound enough to be qualified for admission."

Evidently enjoying his tweaking of the management community, he told another business group whose luncheon he attended at about the same time, "It would be premature to ask your support in the next election, and it would be inaccurate to thank you for it in the past."

Nonbusiness audiences were also reminded of the coolness between president and industry. "Last week, after speaking to the Chamber of Commerce," Kennedy said to an enthusiastic crowd of United Automobile Workers on one occasion, "I began to wonder how I got elected. And now I remember." An AFL-CIO Convention in Miami was informed one day after Kennedy had addressed a New York City meeting of industrialists on a bitter cold day in December, "It's warmer here today than it was yesterday."

In part, Kennedy felt, the business antipathy was nothing more than an unwarranted reflex action on the part of a traditionally Republican constituency toward a Democratic administration. "Many businessmen who are prospering as never before during this administration," the man who defeated Nixon told the Tampa Chamber of Commerce,

> are convinced, nevertheless, that we must be anti-business. When our bill to grant a tax credit for business investment was before the Congress, Secretary of the Treasury Dillon was on a plane to this state, and he found himself talking to one of the leading Florida businessmen about the investment tax credit. He spent some time, he later told me, explaining how the bill would help this man's corporate outlook and income and the businessman was most impressed. Finally, as the plane landed at Miami, he turned to Secretary Dillon and said, "I am very grateful to you for explaining the bill. Now tell me just once more why is it that I am against it?"[23]

There were genuine differences of principle and philosophy, however, and nowhere did the simmering tensions come to a head more graphically than in the case of the New Frontier's anti-inflation efforts. To thwart price level rises, the Kennedy administration had established voluntary wage-price guidelines, which it hoped both management and labor would respect. In March 1962, the Steelworkers Union signed a contract with the major steel producers that justified this hope by not raising wages at all, on the assumption that the companies would similarly not raise their prices.

The assumption was wrong. In April, the United States Steel Corporation announced a six dollars per ton, or 3.5 percent increase in steel prices, and other producers in short order made similar moves. An irate Kennedy went on national television to denounce the "tiny handful of steel executives whose pursuit of private power and profit exceeds their sense of public responsibility." Privately, he said of the Big Steel men, "My father always told me they were sons of bitches, but I never really believed him until now," and these words quickly became public. Faced with an aroused public opinion and presidential pressure, the companies—with Bethlehem Steel now taking the lead—canceled the price boost.

Much of corporate America saw the Kennedy intrusion as the final straw, however, and was slow either to forgive or to forget. Negative communications from the business community flooded the White House (JFK remarked in June that the "nicest" letter that he had received in some time came from a Bethlehem Steel executive informing him, "You are even worse than Harry Truman"). A full year after he had forced Big Steel into its ignominious price retreat Kennedy, upon being informed that the steel industry was all set to present its annual public service award to former President Dwight D. Eisenhower, announced at a Democratic fundraiser, "I was their man of the year last year. They wanted to come down to the White House to give me their award, but the Secret Service wouldn't let them do it."

In the aftermath, too, Joseph Kennedy's son liked to tell the story about a leading business executive who had visited him shortly after the events of April 1962 and had told him how pessimistic he was about the economy. "Things look great," the nation's chief executive had said in response, "Why, if I weren't president, I'd be buying stock myself." And the executive had replied, "If you weren't president, so would I." Kennedy was delighted by a cartoon showing two business executives in their club, one saying to the other, "My father always told me that all presidents are sons of bitches"; he requested the original of it and had it hung on a wall in his secretary's office.

On the other hand, the only president except McKinley to have addressed the NAM never gave up trying to woo executives to his side. Having much in common with the latter through both background and lifestyle, he mixed easily and frequently on a social basis with many of them and could never fully understand why they did not embrace him politically, especially when he felt he was willing to be flexible. He even joked about this: returning to work from a Florida Easter vacation in the second year of his presidency, he told the White House journalists that he had been "back in touch with my constituents and seeing how they felt. And frankly, I've come back to Washington from Palm Beach and I'm against my entire program."

As difficult as dealing with industrialists often was for Kennedy, it was nonetheless child's play for him as compared to some of his encounters with such self-centered and chronically suspicious foreign leaders as Khrushchev, France's president Charles de Gaulle, and Indian Prime Minister Jawaharlal Nehru. JFK and British Prime Minister Macmillan maintained a mutual admiration society, and Kennedy's relations with West Germany's octogenarian chancellor, Konrad Adenauer, were greatly improved by Kennedy's genuine liking for the German. (After Adenauer left office, his successor, Ludwig

Erhard, visited Adenauer after delivering a two-hour inaugural address, and JFK immensely relished Adenauer's greeting to Erhard, "You're only going to be in office two years, and you took almost that long to say what you were going to do.") But Kennedy's interactions with many heads of state were tense and unrewarding. Even here, however, the thirty-fifth president's wit was, by and large, appreciated by the foreigners and quite probably removed some of the acrimony that might otherwise have been present.

Khrushchev, who indeed told several journalists after the Vienna meeting that he liked Kennedy personally especially because of the latter's sense of humor and candor, actually had a definite waggishness himself. He was reported to have told, several times, the "Khrushchev is a fool," revelation-of-a-state-secret story with which JFK was to amuse his campaign audiences. At Vienna, as Kennedy was lighting a cigar, the match slipped out of his hand and landed just behind Khrushchev's chair. The Soviet premier asked, "Are you trying to set me on fire?" and when Kennedy replied that he assuredly was not, Khrushchev rejoined, "Ah, a capitalist, not an incendiary." At this same conference, Kennedy asked Khrushchev if he ever admitted a mistake, and the premier answered, "Certainly. In a speech before the Twentieth Party Congress I admitted all of Stalin's mistakes."

He enjoyed Kennedy's reminder to him at Vienna that the two men had met before, two years earlier, at a Senate Foreign Relations Committee meeting in Washington and that "I remember you said that I looked young to be a senator, but I've aged a lot since then." If Vienna ended so badly as to encourage Khrushchev to trigger the Cuban missile crisis the following year, at least some level of personal bonding had been achieved between the two men that might not have been effected without the mutual kidding, an absence that could conceivably have made a bad Cuban situation even worse.

With the imperious de Gaulle, it was obviously not a question of war or peace. France was firmly in the Western, anti–Communist camp. But de Gaulle resolutely believed that the United States should stay out of European affairs except in situations of dire emergency and that France should not only have its own independent nuclear force but should speak for all of the nations of continental Western Europe—opinions that would have made the French president difficult to deal with even if he were not personally both extremely hard to please and highly conceited.

Nonetheless, the only time that Kennedy and de Gaulle met for face-to-face talks—when Kennedy stopped in Paris en route to his 1961 encounter with Khrushchev in Vienna—the austere Frenchman displayed an unexpected degree of warmth toward his visitor.

This was partially due, as was widely reported, to Jacqueline Kennedy's great success in charming de Gaulle, something that she had also done years earlier as a senator's wife when the Frenchman had visited Washington—so successfully, indeed, that de Gaulle was quoted then as saying, "The one thing I would like to take back to France from America is Mrs. Kennedy." But de Gaulle was also taken with the now-well-honed JFK style. De Gaulle enjoyed Kennedy's reference at a news conference to Jackie's effectiveness in dazzling not only himself once again but also most of his citizenry: "I am the man who accompanied Jacqueline Kennedy to Paris, and I have enjoyed it."

De Gaulle also quite good-naturedly appreciated the American president's answer to a journalist at a ballet that the two leaders attended. During the intermission, de Gaulle let a group of French photographers take pictures of himself and his guest and then brusquely motioned to them to leave. The journalist asked JFK, "Don't you wish you could control your photographers like that?" Kennedy, making implicit reference to the fact that his host had been asked by his nation to head off civil war by returning as president in 1958 after a twelve-year absence from power, replied, "You must remember that I wasn't recalled to office as my country's savior."

Kennedy also scored points with de Gaulle by remarking in a luncheon toast, "Years ago it was said that an optimist studies Russian while a pessimist studies Chinese. I prefer to believe the far-seeing are learning French and English," and by asserting in his informal remarks to employees of the U.S. embassy, "I tried to be assigned to the embassy in Paris myself, and, unable to do so, I decided I would run for president."

Indian Prime Minister Nehru on the surface possessed the same frigid, aloof personality that de Gaulle did, and when he visited the United States in late 1961, he struck many Kennedy advisers as bored and more than a bit condescending. (One such staffer was Schlesinger, who thought that the Indian showed much interest and animation only when he was with Jacqueline. When Schlesinger mentioned this later to the president, JFK replied, "A lot of our visiting statesmen have that same trouble.")

But Kennedy was aware that under the formidable Nehru mien lurked a dry, self-deprecating outlook not unlike his own, and he enjoyed bantering with the intellectual leader. Nehru met Kennedy at the Newport, Rhode Island, naval base, and the two men were then driven to the private Newport estate at which they would confer, over a route that included many of that city's palatial homes: the itinerary was justified to Nehru by the straight-faced Kennedy on the grounds that "I wanted you to see how the average American family lives." Nehru, with equal mock seriousness and full awareness of the title of a book recently authored by the U.S. ambassador to India, Galbraith, replied, "Yes, I've heard of your affluent society."

Nehru had arrived in the United States one day earlier and had as one of his first orders of business appeared on the televised "Meet the Press" program, where host Spivak had interrogated him in an aggressive and rather hostile manner. On the day after his Newport meeting with Kennedy, the two heads of state went to Washington, where at a state dinner that evening the U.S. leader toasted his guest by saying, "We all want to take this opportunity to welcome you to America, Mr. Prime Minister, though I doubt whether any words of mine can embellish the welcome already extended to you by Larry Spivak."

With other foreign dignitaries, Kennedy was no more inhibited. As Julius Nyerere, the Roman Catholic leader of Tanganyika, waited while a drum roll from the U.S. Marine Band proclaimed his entry into the White House reception area, JFK asked him, "Well, Mr. President, how does it feel to go into luncheon with another religious minority politician who made the grade?" When Kennedy overheard his secretary of the Interior, Udall, in conversation with the daughter of Pakistan's president, Ayub Khan, erroneously referring to a mountain that he had climbed as being in Pakistan when it was in fact in adjacent Afghanistan, he said to the woman, "Madam, that is why I named Mr. Udall secretary of the *Interior*." On a visit to Canada, following Prime Minister John Diefenbaker on the speaking program, he announced that he was less loathe to attempt a few words in French after listening to Diefenbaker speak in that language.

Kennedy's ability to view his role in perspective and to take it neither any more seriously nor any less seriously than he believed it should be taken also extended to his more formal speechmaking while on international tour. After receiving honorary degrees, on a visit to Ireland, from both the British and nonsectarian Trinity College and the Irish and Catholic National University, he declared to his audience, "I now feel equally part of both, and if they ever have a game of Gaelic football or hurling, I shall cheer for Trinity and pray for National."

On this same trip to the land of his ancestors, he visited the small town from which his great-grandfather had emigrated to America and with reference to a nearby fertilizer plant announced, "If my great-grandfather had not left New Ross, I would be working today over there at the Albatross Company shoveling fertilizer." At another stop in Ireland, he introduced Dave Powers, who was sitting with seven local first cousins, to the crowd, adding, "Dave looks more Irish than his cousins," and then said, "I also want to introduce Monsignor Michael O'Mahoney, the pastor at the church I go to, who comes from Cork. He is the pastor of a poor, humble flock in Palm Beach, Florida."

At the University of Costa Rica, he began his remarks, "It is a great pleasure to leave Washington, where I am lectured to by professors, to come to Costa Rica where I can speak to students."

The people of Cologne, Germany, were told, "As a citizen of Boston, I find it sobering to come to Cologne where the Romans marched when the Bostonians were in skins." The capital of Massachusetts also received mention when Kennedy made a speech at Paris's ornate city hall: "I am the descendant on both sides of two grandparents who served in the city council of Boston, and I am sure they regarded that as a more significant service than what any of their descendants have yet rendered."

Generally, JFK's reputation for humor preceded him in his travels, and even crowds whose native tongue was not English but who had learned at least the basics of the language tended to laugh appreciatively at these bons mots long before the official translation had been rendered. But a mishap did occur at Kennedy's airport arrival ceremonies in France, when the State Department translator completely failed to convey even a hint of the American president's drollery. Kennedy's Air Force aide, who was fluent in French, subsequently informed his boss of this sin of omission and was told by the latter, "You can't crucify somebody for not being as witty as I might be, but we won't use him again."

Nothing, in fact, could muzzle his badinage for long, not even the worst turns in international relations. When newly installed in his presidency, he had gotten documents concerning the most pressing foreign policy problems in a folder and had mused, "Let's see now, did we inherit these, or are they our own?" Later, he was able to say to his family along the same lines, "I had plenty of problems when I came into office. But wait until the fellow who follows me sees what he will inherit." In addition to letting him deal more effectively with both foreign leaders and the people whom they led, the humor—in international diplomacy as elsewhere—helped him immeasurably in alleviating personal tensions that otherwise might have been unbearable.

The author of the New Frontier did not appear to have developed the inordinate self-absorption that marked many of the foreign leaders with whom he interacted.

He had been elected by one of the smallest margins in American history—he got 49.7 percent of the popular vote compared to Nixon's 49.5 percent—and he often pointed this out to his various audiences. After a newspaper article described one of his aides as "coruscatingly" brilliant, he observed, "Those guys should never forget, 50,000 votes the other way and we'd all be coruscatingly stupid." He once noted to a crowd of Illinois Democrats, "Some years ago in the city of Fall River, Massachusetts, the mayor was elected by one vote, and every time he walked down the street, someone would say to him, 'Say, I put you in office.' I feel a little like that tonight here in Chicago. If all of you had voted the other way—there are about 5,500 of you here tonight—I wouldn't be president of the United States." One week to the day before his assassination, he told an AFL-CIO convention, "Three years ago and one week, by a landslide, the people of the United States elected me to the presidency of this country."

The man politics allowed to go from being an obscure member of the Harvard Junior Varsity to being an honorary member of the Football Hall of Fame had no inflated opinion of his own abilities, either. He often pointed out that he had campaigned in Alaska and failed to carry it, while not going to Hawaii and winning it: "Just think what my margin might have been," he once said, "if I had never left home!" He frequently declared that he had advanced from the rank of lieutenant junior grade in the Navy to commander in chief without any qualifications at all. Three months into his presidency, beset by a badly botched Bay of Pigs Cuban invasion, Russia's man-in-space triumph, and a variety of other widely heralded problems, he told Schlesinger, who was taking notes for a book on his administration, that he had a title for the book: "Kennedy: The Only Years."

When it was suggested that he invite the noted poet Robert Frost, whom he greatly admired, to speak at his inauguration, he said, "Great idea! But with Frost's skill with words, people will remember his speech instead of mine. I think we'd better have him read a poem." At a dinner that included former President Harry Truman, he announced, "I used to wonder, when I was a member of the House, how President Truman got in so much trouble. Now I am beginning to get the idea. It is not difficult."

He could laugh, as well, at his chronic inability to master many of the finer points of economics. Alluding to the several Tuesday nights that as a congressman he and a close friend, *Chattanooga Times* reporter Charles Bartlett, had spent in trying to improve their knowledge of the discipline in a two-man private tutorial with an American University professor, he told Bartlett after his installation in the White House that while he didn't know definitively what had happened to their old instructor, he believed that he "jumped out of the window when he heard I was elected." He had no qualms as he went before Congress in January 1963 prepared to deal with the many criticisms of his economic policies in telling his Council of Economic Advisers chairman, Walter Heller, "Walter, I want to make it perfectly clear that I resent these attacks on you."

He derived enormous enjoyment from an answer that his old friend Paul "Red" Fay gave him shortly after his inauguration, when he visited the Oval Office with his brother Teddy and Fay and asked the latter, "Paul, do you think this is adequate?" Fay's reply, "I feel any minute now that some guy is going to stick his head through one of those doors and say: 'All right, you guys—out of here,'" was tailor-made for Kennedy's funny bone.

He understood that he was the world's most famous person, of course, but he recognized that this was necessarily a mixed blessing. He told a friend when the conversation had turned to the subject of religion:

> I don't mind them taking pictures after mass, but I sure as hell don't want them around after confession. I feel humiliated then, and I know I look it. A Catholic likes to confess to a priest who doesn't know him. It's very disconcerting to sit in the booth and hear the voice from the other side of the screen saying, "Good evening, Mr. President."

Acknowledging the many luminaries from the literary and art worlds he and Jacqueline had invited to dine at the Executive Mansion, he commented, "It's becoming a sort of eating place for artists. But *they* never ask *us* out." Referring to the single most important Democratic state primary of 1960, he told Senator Hubert Humphrey, "If I'd known the job was this tough, I wouldn't have beaten you in West Virginia." Humphrey responded, "If I hadn't known it was this tough, I never would have let you beat me."

The same light touch marked JFK's references to members of his family, in at least one situation doing much to defuse what could have been for Kennedy a definite political negative. In January 1961, to a large extent due to pressure from Joseph Kennedy, the thirty-five-year-old Robert F. Kennedy was appointed by his brother to serve as the nation's attorney general, and the action immediately generated widespread charges of nepotism. In making his selection known to the media, the new president declared that he thought that his sibling might as well get a little experience before beginning the practice of law. He suggested that he had considered making the announcement by opening "the front door of [my] Georgetown house early some morning.... [I'll] look up and down the street and, if there's no one there, I'll whisper, 'It's Bobby.'"

He revealed that just before the real announcement he had said, "Bobby, before we go out there to tell the press that you are to be the next attorney general of the United States, would you mind combing your hair?" As the brothers faced the members of the press, he quite audibly instructed his new cabinet appointee, "Don't smile too much or they'll think we are happy about the appointment."

In office, Robert Kennedy understandably had greater access to his brother than did any other governmental official. Not long after a major national publication had described Bobby as the person with the single greatest influence at the White House, JFK received a telephone call in his office, covered the speaker with his hand, and informed a visitor, "This is the second most powerful man in the nation calling." In person, referring to this same article, he told his attorney general, "Well, there's only one way you can go now—down." When a lawyer some time later wrote the president to suggest that Bobby would make an even better president than he did an attorney general, Kennedy wrote back, "I have consulted Bobby about it, and, to my dismay, the idea appeals to him."

Edward M. Kennedy, the youngest of the Kennedy brothers, ran for the U.S. Senate as soon as he could constitutionally serve in that body—in 1962, when he was thirty years of age—and his public career was noted with the same amiable irreverence that had greeted Bobby's. JFK joked that Teddy was so desirous of succeeding on his own that he had even thought about changing his name. "To what?"

he was asked. "To Roosevelt," the president replied. After Teddy had been nominated by the Massachusetts Democratic convention, he—according to *Time* magazine—had "smiled sardonically," but John Kennedy later disputed this: "Bobby and I smile sardonically. Teddy will learn how to smile sardonically in two or three years, but he doesn't know how yet."

On one occasion, when Teddy accompanied JFK to a Gridiron Club dinner, the latter told the audience in his speech, "I have brought my brother Teddy along this evening. We couldn't find anyone to leave him with." On another, after Teddy had made an especially emotional speech on behalf of JFK about the qualities required in a U.S. chief executive, his brother took the microphone to point out that Teddy was not old enough to qualify under the Constitution to be president. Not long before he died, Kennedy told those in attendance at a Boston Democratic dinner, "My last campaign may be coming up very shortly, but Teddy is around and, therefore, these dinners can go on indefinitely."

Other family members also came in for their share of public attention, often along the age theme: (during the 1960 campaign) "I want you to meet my sister, Pat Lawford, from California. Somebody asked her last week if I was her kid brother, so she knew it was time this campaign came to an end"; and "Master Robert Kennedy, age four, came to see me today but I told him we already had an attorney general."

Jacqueline, however, was the object of comparatively little such facetiousness, possibly because of the fragility of the relationship between the president and his wife, but she was noted jocularly every now and then. Alluding to the total loyalty to him of his personal secretary, Evelyn Lincoln, Kennedy once declared, "Whatever I do or say, Mrs. Lincoln will be sweet and unsurprised. If I had said just now, 'Mrs. Lincoln, I have cut off Jackie's head, would you please send over a box?' she still would have replied, 'That's wonderful, Mr. President, I'll send it right away.... Did you get your nap?'" In reference to the First Lady's dilatory tendencies, he announced to a crowd of supporters, "I appreciate you being here this morning. Mrs. Kennedy is organizing herself. It takes her longer, but, of course, she looks better than we do when she does it." He also was capable of amusing himself by completely fabricating facts regarding his spouse, as when he told an audience of Rhode Island nuns, "You know, Jackie always wanted to be a nun ... she went to a convent school and really planned to take the orders."

Generally, though, the quips that JFK made on the subject of Jacqueline were delivered face-to-face, as when—after his presidential election victory—he told her and Ben Bradlee's wife, both of whom were pregnant, "Okay, girls, you can take out the pillows now. We won!" When a respected physician visiting the White House told him that she could give him an injection that would provide total relief from the considerable pain that his adrenal insufficiency constantly caused him but that it would remove all feeling below the waist, he grinned and said, "We can't have that, can we, Jackie?"

Kennedy was also not averse to using parody and, indeed, drew on it more than any other president before or since.

At the April 1962 White House Correspondents Association dinner, just after he had forced the steel companies to rescind their price increase, he declared:

> The sudden and arbitrary actions of the officers of this association in increasing the price of dinner tickets by $2.50 over last year constitutes a wholly unjustifiable defiance of the public interest.... In this serious hour in our nation's history, when newsmen are awakened in the middle of the night to be given a front page story, when expense accounts are being scrutinized by Congress, when correspondents are required to leave their families for long and lonely weekends at Palm Beach, the American people will find it hard to accept this ruthless decision made by a tiny handful of executives. [24]

Six months after the Cuban missile crisis, he opened his address to the Gridiron Club with many of the same words that he had used in his televised speech to the American public at the time of that emergency: "I have tonight a very grave announcement. The Soviet Union has once again recklessly embarked upon a provocative and extraordinary change in the status quo in an area which they know full well I regard as having a special and historic relationship. I refer to the deliberate and sudden deployment of Mr. Khrushchev's son-in-law to the Vatican."

He also satirized his own inaugural address:

> We observe today not a celebration of freedom but a victory of party, for we have sworn to pay off the same party debt our forebears ran up nearly a year and three months ago. Our deficit will not be paid off in the next hundred days, nor will it be paid off in the first one thousand days, nor in the life of the administration. Nor, perhaps even in our lifetime on this planet. But let us begin![25]

While on the campaign trail, he regularly tailored Robert Frost's famous lines to his locations: "Scollay Square [or Iowa City, or San Francisco, or Jacksonville] is lovely, dark and deep / But I have promises to keep / And miles to go before I sleep."

Even religion was not exempt. To his favorite passage from Ecclesiastes ("a time to weep and a time to laugh; a time to mourn and a time to dance") was insouciantly added on at least one occasion "a time to fish and a time to cut bait."

In such lampooning, essentially anything was fair game. The man who, unable to attend a testimonial dinner honoring his postmaster general, transmitted his regrets together with the notation, "I am sending this message by wire, since I want to be certain that [it] reaches you in the right place at the right time" was not about to let something like the New Testament or his own inaugural address move into the category of untouchables.

Although by no means to the extent that Franklin Roosevelt did, Kennedy sometimes relied on the efforts of others in creating some of his humor. Starting in 1958, his key adviser Sorensen was, as previously indicated, instrumental in developing a file of witty remarks that could be drawn upon for appropriate speech openings and insertions, and Sorensen's influence on JFK's overall use of drollery, while not directly traceable, was well known. (The last time that Sorensen ever saw his boss was on the day before the assassination, when as Kennedy was boarding his helicopter on the White House South Lawn, Sorensen ran out with some suggestions for "Texas humor" that the president had asked him to make.) Nationally known journalists John Bartlow Martin and Joseph Kraft prepared funny lines for Kennedy's delivery at each appearance that the candidate made during the 1960 campaign. Satirist Mort Sahl, forgiven for his comment regarding both presidential candidates in 1960—"I don't see how either of them can win"—also played a hand in authoring some of the humor. So did Special Assistant Schlesinger. At times, Kennedy, like Lincoln, jotted down funny quips and stories that he heard, for future use.

But most of the wryness that was displayed so consistently and so effectively was clearly Kennedy's own creation, a product of his instinctive ability to view life's ironies with detached amusement. The humor formed a point of view that rarely deserted him, at least once he ascended to national power—whether the occasion was a nationally televised press conference, a one-on-one conversation with a foreign head of state, a fundraising banquet, a speech on a college campus, or an appearance at a whistle-stop on the political hustings—and its dual doses of self-mockery and deflation of the self-importance of others came to be expected of him in these appearances.

He reveled in the challenge. Liberated finally when he came to the White House, he could, as Schlesinger said of him, "at last be himself.... The force of his intelligence, gaiety and wit, now displayed without inhibition, made people wonder how two years earlier they could possibly have confused him with Richard Nixon."[26] Like Lincoln, he became more somber under the weight of his awesome responsibilities, but he retained and consistently exhibited his deft humor to the end.

In 1962, Kennedy gave Dave Powers as a birthday present a silver beer mug with the inscription, "There are three things which are real: God, human folly and laughter. The first two are beyond our comprehension. So we must do what we can with the third." He knew those obscure lines, from Aubrey Menen's version of *The Ramayana*, by heart. And he adhered so fully to the message contained in them that at least one qualified observer—*New York Times* reporter Tom Wicker, who saw the youthful president at close range and often—once expressed the view that the inscription should be Kennedy's epitaph.[27]

JFK could do, and did, much with his considerable sense of humor. It allowed him to build enviable media relations and the highly positive image that this in turn gained for him, to achieve excellent rapport with countless groups and individuals, to defuse sensitive issues, to deal relatively painlessly with bores and other undesirables, and to release the enormous tension of his burdensome position. If he was not a great president, he was a hugely popular leader who recognized that his gift for witty understatement could do much to establish a climate in which his underlying goals could be more readily realized. No less than Lincoln, Coolidge, and Roosevelt, his light touch had weighty consequences.

CHAPTER 5

RONALD REAGAN

In 1986, the oldest man ever to be elected president—he would be almost seventy-eight years old when his eight years in the White House ended three years later—paid a visit to Las Vegas. There he told an enthusiastic Republican audience that when he had been in that city on a previous visit his name had been listed on the neon signs outside a major hotel and, since he had neither sung nor danced on this occasion, some people had predicted that he would "never play Las Vegas again." "And what do you know?" he added, "Here I am, and playing to a full house!"[1]

Ronald Reagan was referring to a two-week stint that he had performed in 1954 as a stand-up comedian in America's gambling capital, getting equal billing in his fortnight of appearances with a nondescript quartet called the Continentals. He did not enjoy the experience and was later to describe this venture into nightclub comedy—the only one ever made by any of the nation's chief executives—as the nadir of his long professional acting career. But he was as well served as a politician by his irrepressible sense of the amusing as had been any of his predecessors by theirs.

Regan combined in his public life a genius for witty self-deprecation, which was invariably so cheerful that it reminded many of those who were old enough to remember of Reagan's original political hero, Franklin D. Roosevelt, with a competency in raconteurship that would have done even Lincoln proud.

No more than it had been for Lincoln, Coolidge, Roosevelt, or Kennedy was the sense of humor in any way a secondary facet of Reagan's personality. On the contrary, it was, in the opinion of one of his foremost biographers, Lou Cannon, "a key to his character. He was the resident humorist and gag writer in a White House where ... he engaged in government by anecdote."[2] To economist Alan Greenspan, no slouch at humor himself, the fortieth head of the nation was "psychologically a professional comedian, a professional raconteur." Journalist Owen Ullmann, sounding like Carl Sandburg writing about Lincoln, deemed Reagan to be "the Johnny Carson of national politics, the Joker-in-Chief of the United States."[3] Reagan himself quoted Frank Moore Colby's well-known dictum—"Men will confess to treason, murder, arson, false teeth or a wig. But how many of them will own up to a lack of humor?"—and once told the graduating class at Eureka College, his alma mater, "You can't take life too seriously. And since you have what I hope will be long and productive lives ahead, you'll have a big advantage if you can laugh along the way."

Reagan joked about his undemanding work schedule ("They say hard work never killed anyone, but I figure, why take a chance?") and his age ("I can remember when a hot story broke and the reporters would run in yelling, 'Stop the chisels!'"). He made quips about his conservatism ("Sometimes our right hand doesn't know what our far right hand is doing") and even—during his last White House years—his occasional forgetfulness, which portended his Alzheimer's disease. (He said to one of his primary physicians, "I have three things that I want to tell you today. The first is that I seem to be having a little problem with my memory. I cannot remember the other two.") He found humorous material in the unimpressive C average that he consistently attained during his collegiate years (as president he declared, "Even now I wonder what I might have accomplished if I had studied harder") and his tendency to fall asleep at inopportune times ("I've laid down the law to everyone from now on about anything that happens, that no matter what time it is, wake me, even if it's in the middle of a cabinet meeting"). He saw fodder for humor in the fifty-four more or less forgettable movies that he made between 1937 and 1965, many of which continued to be widely televised even when he occupied the White House. ("I've been asked at times what it is like to sit and watch the late, late show and see yourself. I have one answer. It's like looking at a son you never knew you had.") Minutes after the March 1981 assassination attempt by John W. Hinckley, the badly wounded president was wheeled into the George Washington University Hospital operating room with a collapsed left lung, a loss of a great deal of blood, and a pulse so slight that his nurses had twice failed to locate it. His ability to laugh led him to affably tell the surgeons, "Please assure me that you are all Republicans!" And when a nurse on that occasion said to him, "Keep up the good work," he rejoined, "You mean this may happen several times more?"

He was no less inhibited in his storytelling. He genially told jokes that were unflattering to economists to economists, anti-attorney jokes to lawyers, and anti-bureaucrat jokes to bureaucrats. He offered jokes that made fun of the Soviet Union to Soviet leaders and jokes—often in dialect—about Italian Americans, Japanese Americans, Polish Americans, and Irish Americans more or less indiscriminately to audiences of all ethnicities (although, having incurred some criticism for such efforts, he tended to limit himself to Irish stories later in his career, presumably in the belief that he was safe with these given his Irish ancestry). He was known to tell dirty jokes on occasion. Just like Lincoln—another man whose path to the presidency had its beginnings in humble, small-town Illinois surroundings—practically anything could remind him of a story (he frequently said, "You know, that brings me to a story—almost everything does").

He left office with personal approval ratings that were of Rooseveltian dimensions and by some standards even beyond those of FDR's: his Gallup poll approval rating at his retirement was a striking seventy percent, compared to the sixty eight percent that Roosevelt registered just before his death. In each of his eight years in office, again according to the respected Gallup organization, Reagan was the "most admired" man in the country. His political nemesis, the powerful Democratic speaker of the House, Tip O'Neill, once told him, "In my fifty years in public life, I've never seen a man more popular than you with the American people."

His popularity, indeed, dropped meaningfully below the seventy percent level only once during his presidency, during the 1982 recession. Even at the 1987 peak of the so-called Iran-Contra affair, when Reagan stood accused of having agreed to sell arms secretly to Iran in exchange for the release of American hostages although he had consistently promised never to do this, his personal approval rate held between seventy one and seventy four percent even though seventy five percent of the polled respondents thought that he had not told everything he knew.

This popularity, naturally, translated into votes. In 1980, in a three-way race for the White House against incumbent Jimmy Carter and Independent John B. Anderson, Reagan won by an electoral landslide, getting 489 votes to Carter's 49, and, even with the two opponents, he won 51 percent of the popular vote. In 1984, his electoral total against former Vice President Walter Mondale was the largest in history: he swept 49 states, garnering 525 electoral votes to Mondale's 13 and received an impressive 59 percent of all popular votes cast.

The humor and the popularity were not unrelated. The urbane Democratic governor of New York, Mario Cuomo, had not the slightest doubt, he declared at the 1988 Gridiron Club dinner, that Reagan's trove of good-natured one-liners and gently told stories was "one of the reasons that we Americans love and respect [Reagan]."[4] Veteran humor writer Bob Orben has argued that Reagan's gift of laughter formed the basis for the huge "balance of good will" on which the fortieth chief executive could draw in time of need. Gerald Gardner, a keen observer of the power of humor for presidents and other executives, is convinced that much of Reagan's appeal stemmed from "his ability to flatter a particular constituency with well-tailored wit."[5] Reagan himself—students of his presidency have generally concluded— was well aware that the anecdotes and, especially, the self-mocking quips could advance his popularity immeasurably.

In this regard, Reagan's sunny, grinning, twinkle-eyed delivery was as important as his content. He came across, both in person and on television, as a genuinely decent man, fully justifying his son Ron's comment that he was "almost impossible to dislike"[6] and his wife Nancy's statement that he "never saw anything evil in another human being."[7] Richard Nixon once said of him, when asked what he believed to be the former actor's liabilities, "He may be too nice to be president."[8]

He was eminently likable in his one-on-one relationships, too. Caspar Weinberger, who was secretary of health, education, and welfare in both the Nixon and Ford administrations and then for more than six years served as the Gipper's secretary of defense, has admiringly commented of his last boss, "He had a disarming way about him. People used to say that those who merely disliked him intensely were won over in five to ten minutes, while for those who really hated him it took more like twenty to twenty-five minutes.... He was much less formal and stiff than either Nixon or Ford."[9]

In both his public and his private appearances, the Gipper projected a serene sense of happiness with life, with being president, and with himself. Even his rather extreme political views, which might have been suicidal if voiced by a more peevish personality, accordingly had a minimal downside. Much as the good humor of Roosevelt had done five decades earlier for the liberal philosophy, Reagan's appealing refusal to take life too seriously put, as columnist George Will has phrased it, "a smile on the face of conservatism."[10]

His humor also served the man who became known as the Great Communicator well in other ways. Like Kennedy, Reagan drew on the risible to successfully defuse a sensitive issue that threatened to derail *his* presidential aspirations: in this case, his age. As some of his one-liners offered above have already suggested, he used humor to deflect other sensitive issues as well. Humor allowed him to put people, both in large audiences and individually, very much at ease. "He made people," as Weinberger has put it, "feel relaxed.... He wanted people around him to feel comfortable and he used humor as a very effective means of doing this."[11] Even after the attempt on his life, he used his ability to amuse to help the world relax, reassuring people everywhere that he was all right. Humor served as an eminently useful vehicle with which he could make his points, and it let him more easily confront adversity. On occasion it enabled him to evade facts that either might be embarrassing or—more often— that he simply did not know and to avoid the confrontations that his chief of staff once said he disliked "more than any man I have ever known."[12]

"With his background as an actor," his secretary of state George Shultz, declared, "he thought a lot about how you could communicate with people. And the use of humor, at which he was so adept, was an important part of his answer."[13]

"Politics," Reagan once declared, "is just like show business. You need a big opening. Then you coast for a while. Then you need a big finish." As a politician, he tended to deviate from this maxim only in injecting some additional humor into the coasting period: the man whom biographer Cannon thought engaged in government by anecdote could be counted upon to open not only most of his speeches but even the cabinet and other small-group meetings over which he presided, as well as his scheduled get-togethers with individuals, with a quip or an anecdote and to close those events with a similar effort.

The former entertainer rarely ran short of material. Similarly to both Lincoln and FDR, he drew many of his anecdotes from a carefully collected and constantly expanding file. He had picked up countless sports-related jokes and stories as a major league baseball and Big Ten football radio sportscaster in Iowa in the 1930s, and during his acting days over the next three decades he exchanged jokes with some of Hollywood's foremost comedians, mentally filing their choicer stories and witticisms for future reference.

In the White House, presidential assistant Michael Deaver and

Vice President George Bush got together daily before their 9 A.M. meeting with Reagan to think of a fresh humorous tale to tell him, and after Deaver left Reagan's staff, White House Chief of Staff Donald Regan joined with Bush to continue this custom. (In turn, Bush regularly asked his own staff and even his own sons for funny material to bring in to his superior and phoned his contacts across the country with the same objective.) Other fertile sources of humor for Reagan as president were Shultz, who frequently inserted jokes in cables that he sent to Reagan from abroad; U.S. Information Agency chief executive Charles Wick, who had, like Reagan, worked in Hollywood before coming to Washington; the witty National Security adviser, William P. Clark, who once said that William J. Casey (who tended to mumble) was so difficult to understand that he was the only Central Intelligence Agency director in history who didn't need a scrambler on his telephone; and—a bit surprisingly—Reagan's mother-in-law, Edith Davis, who telephoned Deaver as often as once a week and gave him a raunchy story to relay to the nation's chief executive (according to Deaver, Reagan would regularly hold his sides when he heard her jokes).

Two professional speech writers were also enlisted in this cause. Landon Parvin usually submitted from three to five pages of jokes to Reagan for a given event so that the president could have a wide selection. Aram Bakshian was also assigned the writing of funny lines on a regular basis.

Nor did the Great Communicator hesitate to draw on the witticisms of such long-dead notables as Mark Twain (he was especially fond of Twain's "Do what's right and you'll please some of the people and astound the rest") and Oscar Wilde (Reagan more than once quoted the Irish playwright's dictum that the only way to get rid of temptation was by yielding to it). Other men who posthumously provided him with material were Bismarck (whose "If you like laws and sausage, you should never watch either one being made" tickled the lighthearted chief executive's fancy) and the German poet Heinrich Heine (whose observation regarding a certain ambassador— "Ordinarily, he is insane, but he has lucid moments when he is only stupid"—aptly described, Reagan disarmingly asserted in a speech at Oxford University, the way that some foreign affairs experts regarded *him*).

In his storytelling, he sometimes injected tales—generally with attribution—that Lincoln had recited twelve decades and more earlier. He believed that his White House predecessor was almost in a league of his own as a raconteur and on several occasions remarked of a portrait of the Great Emancipator that hung in the state dining room during his presidential years, "He seems to have a twinkle in his eye; he looks as if he's just finished telling a story."[14]

House Speaker O'Neill was a prolific source of Irish jokes and folk stories, even though the two powerful leaders were almost total opposites in their political beliefs, and O'Neill once told Reagan that, while they could be friends after six o'clock in the evening, "before six it's politics." Reagan, never one to let partisanship stand in the way of friendship, at some point began telling the Democratic legislator whenever he ran into him, "Look, Tip, I'm resetting my watch. It's six o'clock."

Even newspaper comic strips could serve as potential material. Reagan, who read many newspapers as he traveled, always turned to the comics first, then looked at the front page and the rest of the paper. (Deaver once wrote, "We would land in a city and his reaction would be, 'Ah, Cincinnati, they have good comic strips here.'"[15]) A particular favorite was "Doonesbury," even though it at times satirized Reagan with tongue-in-cheek expositions of—for example— "Reagan's brain." Garry Trudeau's creation was frequently the personally secure Reagan's first reading of the morning.

In addition to all of these contributions from others, the former resident of Hollywood also was capable of as much spontaneity in his humor as Lincoln, Coolidge, Roosevelt, and Kennedy.

As governor of California from 1967 to 1975, Reagan was often the object of protests against the highly unpopular Vietnam War. On one occasion, when college students surrounded his limousine and chanted, "We are the future," he scribbled a message on a piece of paper, which he then held up to the automobile's window: "I'll sell my bonds." When, during another student protest, a group of unkempt antiwar advocates promised him a "blood bath," his response to them was that it would be much more appropriate if they themselves simply took a regular bath. As for a common student-radical slogan of the day, "Make Love, Not War," he once offered the apparently off-the-cuff opinion that many of the people holding up the signs containing this slogan didn't look like they could do either.

With the 1968 Republican presidential nomination very much up for grabs he was an undeclared if fully recognized entrant in the race. At one point his popularity in the polls seemed to be slipping a bit, and he was asked by a reporter for an explanation. He replied,

"I regard that as a tribute to my efforts to convince people I'm not a candidate." Asked about rival Nelson Rockefeller's presidential chances, he answered, "You're asking the wrong noncandidate. Ask him."

Vying for the 1980 GOP nomination with the patrician George Bush, he told a member of his staff regarding the latter, "I never feel comfortable around him. Whenever he talks to me, he seems to be staring at my necktie." Although this attribution may apocryphal, he reportedly also said of his future vice president, "George Bush is the kind of man who washes his hands *before* he goes to the bathroom."

During the 1980 presidential campaign, a wire service reporter asked Reagan to autograph a Hollywood studio public relations photograph taken from the 1951 Reagan film *Bedtime for Bonzo* which showed Reagan with the chimpanzee Bonzo. The journalist received from the Republican standard-bearer the inscription, "I'm the one with the watch." After informing a crowd in this same campaign that incumbent President Carter had promised "tax increases" when he (Reagan) had meant to say "tax decreases," the man who would succeed Carter quipped, "I've been talking about Carter so long that I make mistakes like he does." Just before he was inaugurated for the first time a few months later, he was briefed by a foreign policy advisor who joked about Carter's sentimentally kissing Soviet leader Leonid Brezhnev after they had signed the second Strategic Arms Limitation Talks pact in Vienna. The advisor kiddingly told the incoming president, "We don't ever want to see a picture of you kissing Brezhnev," and Reagan responded in an implicit reference to the less-than-ravishing appearance of the Soviet boss's spouse, "You won't even see me kissing Brezhnev's wife!"

As president, Reagan once attended an anti-abortion banquet at which industrialist Peter Grace erroneously talked about the need to protect the life of the "feces." Compounding his mistake, Grace announced, "I was once a feces. You were feces." After the dinner, the organizers of the event went over to Reagan and, apologizing, asked him if he had been embarrassed. He said, "Oh, no. But I'm afraid the feces really hit the fan tonight." An aide in the Oval Office observed that Reagan's new puppy, Lucky, a huge Belgian cattle dog that the chief executive had been given, clearly had to relieve himself and excitedly said to his boss, "Mr. President, you need to get that dog out of here. He's going to end up pissing on your desk." Reagan responded, "Why not? Everyone else does." When he was told at a meeting of his cabinet that the federal government's congressionally mandated program of dairy industry subsidies and the consequent governmental stabilization of market prices by purchases of butter from producers had led to federal warehouses currently containing 478 million pounds of surplus butter, he cried, "Four hundred and seventy eight million pounds of butter! Does anyone know where we can find four hundred and seventy eight million pounds of popcorn?"

The fortieth president once explained to his biographer Cannon at some length how his (and Kennedy's) friend Jack Benny had "used self-ridicule as the foundation of his comedy, emphasizing that it was Benny's self-security that made his art possible."[16] But Benny's professional hallmark of stinginess—upon being accosted by a robber and told, "Your money or your life!" he paused for many seconds before replying, "I'm thinking it over!" and after he had given a beggar a quarter to "buy yourself a pair of shoes" and been disdainfully asked by the recipient, "Wow, a quarter?" he answered, "You'll need laces, won't you?"—was staged. He was actually very generous in real life. Reagan, no less comfortable with himself than was Benny—author Garry Wills once wrote that Reagan had an "almost preternatural" inner security[17]—consistently made fun of a subject that was entirely factual: his age and its accompanying infirmities.

In the harsh terrain of politics, the issue could not have been avoided in any event. Cartoonists regularly drew the former actor as a mass of wrinkles, and it was well known that he began wearing a hearing aid in his right ear halfway through his first White House term and another in his left ear two years later. Even at the beginning of his eight-year presidency, the British humor magazine *Punch* reported a Reagan aide racing into the Oval Office exclaiming, "Mr. President, Soviet troops are massing on the Yugoslav border" and Reagan answering, "About a quarter to six." On the cover of political satirist Gardner's book *Who's in Charge Here?* a reporter is telling Reagan, "You said that you'd resign if your memory ever started to go," and Reagan is responding, "When did I say that?"

Reagan, operating on the premise that the best defense was a good offense, regularly and successfully dealt with the topic by ridiculing it with amiability and charm.

He started doing this, for that matter, some time before he became president. He told an audience in 1978, for example, "You know, I've already lived some twenty years longer than my life expectancy was at birth. And that has been a source of annoyance to a number of people." He informed a group of history students in the late 1970s, "History's no easy subject. Even in my day it wasn't, and we had so much less of it to learn then." In the 1980 campaign he declared that there was no truth to the rumor that he looked younger "because I keep riding older and older horses." A San Francisco lawyer who sent Reagan a picture of the two of them taken two decades earlier got a thank you note that said, "I have just received your photograph, and am certain it is a fake. We were never that young."

Once installed in the White House, he seemed almost addicted to the subject. He was given to quoting Thomas Jefferson's advice not to worry about age and then saying, "Ever since he told me that, I stopped worrying." He reminded listeners on many occasions that William Henry Harrison "spoke at his inauguration for nearly two hours, caught pneumonia and died within a month. I told him to keep it short." Other notables with whom, he liked to announce, he had conducted face-to-face conversations were Benjamin Franklin and Andrew Jackson.

On the other hand, he sometimes *denied* that he had traveled in such high company, as when he jauntily asserted, "I do have to correct one thing I said. I really did not know Thomas Jefferson. I couldn't possibly have. You see, we lived in different states!" In his 1982 State of the Union address, he said:

> President Washington began this tradition in 1790 after reminding the nation that the destiny of self-government and the "preservation of the sacred fire of liberty" is "finally staked on the experiment entrusted to the hands of the American people." For our friends in the press, who place a high premium on accuracy, let me say I did not actually hear George Washington say that.[18]

Variations on the theme could be achieved without the dropping of early American names. In a speech before the Washington Press Club, Reagan noted that it was founded in 1919 and sighed, "It seems like only yesterday." The Gridiron Club's members were reminded that *their* organization had been graced by prominent speakers since its establishment in 1885 and learned that Reagan was disappointed "when you didn't invite me the first time." On the eve of the 1984 presidential campaign, a gathering of senior citizens was told that the incumbent chief executive planned to "campaign in all 13 states." Another mid–1980s audience was informed that "there are some people who currently have plenty of time to run for office, but they don't seem to have any time for new ideas. Most of them are younger than I am. Everybody is." On the occasion of his seventy-third birthday, in early 1984, he told a Eureka College convocation, "I have what every man who has that many candles on his birthday cake needs around him—a large group of friends and a working sprinkler system."

Nor were foreigners exempted from the Reagan age treatment. Those in attendance at a state dinner for visiting Chinese President Li Xiannian heard that "President Li comes from a nation where people are well known for their traditional respect for their elders. President Li, I can assure you I'm doing my best to reestablish that tradition in our own country." In a speech at London's five-hundred-year-old Guildhall, the U.S. president declared that it was comforting to be near anything that much older than himself and that some people even viewed his election to the presidency as America's attempt "to show our European cousins that we too have a regard for antiquity."

But on October 21, 1984—in his second nationally televised debate with his Democratic challenger for the presidency, former Vice President Walter Mondale—Reagan used his lighthearted approach to the subject to maximum advantage.

The septuagenarian White House incumbent had registered an unimpressive performance in the first debate, held two weeks earlier. He had appeared to lack not only energy and quick-wittedness but lucidity in dueling with his much younger opponent, and he had given a general impression of a man whose best years had long since passed. The nightclub and television humorist Mark Russell had said of him immediately afterward, "He's an actor and he acted his age,"[19] and the syndicated humor columnist Art Buchwald almost simultaneously had written, "The president's advisors know that if he goes to sleep for even five minutes during the second debate, he'll be in trouble."[20]

Early in the second debate, *Baltimore Sun* senior journalist Henry Trewhitt addressed the following question to Reagan: "Mr. President ... You already are the oldest president in history, and some of your staff say you were tired after your most recent encounter with Mr. Mondale. I recall that President Kennedy had to go for days on end with very little sleep during the Cuban missile crisis. Is there any doubt in your mind that you would be able to function in such circumstances?" With not a moment's hesitation, the man who had fared so poorly on October 7, replied, "Not at all, Mr. Trewhitt. And I want you to know that also I will not make age an issue of this campaign. I am not going to exploit for political purposes my opponent's youth and inexperience."

Trewhitt's rejoinder—"Mr. President, I would like to head for the fence and catch that one before it goes over"—was consistent with that of the studio audience, which erupted in highly appreciative chuckles and applause. The next morning's newspapers were equally positive, with many of them echoing the statement of influential *Washington Post* columnist David Broder, "It well may have been that the biggest barrier to Reagan's reelection was swept away in that moment."[21]

Knowing a winner when he had one, Reagan kept making fun of his age until the end of his White House tenure. Often, when presented with an honor, he would announce to the awarding organization's membership, "Tonight is a very special night for me. Of course, at my age every night is a very special night." During the 1988 campaign, he said at a Gridiron Club banquet: "I heard one [presidential] candidate say that what this country needed was a president for the '90s. I was set to run again. I thought he said a president in his 90s." On the last day of his presidency, at a welcoming ceremony in Los Angeles, he told the crowd that he had been asked to appear in a remake of his movie *Bedtime for Bonzo*, but this time in the part of the chimpanzee.

Even as late as February 1994, for that matter, when the cruel ravages of his Alzheimer's had already extracted some toll, he could assert—at his eighty-third birthday celebration—"Now, as most of you know, I'm not one for looking back. I figure there will be plenty of time for that when I get old!"

Reagan was not the hardest working of chief executives. He rarely arrived in his office before 9 A.M., like Coolidge regularly took an afternoon nap (which his official schedule listed as "personal staff time"), and almost always ended his working day by 5 P.M. He frequently spent long nonworking weekends at his Camp David retreat in nearby Maryland, and during his eight presidential years was for the equivalent of almost one of those years on vacation at his California ranch.[22]

When a national magazine was researching the topic of "A Day in the Life of President Reagan," the White House press corps joked that the fake schedule that Reagan's assistants had constructed as an outline to guide the researcher was in actuality a month in the life of President Reagan. Early in his first term, *Newsweek* magazine wrote, "Jimmy Carter gave hard work and attention to detail a bad name. Ronald Reagan will not make that mistake,"[23] while columnist Buchwald reported that the new president had spent "many sleepless days over the Middle East," and television comedian Johnny Carson announced that Reagan liked to take a "working nap" in the White House.

Tip O'Neill liked to tell the story of what happened on inauguration day in 1981, when the just-installed president went to the speaker's office to change clothes following the Capitol Hill ceremony. Reagan admired O'Neill's magnificently handcrafted oak desk, told the speaker so, and learned from O'Neill that the desk had belonged to Grover Cleveland when he had held the presidency. Reagan replied, "That's very interesting. You know, I once played Grover Cleveland in the movies." O'Neill responded, "No, Mr. President, you're thinking of Grover Cleveland *Alexander*, the ball player"—a reference to the role that Reagan had in fact played in the film *The Winning Season*. When O'Neill later told this story to one of his fellow congressmen, the latter deadpanned that possibly Reagan labored under the false assumption that Grover Cleveland's presidential schedule had been as untaxing as his own and that he had consequently spent many of his afternoons pitching for the Washington Senators baseball team.

Nor did the afternoon nap and generally restful approach to the job seem to be quite enough. Reagan not infrequently dozed off at staff meetings. On at least two memorable occasions—during a June 1982 talk in the Vatican with Pope John Paul II and at the Moscow Summit Conference in May 1988—he very publicly fell asleep (the Soviets, showing considerable tact, told reporters on the second occasion that the nap was entirely understandable because, except for the American president's own address, all of the speeches were "a bore").

He often devoted so little time and energy to his duties that in a 1983 meeting with leaders of U.S. automobile companies he took the wrong collection of index cards to the session and consequently read from the wrong notes until he finally caught on. The night before he was to preside over an important economic summit in Williamsburg, Virginia, his chief of staff, James Baker, gave him a painstakingly assembled briefing book to absorb. The next morning, Reagan confessed that he had essentially not read any of it and explained to Baker, "Well, Jim, *The Sound of Music* was on television last night."

In actuality, Reagan was not so much a lax administrator as he was a contented person, who was quite willing to let matters take their own course so long as no major problems arose. He was a firm believer in delegation, who once asserted, "Show me any executive who doesn't delegate and I'll show you a failure." He granted so much authority to his chiefs of staff that he could jest, "The other day when I told Don Regan [his staff chief at the time] I was opposed to dictators whoever and wherever they are, he asked if he should start packing."

Reagan's languor could well have spelled disaster in his public standing. But with the abundant aplomb that never seemed to desert him, he proceeded to counter this negative every bit as effectively as he had done with the issue of his age and by the same mechanism: defusion by humorous self-deprecation.

He frequently declared that his chair in the cabinet room might someday bear the label "Ronald Reagan Slept Here" and similarly sent a photograph of his sleeping press secretary, Marlin Fitzwater, aboard Air Force One with the autographed inscription, "Hey, Marlin, we're only supposed to do this in Cabinet meetings." Referring to a particularly busy, if short-lived, period in his presidency, he cracked, "I've really been burning the midday oil." Of another rare few days of heavy scheduling, he said, with an understatement worthy of Coolidge, "I have no time to be president."

Just like the humor related to his age, this kind of self-mocking seemed to be a start-to-finish constant in his litany of quips, too.

Immediately before his first inauguration, after being briefed by his foreign policy advisers on the myriad problems that he would be inheriting (among them, the threat of war in parts of both Latin America and the Middle East, Soviet designs on Poland, and ongoing trouble with Iran), he responded, "I think I'll demand a recount!" On the morning of January 20, 1981, an aide walked into Washington's Blair House to help him get ready just before 9 A.M., was informed that the president-elect was still in bed, anxiously reminded him that he was going to be inaugurated in two hours, and was asked by Reagan, "Does that mean I have to get up?" After his first full day on the job, Reagan cheerfully said, "It's been a very wonderful day. I guess I can go back to California. Can't I?" Less than a month into his presidency, when a friend from California visited him in the White House and then said his goodbyes, Reagan reportedly responded, "Wait until I get my hat. I'll go with you."

Midway through his tenure, he told a press conference audience,

"Mike Deaver said that I have a short attention span. I was going to reply to that, but what the hell, let's move on to something else." To the Gridiron Club membership, he said, "Do you remember when I fell asleep during my audience with the Pope? ... Boy, those were the good old days."

Not long before his second term was over, he met with a group of journalists, proudly outlined what he considered to be the major accomplishments of his administration, and then asserted, "All in all, I must say, not bad for a fellow who couldn't get his facts straight and worked four hours a day." Another assemblage of media people, asking him about his future plans, was informed, "As soon as I get home to California, I plan to lean back, kick up my feet and take a long nap. [Long pause.] Ah, come to think of it, things won't be all that different after all!"

Reagan was also well aware that his three decades as a professional actor, following five years as a radio announcer, might in some quarters be attacked as unimpressive preparation for the mightiest job on the planet. He was, accordingly, no less willing to bring up *this* topic before others did, and he used the same jocular self-abasement that he had bestowed on his age and relaxed approach to the duties of his office.

He volunteered lighthearted reminders of his Hollywood past, in fact, from the very beginning of his political career. Asked what kind of governor he thought that he would make, he rejoined, "I don't know. I've never played a governor," and he was fond of telling crowds what his studio boss, Jack Warner, had supposedly exclaimed when he learned that his old B-movie star was thinking of running for California's top elected job: "No, no. Jimmy Stewart for governor; Reagan for best friend." He regularly said, "I'm an actor, not a politician." On one occasion, he asserted with a Coolidgean deadpan when asked about Democratic White House candidate Gary Hart, "This country would never accept a president who looks like a movie star." Sworn in as governor a few minutes after midnight on January 3, 1967, and assigned to walk into the state capitol rotunda next to his fellow former actor, Senator George Murphy, he turned to Murphy and commented in a statement that was subsequently repeated many times by the media, "George, here we are on the late show again."

When he was asked, following his debate with Carter in 1980, if he had been nervous in his widely watched contest with an incumbent president, he replied, "No, not at all. I've been on the same stage with John Wayne." (It was an answer which, with slight modifications, he was to repeat many times over the next eight years—for example, when he seemed to let Mikhail Gorbachev get the credit for a landmark arms control treaty and informed journalists, "I don't resent his popularity. Good Lord, I co-starred with Errol Flynn once.")

In the White House, he was frequently asked how an actor could be president and generally gave the question the same answer: "I've sometimes wondered how you could be president and not be an actor." His opening line to banquet audiences sometimes was, "In the business I used to be in, if you didn't sing or dance, you wound up as an after-dinner speaker, so here I am." On at least one occasion, he announced that one of his greatest moments as an actor had come quite early—in his junior year at college, when he had played a Greek shepherd boy who was strangled and had won a prize for his portrayal. He had been thrilled, he said, "No actor can ask for more. Dying is the way to live in the theater." He publicly reminisced about the time, in his early Hollywood years, that his agent wired him: "WARNER'S OFFER CONTRACT SEVEN YEARS, ONE YEAR'S OPTION, STARTING AT $200 A WEEK. WHAT SHALL I DO? He immediately telegraphed back: "SIGN BEFORE THEY CHANGE THEIR MINDS."

Due in no small part to his constant references to it (for example, "I saw *Knute Rockne* on television one night, and it was so hacked up that my eighty-yard run was a five-yard loss"), so many people knew of what had been perhaps his most prominent movie role that many decades after the film about the legendary Notre Dame coach was produced (and almost two years after he stepped down from the presidency) he remarked at a University of Southern California–Notre Dame luncheon:

> In closing, I know some of you are wondering if I'm going to say that line from the certain movie. But I know better than to take sides. So I've come up with what I hope will be a good compromise. As you may know, tomorrow I will flip the coin to officially start the game. So if you'll permit a little modification: Will you tell your teams to go out there and win one for the Flipper?[24]

At no time in his entire political career did the man whom syndicated columnist George Will once called the "most cheerful of all Presidents"[25] use humor to better advantage than in the immediate aftermath of the near-fatal 1981 assassination attempt. In his widely publicized and enormously reassuring comments and handwritten notes at the George Washington Hospital, he was—as Deaver later said—"like an old trooper who had found the world's most appreciative audience, which in a sense he had."[26]

Just before he was wheeled into surgery, he quipped to Nancy (in a line similar to the famous remark that prize fighter Jack Dempsey had made to *his* wife after losing the heavyweight championship to Gene Tunney in 1926), "Honey, I forgot to duck." Soon after emerging from the anaesthesia, he was informed by an aide, "You'll be happy to know that the government is running normally, and he immediately responded, "What makes you think I'd be happy about that?" In the postoperative room, he told his doctors (one of whom had already told him in answer to his "Please assure me that you are all Republicans" plea, "Today, we're all good Republicans, Mr. President") an off-color joke.

To Deaver, he cracked, "I really screwed up the schedule." In a note to his aides, he wrote, "If I had had this much attention in Hollywood, I'd have stayed there." In another note, this time to his nurses, he quoted Winston Churchill's dictum that there "is no more exhilarating feeling than being shot at without result." In still another note, he paraphrased the well-known statement of W. C. Fields, "All in all, I'd rather be in Philadelphia." In yet a fourth missive, referring to the Washington Hilton Hotel out of whose front door he was walking when Hinckley started shooting, he wrote, "I'd like to do this scene again—starting at the hotel."

He straightfacedly asserted, "I knew from the manner in which I was unclothed that I probably wouldn't wear that suit again," and he told his daughter Maureen when she visited him in the hospital a day after the shooting that the suit had been a brand-new one, that he understood that Hinckley's family was quite wealthy, and that he wondered accordingly if the Hinckleys would buy him a new outfit.

Two days after the surgery, television comedian Carson informed his audience at the Academy Awards presentation in Los Angeles, "I was tempted to call [the president] and ask if he had any more of those one-liners *I* could use!"[27]

Of the entire in-hospital performance, *Washington Post* columnist Broder was typical of many admirers in writing, "During his [previous] sixty-nine days in office President Reagan had shown wit and grace. When he displayed that same wit and grace in the hours after his own life was threatened, he elevated those appealing human qualities to the level of a legend."[28]

With accolades such as these, Reagan was loathe to shelve his near-death experience as grist for his humor mill. Four weeks after the shooting, he went to Capitol Hill to address a joint session of the Democratic-controlled Congress, received a huge standing ovation as he was introduced, and began his speech by saying, "You wouldn't want to talk me into an encore, would you?"

Almost exactly one year to the day after the attack on him, he returned to the Washington Hilton to address the same group (the AFL-CIO's Building and Construction Trades Department) that he was speaking to just before Hinckley's attempt and announced, "I know you all understand how happy I am to be back—standing before you today. If it's all the same to you, though, when I finish speaking, I think I'll slip out the back door this time." Asked by a journalist on this occasion if he was afraid, he answered, "No, but I'm wearing my oldest suit today."

Almost two years later, with his popularity temporarily a bit on the wane, he told his chief pollster, "Dick, I know what we can do. I'll just have to go out and get shot again."

Even as late as November 1985, when he returned from a meeting in Geneva with Soviet leader Gorbachev and spoke to another highly enthusiastic congressional joint session, he declared, "I haven't gotten such a reception since I was shot."

Reagan once told a group of Republican officials a story involving a congressman

> who was sitting in his office one day when a constituent comes by to tell him why he must vote for a certain piece of legislation. The congressman sat back, listened, and when he was done he said, "You're right. You know, you're absolutely right." The fellow left happy. A few minutes later, another constituent came by and this one wanted him to vote against the bill. The congressman listened to his reasons, sat back and said, "You know, you're right. You're right. You're absolutely right." Well, the second constituent left happy. The congressman's wife had dropped by and was sitting outside the office when she heard these two conversations. When the second man left, she went in and said, "That first man wanted you to vote for the bill, and you said he was right. And the second one wanted you to vote against it, and you said he was right, too. You can't run your affairs that way." And the congressman said, "You know, you're right. You're right. You're absolutely right."[29]

The one-time nightclub comedian did not himself go to this extreme in his conduct of the nation's business. He could, on the contrary, be quite unyielding when he felt that his basic principles were being threatened. But his day-to-day behavior was marked by an extreme amiability and consideration for the desires of others that few of his Oval Office predecessors had ever demonstrated on a consistent basis.

The good disposition and quite visible decency let him go through life expressing—at least according to his presidential press secretary, Larry Speakes—genuine animosity for only two living creatures: Israeli Prime Minister Menachem Begin (Reagan thought him, not without justification, to be both insensitive and arrogant) and Reagan's one-time movie co-star, the chimpanzee Bonzo (Bonzo once pulled the future president's tie so tightly that it had to be cut off with a pair of scissors).[30] The same qualities allowed Chief of Staff Regan to note in his memoirs that he could not remember a single occasion on which Reagan had either postponed or cancelled an appointment or even complained about an obligation on his schedule.[31] And these qualities invariably permitted the former California Governor to get away with much more in his humorous efforts than would otherwise have been the case.

Reagan, for example, amiably told some economists that "if all of the economists in the world were laid end to end, they still wouldn't reach a conclusion," that economists are the sort of people "who see something happen in practice and wonder if it would work in theory," and that "an economist is a person with a Phi Beta Kappa key on one end of his watch chain and no watch on the other." He received appreciative chuckles in return.

Similarly, each of his three top economic advisers heard the following story from their boss when they came aboard his team, and there is no evidence that any of them took umbrage at it. An engineer, a lawyer, and an economist are arguing about whose profession is the oldest. The engineer points out that God created the universe out of chaos and that "this was an engineering job." The lawyer rejoins, "Wait a minute. The Bible says that in the beginning, before chaos was 'the Word,' 'the Law.' So lawyers clearly came first.'" The economist then asks, "Who do you think created the chaos?"

Federal Reserve Board chief Alan Greenspan enjoyed at least one anti-economist joke that he first heard from Reagan so much that he often retold it in his own speeches. Brezhnev is viewing the traditional May Day parade of Soviet armed forces strength at the Kremlin. Among the state-of-the-art missiles, formidable-looking tanks, and thousands of smartly marching members of the military is a vehicle that is transporting an assemblage of quite unimpressive-looking civilians. An assistant apologizes to the Soviet leader for their inclusion, declaring that he has no idea what they are doing in the ceremony. "Calm down, comrade," Brezhnev replies. "Those are my economists, an integral part of the military might of the Soviet Union. I put them in the parade. You have no idea how much damage they can do."

Lawyers, both singly and in groups, were told, among other often-recounted anti-attorney anecdotes, one that Reagan had early in his political career correctly judged to be a sure-fire winner:

> A pope and a lawyer arrive at St. Peter's gate simultaneously. The pope is assigned a respectable but modest condominium in a courtyard while the lawyer is given a beautiful Tudor mansion overlooking a golf course. "How can this be?" the lawyer asks St. Peter, "The father of Christendom merits only a nice condominium and I have been given this magnificent mansion." St. Peter replies, "Well, we have thirty-nine popes here, but you're the first lawyer."[32]

One audience of attorneys responded with sympathetic laughter when, in 1985, Reagan told them that he was disappointed that the White House counsel wouldn't let him accept the offered honorarium: "I was really looking forward to the first time I ever talked to a group of lawyers and came home with the fee."

Washington bureaucrats could grin and not only bear but actually enjoy it when they heard from the president's engagingly sunny lips that a governmental bureau was "the nearest thing to eternal life that we'll ever see on this earth," that the ten most dangerous words in the English language were, "Hi, I'm from the government, and I'm here to help," and that the District of Columbia was "an island, surrounded on all sides by reality." Democrats found it hard to take personal affront at Reagan's affably communicated assertions that the difference between his Republican party and the Democrats was that "we want to check government spending and they want to spend government checks," that the leaders of the Democratic party had "gone so far left that they've left the country," and that it wasn't "so much that [Democratic party] liberals are ignorant. It's just that they know so much that isn't so."

Portly House Speaker O'Neill, an old-fashioned tax-and-spend liberal in the eyes of many, enjoyed it when he learned that Reagan had said in a recent speech, "There are some things that are current today and sweeping the country that I haven't had time to get familiar with: Pac-Man, for example. I asked about it and somebody told me that it was a round thing that gobbled up money. I thought that was Tip O'Neill." The quip was made with no more bite than when Reagan, at a celebration in honor of his friend Bob Hope, said of the honoree, "He's entertained six presidents. He's performed for twelve," or when the fortieth president affectionately remarked that the notoriously loquacious but eminently likable Senator Hubert Humphrey had "never had an unuttered thought."

His obvious absence of malice even let the former actor get away with kidding statements that could well have spelled political death for a more wrathful person—a Nixon, say, or a Lyndon Johnson. Campaigning in New Hampshire in early 1980, he announced, "How do you tell who the Polish fellow is at a cock fight? He's the one with the duck. How do you tell who the Italian is at the cock fight? He's the one who bets on the duck. How do you know the Mafia was there? The duck wins." Mildly criticized for this, Reagan jovially declared that he had told the story "as an example of jokes that politicians shouldn't tell."

In like vein, he suffered no dire consequences when, just before delivering one of his weekly radio addresses in mid–1984, he said into what he erroneously believed to be a dead microphone, "My fellow Americans, I am pleased to tell you today that I've signed legislation that will outlaw Russia forever. We begin bombing in five minutes." (The humorist Mort Sahl at the time quoted a Reagan supporter as having asserted, "I hope this isn't just another empty campaign promise.") After Reagan had publicly joked about the Bureau of Indian Affairs employee who was seen sobbing at his desk because he had just learned that "my Indian died," his defenders credibly pointed out that this was not a racist joke at all but rather just another of Reagan's constantly rendered jibes against what he perceived to be Washington's hugely bloated bureaucracy. Reagan remarked, in a Gridiron Club speech delivered during a major period of national agricultural recession, "Perhaps we should keep the grain and export the farmers," and he emerged without any meaningful damage from the agricultural sector, one of the Republican party's most consistently counted-upon bases.

Even a particularly ill-advised Reagan remark, made during the 1988 presidential campaign and based on unfounded rumors that the Democratic candidate, Michael Dukakis, had in the past undergone psychiatric treatment, did no lasting damage. Attempting to be funny, Reagan had referred to Dukakis in a conversation with reporters as an "invalid"; both Dukakis and the public seemed to quickly overlook this lapse from both good taste and fact. Reagan's geniality also allowed him to escape entirely unscathed when he told Gorbachev at the third (and most successful) Reagan-Gorbachev summit, in late 1987 in Washington, about an American en route to the USSR who on his way to the airport asked his taxi driver, a college student, what he planned to do after graduation and was informed by the latter, "I haven't decided yet." When he arrived in Moscow, he asked his taxi driver there—also a college student—the same question and received the answer, "I haven't been told yet."

Reagan came to be called the Teflon President, as his many attractive qualities made him almost immune from effective attack. Humorist Russell once announced that a group of demonstrators had "burnt Reagan in effigy outside the White House, but the effigy kept blowing out the flame," and while there was obvious hyperbole there, the tribute to Reagan's remarkable resilience did not go unnoticed—a resilience which Reagan could credit to some degree to his constant exudation of good will.

Gorbachev, with whom Reagan developed a mutual admiration society and the possessor of a highly developed sense of humor himself, was not taken by surprise by the anti–Soviet tone of the taxi driver joke, either. When the two men had first met, in Geneva in late 1985, Reagan had cheerfully told Gorbachev about the American who said to a Russian that the United States was so much a land of freedom that he could stand in front of the White House and shout, "To hell with Ronald Reagan!" and was informed by the Russian, "That's nothing. I can stand in front of the Kremlin and yell, 'To hell with Ronald Reagan!' too." The author of *glasnost* and *perestroika* had reportedly laughed quite heartily.

Gorbachev also seemed to like a tale that Reagan told him involving a Russian who was walking down a street in Moscow one evening when a soldier yelled, "Halt." The man started to run, and the soldier shot him. Another Russian said to the soldier, "Why did you do that?" The soldier replied, "Curfew." The civilian pointed out that it was not curfew time yet. And the soldier responded, "I know. He's a friend of mine. I know where he lives. He couldn't have made it."

Reagan's high standing with Gorbachev appeared not to suffer at all from the former's propensity to tell audiences a variety of other anti–Soviet jokes as well. One of these, frequently repeated by the U.S. president, was a short question-and-answer one: "Question: What are four things wrong with Soviet agriculture? Answer: Spring, summer, fall, and winter."

Another Reagan favorite featured a lost parrot and its Russian owner, who told the Soviet KGB secret police: "In case that bird is found, I just want you to know that I disagree with everything it says."

Still another dealt with a visit that Gorbachev, who had launched a vigorous anti-drinking crusade, supposedly paid to a factory. While there, he was confronted by an irate employee who insisted that Gorbachev defend his program. "Well, look at it this way," the head of state asked, "If you had one glass of vodka before coming to work, would you be able to handle this complex machinery?" The worker responded that he had never thought about it. "And if you had two glasses of vodka before you came, would you be able to discharge any of your responsibilities at all?" The worker, again, said that he had never given the matter any thought. "And," Gorbachev persisted, "If you had three glasses of vodka before coming to work, would you even be able to come to work?" "Of course," the man answered with some disdain, "I'm here, aren't I?"

Another story often told by Reagan focused on a Communist party official who asked a farmer how things were going and received in reply the comment that the harvest was so bountiful that if the potatoes were stacked on top of each other they would reach the foot of God. "But this is the Soviet Union," the political dignitary responded. "There is no God here." "That's all right," the farmer countered. "There are no potatoes, either."

Yet another tale that Reagan frequently repeated involved an elderly man who asked a clerk in a Moscow grocery store for a kilogram of beef, half a kilogram of butter, and a quarter kilogram of coffee. Informed that the store was out of all of them, the man left. Another customer, having witnessed the scene, thereupon observed to the clerk, "That old man must be crazy," and the clerk responded, "Yeah, but what a *memory!*"

Reagan also often told about the Russian who, having ordered an automobile at the Soviet Bureau of Transportation, was told that—although he would have to pay in full as of the ordering date—there would be a ten-year wait. The man dutifully filled out the requisite forms, plunked down his money, and was directed, "Come back in ten years and get your car." The man asked, "Morning or afternoon?"

The government official said, "We're talking about ten years from now. What difference does it make?" And the man answered, "The plumber is coming in the morning."

Reagan's highly positive opinion of Gorbachev rested partly on the fact that the latter could, unlike most of his Kremlin predecessors, enjoy such narratives as these and not take his nation, or himself, overly seriously. It also in part stemmed from Gorbachev's essential forthrightness, which led the American president on many occasions to say that the Soviet was "someone you can do business with" and at least once to pay him the ultimate compliment, especially considering the source, of announcing that Gorbachev could be a successful politician in the United States because he was "such a likable person."

Reagan could even do business with the Communist leader on the level of prank playing. At the 1985 Geneva summit meeting, he got Gorbachev to join him in a widely televised, playful protest against the tardiness of their two wives. Raisa Gorbachev had been invited by Nancy Reagan to have coffee with her upstairs at the Reagan temporary residence and, despite an official schedule that called for the two women to rejoin their husbands outside at an appointed time, the first ladies were already fifteen minutes late. When they finally did appear, the two heads of state, with their suit sleeves pushed back, were busily tapping their wristwatches with mock impatience.

Despite his personal liking for Gorbachev, Reagan never underestimated the Soviet leader's considerable bargaining skills nor did he leave anything, once negotiated, to Gorbachev's apparently quite sincere declarations of good intentions. Immediately after the two men had met for the first time, Reagan emerged from a restroom with his left arm concealed so well that his jacket sleeve was hanging limply, looked down, and asked, "Where's my arm? It was here this morning before I met with Gorbachev." In the wake of all of the agreements struck with the Soviet at the summit conferences, he regularly announced, "It's still trust but verify. It's still play but cut the cards."

The Soviet Union was not the only nation that Reagan poked fun at for its governmental inefficiencies. The U.S. government also came in for regular verbal jabbing as the one-time stand-up comedian addressed *its* tendency to be too big, too inefficient, and too wasteful of taxpayer dollars.

American government, he liked to say, was like a baby: "It has an alimentary canal with a big appetite at one end and no sense of responsibility at the other." He had never been very good himself, he told audiences, at fundraising and that's why he got into government, "because we don't ask for it, we just take it." Feeding more tax dollars to the government, he announced, was "like feeding a stray pup. It just follows you home and sits on your doorstep asking for more." "The best view of government," he told a Spirit of America rally in Atlanta in 1984, "is in the rearview mirror as we leave it behind." As for lowering the crime rate, he argued that one way to make sure that crime didn't pay was to let the government run it, and he told a joint session of Congress in his final State of the Union message, "Some years ago, the federal government declared war on poverty and poverty won."

The one-liners were supplemented by stories. He said that governmental programs sometimes reminded him of the country preacher who went to a revival meeting at a town one hundred miles from his own. En route to the church where he was scheduled to conduct the festivities, he spotted a man from his hometown, who was well known for his drinking, seated on the porch of a little country store. The minister asked the man why he was so far from home and received as the answer, "Preacher, beer is five cents a bottle cheaper here." The minister responded that it really didn't make much sense to travel one hundred miles just to save that kind of money, and the drinker thought for a moment and then said, "Preacher, I'm not stupid. I just sit here until I show a profit."

Governmental units weren't very ambitious even with their ill-gotten tax gains, he thought. Some of them were like the two hikers who suddenly saw a grizzly bear coming over the hill, headed right for them. One of the hikers, according to Reagan, quickly reached into his backpack, took out a pair of tennis shoes, and began putting them on his feet. The other hiker asked his friend, "You don't really think that you can outrun a grizzly bear, do you?" And the man with the tennis shoes answered, "I don't have to outrun the bear. I just have to outrun you."

Regarding individual government employees, Reagan enjoyed telling about the man who

sits at a desk in Washington. Documents come to him each morning. He reads them, initials them, and passes them on to the proper agency. One day a document arrived he wasn't supposed to read, but he read it, initialed it, and passed it on. Twenty-four hours later it arrived

back at his desk with a memo attached that said, "You weren't supposed to read this. Erase your initials, and initial the erasure."[33]

Similarly, the man from Illinois told at least one organized labor
audience that a neighbor of his in California who was building his
own home got so fed up with all the paperwork and the regulations
required that "he pasted them all together into one strip of paper,
put up two poles in front of the half-finished house, and strung them
up across there. The strip of paper was 250 feet long."

It was almost irrelevant that the last two of these stories
appeared to be as fictitious as the first two. They were, as Reagan's
anti–Soviet anecdotes, related with such cheeriness and good will that
it would have been almost indecent to register objections.

There was nothing contrived about Reagan's trademark good
nature. On the contrary, the man whose senior year high school year-
book printed under his name, "Life is just one grand, sweet song,
so start the music," exhibited it throughout his political career.

When, as both gubernatorial candidate and then governor,
he was heckled by student protesters who repeatedly shouted such
questions as "What about Vietnam?" at him, he frequently
responded by genially asking, "Is there an echo in here?" Invariably,
applause and laughter constituted the audience response. (He used
the same line as president at least once, when in mid–1982 he was
addressing the West German Bundestag, and two left-wing mem-
bersof that parliamentary body kept shouting, "What about El Sal-
vador?")

He could laugh off mispronunciations of his last name—a common happening in his pre-presidential days—and enjoyed telling
a story about a man who didn't know him but was asked to introduce him soon after he was elected governor. The man was not sure
whether the name should be announced as *Ray*gan or *Ree*gan and,
turning this dilemma over in his mind, went for a stroll, in the course
of which he met a neighbor who was walking his dog. "I've got
a problem," the first man confided to the other. "I've got to introduce the new governor at a meeting tomorrow and I don't know how
to pronounce his name. Is it *Ray*gan or *Ree*gan?" It's *Ray*gan,"
the neighbor replied. "Are you sure?" the first man asked. "I don't
want to say the wrong thing." "Believe me," said the neighbor "It's
*Ray*gan. I've known the guy for years." "Gee, thanks," the first man
declared "Now I can sleep. And by the way, that's a nice dog you've
got there. What breed is it?" "It's a bagel," responded the neighbor.

When he ran for the presidency in 1980, Reagan's good disposition was particularly tested in a late October televised debate with the incumbent chief executive, Carter (who had been advised by one of his strategists to exhibit a bit of humor himself during the event but had apparently dismissed this suggestion out of hand). Carter, trying to show the one hundred million–person TV audience that Reagan's foreign and domestic views were not only "disturbing" (he used this word seven times in referring to his opponent) but even "dangerous" (he tossed in this adjective four times), at one point in the debate made the unwarranted charge that Reagan "began his political career campaigning around this nation against Medicare" and was now against national health insurance of any kind. Reagan listened with an amused forbearance, then gently shook his head, and, with mock sadness calmly protested in words that many observers thought won him the debate, "There you go again!"

As president, he was capable of dealing with the aggressive and rather rude journalist Lester Kinsolving, who had plagued the nation's chief executives at press conferences from the days of Richard Nixon. Kinsolving, representing a relatively unknown operation called the Globe Syndicate, tended to disregard the niceties of waiting until he was recognized by the president and instead simply shouted out his question no matter which of his colleagues had been acknowledged. Reagan finally announced at one press conference, "My finger must be crooked—every time I point at somebody, Lester Kinsolving starts asking a question."

Another potential thorn in Reagan's side, the American Broadcasting Company's highly respected but no less aggressive newsman Sam Donaldson, was also disarmed by the Great Communicator's amiable brand of humor. Reagan declared on one occasion, "Somebody asked me one day why we didn't put a stop to Sam's shouting out questions at us when we're on the South Lawn. We can't. If we did, the starlings would come back." Another Donaldson-related statement by Reagan was based on the widely believed but not really valid theory among journalists covering the White House that women with red dresses tended to get recognized by the president at his press conferences: "At my last press conference I thought that gimmick of wearing a red dress to get my attention went a little too far. Nice try, Sam." During the 1984 campaign, Donaldson yelled out to Reagan over the din of a helicopter on the White House lawn, "What about Walter Mondale's charges?" He received the affable answer, "He ought to pay them." During the Iran-Contra affair, Reagan announced with a grin,

"I have to admit we considered making one final shipment to Iran, but no one could figure out how to get Sam Donaldson in a crate."

Donaldson, who has been covering presidents since 1961, has nothing but praise for Reagan's use of humor. "It helped project his deserved image as a nice, friendly guy," he says, "took the edge off the negatives, and helped deflect those embarrassing moments when he didn't have the facts. His humor was almost never mean-spirited, unlike that of Jimmy Carter, who almost always had to have someone as the butt."[34]

The veteran ABC commentator has his own favorite Reagan-Donaldson story:

> Just before a nationally televised event, which was going to be shown live nationwide and the TV cameras were already rolling, Reagan, Nancy Reagan and [presidential White House aide] David Gergen came into the press room with a birthday cake—it was somebody's birthday—and everyone sang "Happy Birthday." I was offered a piece, and I told Reagan, "Mr. President, I'm not going to sell out for a piece of cake." Reagan immediately responded, "Oh, Sam, you've sold out for a lot less!"[35]

Nor did Kinsolving and Donaldson offer Reagan his only chances to poke fun at members of the Fourth Estate. Although he enjoyed a treatment by the press that was every bit as favorable as that received by Coolidge, Roosevelt, and Kennedy, Reagan once feigned concern with some atypically hostile media coverage and cracked, "If this has been a honeymoon, then I've been sleeping alone." At an annual dinner of the White House Correspondents Association (just like JFK, he attended almost all of these during his presidency as well as the equally lighthearted journalistic dinners of the Gridiron Club and the Alfalfa Club, and seemed to genuinely enjoy them), he said of a disgraced White House predecessor, "I thought it was extraordinary that Richard Nixon went on "Meet the Press" and spent an entire hour with Chris Wallace, Tom Brokaw, and John Chancellor. That should put an end to that talk that he's not been punished enough." At another such banquet, he announced, "Now I've been told that this is all off the record and that the cameras are all off. Is that right? Because I've been waiting years to do this," and he thereupon placed his thumbs in his ears and wiggled his fingers at the assemblage.

At a Gridiron Club dinner, he was kiddingly accused of reading important briefing papers during the commercial breaks that took place while he watched television, and he amiably retorted, "That's not true. I *watch* the commercials. I read my papers while the *news* is on." Another Gridiron Club audience learned from its chief of state:

> As you know, historians trace the presidential press conference back to a chief executive who was quite reticent with the press, John Quincy Adams. He didn't hold press conferences. But it seems that every morning before dawn, Adams would hike down to the Potomac, strip off his clothes, and swim.... And one summer day, a woman of the press, under orders from her editor, followed him. And after he'd plunged into the water, she popped from the bushes, sat on his clothes and demanded an interview. And she told him that if he tried to wade ashore, she'd scream. So Adams held the first press conference up to his neck in water.[36]

He knew, Reagan told the crowd, just how Adams felt.

Another Reagan speech to reporters contained the following tale, designed to illustrate how hard the media was to impress:

> In the old days of vaudeville ... ambitious young vaudevillians would go into an old empty theater and try out in front of a blasé booking agent who'd be sitting there in one of the front seats with a cigar, all alone in the theater, watching them do their act—and he was very hard to please.
>
> One young fellow walked out to center stage. The agent asked him what he did, and the kid just took off and flew around the whole theater—made a couple of circles clear up to the ceiling, came back down, and landed back at the center of the stage.
>
> The agent says, "What else do you do besides bird imitations?"[37]

The favorable press coverage that Reagan got was certainly not due to the frequency of his press conferences. During his first year in office, he held a grand total of six of these, the fewest of any modern president, and in his entire eight years in the Presidency he held only 151 conferences with the White House press corps (in contrast, FDR, as noted earlier in this volume, held 337 of them in his first term alone). Nor did it stem from his display of knowledge concerning specific issues that he was asked about at these presidential appearances, because such knowledge was often conspicuous by its absence. His hearing problems didn't gain him any points in these sessions either. But his buoyant, self-deprecating sense of humor together with his obvious niceness more than made up for these defects. There was, as Tip O'Neill once said of him, "just something about the guy that people like. They want him to be a success." Reporters, who—as Deaver asserted— "responded to his decency,"[38] were no different than anyone else. At least one ranking Reagan aide was convinced that his boss "enjoyed the most generous treatment by the press" of any president since FDR, and even liberal publications which might have been expected to be quite hostile to a conservative like Reagan, were surprisingly friendly: *Washington Post* editor Ben Bradlee, for example, thought that his paper was kinder to Reagan than to any other president he could remember.[39]

The good nature and the humor helped defuse potential problems for Reagan underlings as well. A junior aide, John F. W. Rogers, finding himself alone in the Oval Office with Reagan for the first time after Nancy Reagan and Deaver had moved to the next room to discuss Executive Mansion furnishings (a topic in which the president found it difficult to become interested) was understandably uncomfortable and diffident. Reagan quickly relaxed him. He pointed to a portrait of George Washington in which the first president had a hand thrust inside his coat in a manner reminiscent of Napoleon and asked the young employee, "What do you think he's doing with his hand?" After Rogers had said that he didn't know, Reagan suggested, "I bet he's in there scratching himself."

When Defense Secretary Caspar Weinberger was in some trouble because of an embarrassing leak from the Pentagon of a letter from Weinberger to Reagan urging him to make no arms deals with Gorbachev at Geneva, a reporter asked Reagan if he planned to fire the defense secretary for this gaffe. Reagan responded with a question of his own: "Do you want a two-word answer or one?" The reporter replied, "Two." Reagan rejoined, "Hell, no."

At another press conference, commenting on an accusation that Reagan's press secretary, Speakes, had invented quotations and attributed them to the president, Reagan quipped: "That's the nice thing about this job. You get to quote yourself shamelessly, and if you don't, Larry Speakes will."

Even the deeply felt rancor that existed between the First Lady and Chief of Staff Regan was not immune from Reagan's defusion-through-humor efforts, as in "Nancy and Don at one point tried to patch things up. They met privately over lunch. Just the two of them and their food tasters." In this case, however, the efforts failed: Regan was forced, ultimately, to resign.

Among the many stories that the former resident of Hollywood told, one in particular epitomized his general approach to life, and he tended to share it with listeners often. It featured two small boys, one a consistent pessimist and the other a highly optimistic child. A psychiatrist suggested to both sets of parents that to make the first boy more of an optimist and the second one more of a realist the former be locked in a room containing a large number of attractive new toys and the second be enclosed in a room that had stacks of horse manure. When the parents came back, the pessimist was in tears and refusing to play with any of the toys because he was worried that they might break. The optimist, on the other hand, was cheerfully shoveling the manure as he announced to his amazed parents, "With this much manure around, I know there's a pony in here someplace."

The "every cloud has its silver lining" moral of that tale was obvious, and Reagan much of the time did draw from his rich collection of anecdotes—his "parables," as he called them—to make points. In words not far removed from Lincoln's, he said, "I believe an illustration, like a picture, is worth a thousand words. Jesus used parables to make his points and help people understand."

Thus, to poke fun at fellow Republicans who seemed to him to be too self-satisfied, he on several occasions relayed the story of a man who was badly injured in a street accident and quickly surrounded by a host of bystanders. An older gentleman bent over the victim in an effort to help, but another man pushed the first individual out of the way and yelled, "Let me at him. I have first aid training." The older man did as requested and the more aggressive newcomer began doing the various things that he had been taught in his first aid class. After a few minutes of this, with no visible improvement in the injured person having resulted from the newcomer's intervention, the elderly man tapped the man who had taken first aid training on the shoulder and gently said, "When you get to the part about calling the doctor, I'm right here."

At least one dignitary in attendance at a White House Presidential Citizens Medal presentation, the noted nuclear scientist Edward Teller, felt that Reagan told another story to underscore his belief that his guests should be satisfied with their already-won accolades and not worry if they were not asked to do anything more. In this tale, a "cantankerous old woman" went to a judge and informed him that she wanted a divorce. The jurist asked, "How old are you, madam?" and she responded that she was ninety. He asked the age of her husband, and she replied, "Ninety-two." Asking her how long the two of them had been married, he learned that they had been husband and wife for seventy-three years. When he queried her as to whether there were any children, she said, "Oh, yes, Your Honor. Six children and they are all right. Twenty-six grandchildren, five great-grandchildren, and one more coming." "Madam," asked the judge as he assimilated all of these facts, "do I understand you want to be divorced?" "Yes, Your Honor," the woman declared. "Enough is enough."

The fortieth chief executive sometimes favored a tale from the sports world when he advanced his abiding opinion that government officials were too slow to accept blame for anything and too quick to blame others. It involved the legendary baseball manager Frankie Frisch, who one day sent a rookie on his team to play center field. The rookie immediately dropped the first fly ball that was hit to him. Soon thereafter, he let a ground ball go between his feet, and he then threw the ball to the wrong base. Frisch raced out of the dugout, took the disgraced player's glove away from him, and yelled, "I'll show you how to play the position." The next batter belted a line drive directly over second base. Frisch ran toward it, missed it completely, lost his balance and slipped when he tried to chase it, threw down his glove, and shouted at the rookie, "You've got center field so screwed up nobody can play it."

On signing new legislation in 1983, Reagan expressed his hope that the law would achieve its intended purpose, but pointed out at the same time that faith was not quite the same as certainty, by recounting a story about a man who fell off a cliff. As he was falling, he grabbed a tree branch that was sticking out of the side of the cliff and looked down three hundred feet to the canyon floor below. He then looked up and said, "Lord, if there's anyone up there, give me faith. Tell me what to do." A voice from the heavens said, "If you have faith, let go." The man looked down at the canyon floor and then took another look up and said, "Is there anyone else up there?"

Reagan got much laughter and applause at the USSR's Moscow State University in 1988 by telling an anecdote to buttress his already-offered judgment that bureaucracies were a problem around the world, knowing no national boundaries. There was an old story about a town which "could be anywhere," he said, with a bureaucrat "who was known to be a good-for-nothing, but he somehow had always hung on to power." One day at a town meeting an old woman rose to her feet and told the bureaucrat that where she came from there was a folk legend that whenever a baby was born an angel descended from heaven and kissed the newborn on one part of its body. If the baby was kissed on his hand, he would grow up to become a handyman. If the kiss was placed on the baby's forehead, the child would become intelligent and clever. "And," she said, "I've been trying to figure out where the angel kissed you so that you should sit there for so long and do nothing."

To illustrate his strongly held belief that neither intelligence nor common sense correlated to years of formal education, he relayed to a Conservative Political Action Conference banquet audience an anecdote about a farmer and a lawyer. Having gotten into a bad traffic collision, both came out of their cars. The farmer took a look at the lawyer, went back to his car, and reappeared with a bottle. "Here," he told the attorney, "you look pretty shook up. I think you ought to take a nip of this; it'll steady your nerves." After the lawyer had taken the suggestion, the farmer said, "You still look a little bit pale. How about another?" The lawyer took a second swallow. At the urging of the farmer, he took several more swallows and finally announced to the farmer that he was at this point feeling rather well and asked the farmer if he didn't think that maybe *he* should take a little nip, too. The farmer thereupon replied, "Not me, I'm waiting for the state trooper."

Some of Reagan's stories, on the other hand, seemed to have absolutely no point at all. Thus, a visiting foreign statesman who had just made an emotional pitch for arms control was immediately asked by Reagan, "Say, have you heard the one about Brezhnev and the Warsaw hotel?" Congressional visitors with serious matters of state on their minds were apt to be detoured by completely irrelevant tales about "Murphy the spy" or some long-forgotten pitcher for the Chicago Cubs or what Jack Warner said to one of his leading actresses in Reagan's Hollywood era. Cabinet members heard jokes that—while invariably told with Reagan's great gifts of timing, verbal inflection, and gesturing—often seemed to have nothing to do with anything on the agenda. A rough estimate by one of the ex-actor's closest aides was that only about half of his stories bore any visible relationship to what had just been, or was about to be, discussed.

Even when a connection could be made, it sometimes was, at best, a strained one. The Great Communicator liked to tell a joke, for example, "about communication and some of the basic rules of communication" that served as a lead-in to the redundant line, "So, I'm going to try to communicate a little bit today." A young baseball star's wife, busy preparing dinner one evening while her husband relaxes in the living room, hears their baby cry and says to her husband, "Change the baby." The ballplayer responds, "What do you mean, change the baby? I'm a ballplayer. That's not my line of work." Irate, the wife answers, "Look, buster, you lay the diaper out like a diamond, you put second base on home plate, put the baby's bottom on the pitcher's mound, hook up first and third, slide home underneath, and if it starts to rain, the game ain't called, you start all over again."

Similarly stretching things a bit, since it generally was triggered by nothing more than a self-mocking reference to his age, was another favored story—an ironic one, in this case, given his own fate. In this scenario, an elderly couple is getting ready to go to bed, and the wife suddenly announces that she has a burning desire for ice cream and that there is none in the house. The husband offers to go to the store and get some. She says, "Vanilla, with chocolate sauce," and he repeats it, "Vanilla, with chocolate sauce." She then adds, "With whipped cream and a cherry on top," and he now confirms the entire request, "Vanilla with chocolate sauce, whipped cream and a cherry on top." He goes out to do the errand, and when he gets back he finds her already in bed. He hands her a bag and, discovering a ham sandwich when she opens it, she tells him, "I told you to write it down. You forgot the mustard."

Nor could the most astute verbal sleuth, most likely, find any relevancy between an anecdote involving Brezhnev and the rest of a 1982 speech that Reagan gave at a Eureka College Alumni Association dinner, beyond the fact that Brezhnev had already been mentioned. Here, the Soviet leader, having just been installed as president, invites his aged mother to come up and see his suite of offices in the Kremlin. He then puts her in his expensive limousine and has his chauffeur drive her with him to his luxurious Moscow apartment, following which he takes her in his helicopter to his magnificent country home. As a final bit of showing off, he flies her in his private jet to view his palatial home on the Black Sea. Throughout the lengthy itinerary, Brezhner's mother is strangely silent. Finally, as the schedule nears its completion, the woman utters what are almost her first words of the entire day: "Leonid, what if the Communists find out?"

Similar non sequiturs and relative non sequiturs also at times marked Reagan's conversations when he was not telling stories. Soon after he became governor, he presided over a lengthy and rather technical meeting that dealt with state mental hospital budgetary cuts and at one point, apparently in an attempt to lighten up the proceedings, asked, "Do you know how hard it is to mispronounce 'psychiatric' once you know how to do it right? I had to do it in *King's Row* and at first I couldn't do it. It's like deliberately singing a flat note." As president, with Lebanon in chaos, he affably told the visiting Lebanese foreign minister after an elaborate briefing by the latter, "You know, your nose looks just like Danny Thomas's."

Because of his propensity for stories and badinage like these it was sometimes said by his opponents that Reagan was in his "anecdotage." It was also because of such behavior that Reagan's White House predecessor, Gerald Ford, said of him, "He is one of the few political leaders I have ever met whose public speeches revealed more than his private conversations." Oregon Senator Robert Packwood, reporting on a recent visit of Packwood and other senators to the Executive Mansion, observed of the former California governor, "He's on a different track. We just shake our heads."[40]

On the negative side, too, for Reagan, was an opinion in some quarters that the lighthearted approach to the presidency and Reagan's heavy reliance on his sizable trove of anecdotes and one-liners indicated a lack of both knowledge and general intelligence. While scholars have generally credited the ex-actor with the possession of ample amounts of both, many of his detractors thought of him as an amiable dunce, a leader who fell back on the jocular to disguise both an unwillingness and an inability to master the complexities of the most important job on the planet. Not unlike Lincoln in this regard, too, he was viewed by some as a man who was insufficiently attuned to the seriousness of his professional environment and whose unwritten motto despite Communist threats and major weaknesses in the domestic economy, seemed to be "Anything for a laugh."

On these grounds, Speaker O'Neill, for all of his admiration for Reagan's charm and popularity, also thought that the fortieth chief executive of the United States knew less than any president he'd ever known.

Reagan's budget director, David Stockman, who left the White House in 1985, subsequently lambasted his former superior in a widely publicized book for having neither the aptitude nor the desire for details and for his habit of wandering in circles with all kinds of anecdotes.[41] Reagan scholar Wilbur Edel, in his book, has faulted his subject for a conspicuous lack of originality except in his off-the-cuff witticisms and—citing such incidents as the "bombing of Russia"—has pointed out that even here Reagan could potentially have paid a heavy price for them.[42]

Even a story that Reagan told more than a few times, when asked how he could hold up so well in the face of all of his foreign and domestic problems, while it clearly contained the usual Reaganesque heavy injection of self-mockery, also seemed to some people to contain a significant germ of truth. There once were two psychiatrists, one of them young and one of them old, Reagan would say to the person who had posed him the question, and they had offices across the hall from each other. Each morning, they would meet in the elevator, each well-rested and energetic, but by late afternoon, when they saw each other again as they left their offices, the young psychiatrist looked fatigued and in some disarray while the older man appeared to be as relaxed and well-scrubbed as he had been when he came to work. One day, the young psychiatrist asked his colleague just how this could be, telling him, "You look so fresh all the time. I hear these terrible stories from my patients every day. How do you put up with it? What's your secret?" And the older psychiatrist looked at the young one and said, "I don't listen."

Potentially even more damaging to Reagan was his chronic inability to resist saying things in private that were replete with political incorrectness or bawdiness to trusted confidants who presumably wouldn't repeat these utterances publicly.

A favorite joke that he told throughout his political career involved a man who for some reason harbored a strong prejudice against Italians. One day, taking a walk with a friend, he came upon an Italian organ grinder and his monkey and proceeded to place the considerable sum of five dollars in the monkey's hat. The friend, amazed, said, "You've been telling me for years how much you hated Italians, and here you do that." And the man who disliked Italians replied, "Well, they're so cute when they're little."

When, as governor he appointed a Japanese American, the famed semanticist S. I. Hayakawa, to the presidency of the violence-racked and then completely closed-down San Francisco State University, he informed at least one close associate, "If Hayakawa can get that college straightened out, we'll forgive him for Pearl Harbor."

In private, also, he did what Press Secretary Speakes deemed "a very good gay imitation" which often included a lisp and wrist flicking ("If those fellows don't leave me alone, I'll just slap them on the wrist"; "I washed my hair last night and I just can't do a thing with it").

Again, away from the public eye, he sometimes told off-color jokes that similarly might have caused him problems if he told them to anyone but intimates. One such tale—frequently related by Reagan—involved the great Winston Churchill's going to the men's room while a guest at a London social event and finding his old political rival Clement Atlee standing at the urinal next to him. Churchill, as Reagan told the story, quickly moved a few places away and was asked by the surprised left-wing leader, "My, my, Winston, are we being modest?" Churchill replied, "Not at all, Clement. It's just that whenever you see something that is large, privately owned, and working well, you want to nationalize it."

By most informed accounts, Eureka College's most illustrious graduate was as devoid of racial or other prejudice as any man of his generation. His father had refused to let his two sons see the film classic *The Birth of a Nation* because it glorified the Ku Klux Klan and later wouldn't stay at a hotel that banned Jews. In the second situation, the future president's parent had told the desk clerk, "I'm a Catholic, and if it's come to a point where you won't take Jews you won't take Catholics." The young Ronald was influenced greatly by this attitude, and he further developed a liberal outlook in his personal friendships (if not in his politics) from his years in Hollywood. As for his bawdy anecdotes, these were invariably told only in private (and, indeed, almost never in mixed company). His compulsion to be funny could nonetheless have caused serious problems for him had such remarks as the ones noted become public, and, as it was, his advisers were often worried that his spontaneous comments might do him political harm. Speakes, in particular, regularly tried to discourage him from ad-libbing, and frequently, as Reagan was getting set to deliver a speech, Chief of Staff Regan would say, "No ad libs!" and shake a finger at his boss.

On balance, however, the man whom Federal Reserve chief Greenspan called "psychologically a professional comedian" reaped, as had his four White House predecessors who allowed their senses of humor full rein, far more than he lost by his refusal to take either his professional or his personal life overly seriously.

As other presidents discussed in this volume, he often used his self-deprecating comedic talents to narrow the large psychological distance that might otherwise have existed between a person in his position and the average American. He utilized them to disarm listeners of *all* social and professional strata; being with him was like, as Nancy Reagan's press secretary once declared in admiration of his ability to break down interactional barriers, "being with a favorite uncle."[43] He drew on humor to buttress his messages, to take the wind out of the sails of political opponents, and to relieve tension, his own or that of others. And he used it to defuse or sidetrack issues that at times could have been politically fatal and at other times were matters that he simply did not care to bone up on.

Reagan, with his smiles, banter, and stories, softened up the most hard-bitten of politicians, put matters in their proper perspective, and brought people closer together. Probably more than any other factor, it was Reagan's completely unfeigned appreciation of the funny and his constant resort to humor that let him ride out the various crises that arose during his presidency as few White House residents have.

Of all of the dividends allowed Reagan by his deeply embedded instinct to amuse, however, perhaps most important was the fact that his kindly, never hurtful, brand of joking was a vital ingredient in gaining for him the affection of his nation. He was the living embodiment of Gardner's maxim, "Our chief executive must please as many and offend as few as possible. And humor is one of the most reliable ways in which to please."[44] Americans, as Schieffer and Gates have written, "had not just loved Ronald Reagan but been entertained by him.... It was as fine a compliment as an actor could receive."[45] But the love stemmed in no small part from the entertainment.

CHAPTER 6

PRESIDENTIAL CANDIDATES

Although the number of American presidents who have realized considerable gains from the exercise of their senses of humor can literally be counted on the fingers of one hand, that number could easily have been larger. Several losing candidates in presidential races also had well-developed funny bones. While by definition it must remain conjectural as to how this characteristic would have played out for *them* had the electorate seen fit to make them winners, there is no reason to think that they would in office have been any less well served by their ability to poke fun at themselves and at others than were the five jocose men who did make it to the White House.

Into this also-ran category, certainly, falls Adlai E. Stevenson, the Democratic standard-bearer who lost twice—in 1952 and 1956— to the enormously popular World War II hero Dwight D. Eisenhower. Stevenson, who had been a well-liked governor of Illinois, was by all accounts capable of a high level of off-the-cuff humor. "He had," as his close associate John Kenneth Galbraith saw him, "a great enjoyment of life and of good speech. He could turn a wicked phrase."[1]

During the 1952 campaign, Stevenson was a featured speaker at a Baptist convention in Texas and in introducing him his host told the audience that the man from Illinois had been invited there "just as a courtesy, because [church leader] Dr. Norman Vincent Peale has already instructed us to vote for your opponent. Ladies and gentlemen, Governor Stevenson." Without batting an eyelash, the Democratic nominee strode to the microphone and started his remarks by saying, "Well, speaking as a Christian, I would like to say that I find the Apostle Paul appealing and the Apostle Peale appalling." In that same campaign, informed by a group of professors that he had "the support of all thinking Americans," he responded, "That's not enough. I'm going to need a majority." Once, when vigorously heckled by a highly emotional archconservative in Dallas, he calmly announced to the crowd, "I still believe in the forgiveness of sinners and the redemption of ignorance."

Stevenson made crisp observations about the media, too. "An editor is a person who separates the wheat from the chaff and then proceeds to print the chaff" and "Accuracy to a newspaper is what virtue is to a lady, except that a newspaper can always print a retraction" are among his more famous ones. Of the endorsement of Eisenhower by Republican senators Joseph R. McCarthy of Wisconsin and William Jenner of Indiana, he said, "This is the first time I've heard of a party campaigning on the slogan, 'Throw the rascals in.'"

He once told an audience of lobbyists, "Now, as I understand our respective roles, I am to contribute a speech—and you are to contribute something more tangible. This is a nice division of labor, much like the relationship of Big Ben to the Leaning Tower of Pisa. That is to say, I've got the time, if you've got the inclination."

In the best traditions of his fellow Illini Lincoln and Reagan, Stevenson was also a masterful storyteller. He regaled listeners with such tales as one about two prisoners in a jail cell, one rather smugly informing the other, "I'm going to study and improve myself and when you're still a common thief I'll be an embezzler." Another favorite Stevenson anecdote involved French statesman Georges Clemenceau being addressed at great length inside a railroad station by an extremely boring political supporter. Clemenceau noticed a man on the other side of the platform yawning, and he quietly commented, "I'm afraid we are overheard." Eisenhower's opponent also liked to tell a story about a visit that Argentinean First Lady Evita Perón made to Spain, during which she complained to the military figure seated beside her in the open limousine that someone in the crowd had called her puta ("whore").The man responded, "Think nothing of it, Madam. I've been retired for twelve years and they still call me General."

Senator Barry Goldwater of Arizona, nominated by the Republicans to take on incumbent President Lyndon Johnson in 1964, also deserves a place in this pantheon. He often declared that where he came from "we have so little water that the trees chase the dogs," and of his attempt to learn how to play the bagpipe he quipped, "I can't figure out how to hold the doggone thing. It's like making love to an octopus." His senatorial colleague and friend Hubert Humphrey talked so fast, he said, that listening to him was "like trying to read *Playboy* magazine with your wife turning over the pages." "Hubert," he straight-facedly averred, "has been clocked at 275 words a minute with gusts up to 340."

During the campaign, Goldwater frequently poked his fingers through a pair of horn-rimmed eyeglasses that had no lenses and announced to audiences, "These glasses are very much like President Johnson's programs. They look good, but they don't work."

Always good copy primarily because of bons mots like these, Goldwater was a favorite of the journalists who covered his White House race, despite his deeply rooted conservatism and his tendency to make militantly anti–Communist remarks. The press affectionately referred to his campaign airplane as the Enola Gay (after the aircraft that dropped the atomic bomb on Hiroshima) and to his warlike convention acceptance speech as "10–9–8–7–6..." One pundit said that his motto was "Ready! Fire! Aim!" On his part, in his dealings with the Fourth Estate, he good-naturedly lampooned his conservatism. In response to a press conference question as to what he would do in the event of a Soviet nuclear attack, he announced that his first action would be to "circle the wagons"; at another press conference he said that a movie would be made about his life and that it would be produced by "18th Century–Fox." He also confided to a group of journalists that he had a position awaiting him in industry should his presidential bid fail: "I've been offered a job as consultant on the 'Flintstones' TV show."

The modest Goldwater, who privately doubted that he was genuinely of presidential calibre and once said, "You know, I haven't really got a first-class brain," did not, however, utter one remark that has been often attributed to him. The alleged statement dealt with Goldwater's supposedly seeking membership in a Phoenix country club that had the reputation of being anti–Semitic but that also possessed an excellent golf course. Although it was reported that Goldwater said, "Since I'm only half–Jewish, can I join if I only play nine holes?" he never did. He told an interviewer who asked him about it, "It's a damn funny story but unfortunately not true."[2]

Three days after his 1996 defeat at the hands of William Jefferson Clinton, Senator Robert Dole of Kansas appeared on David Letterman's late-night television show, seemingly very much at ease. When the sometimes caustic Letterman commented that Clinton was "fat" and weighed "three hundred pounds," the man who came in second responded, "I never tried to lift him. I just tried to beat him." Asked about his future plans, he said, "My slogan was 'A better man for a better America.' But I'm going to head for Florida. My slogan

is going to be, 'A better tan for a better America.'" Pointing out that
he had originally announced his candidacy (unofficially) on Letterman's show in early 1995, Dole told his host that he wanted to know
what had gone wrong: "You said if I came on the show, everything
would be fine. But at least I get two hundred bucks for being here
tonight. First work I had."[3]

Fellow Letterman guest Ted Koppel, the host of the network
television program "Nightline," declared when he came on, "If Bob
Dole had only showed that side of himself a little more often." Letterman added, "He is genuinely very, very funny as a man," and
Koppel agreed, relating what had happened when he had traveled
with Dole on a bus caravan trip during the campaign. Initially, said
Koppel, the people on the first bus felt that they were all alone, but
when the bus went over an overpass, the first bus's passengers (Dole
included) could see that there were forty five or fifty other vehicles
in the caravan. Dole, Koppel reported, looked out the window and
said, "God, it looks like the funeral procession of a really great
man." Koppel then paused to let the audience laugh before adding,
"He was right."[4]

"If the use of rapierlike wit was an Olympic sport," former Congressman Morris Udall had written some years earlier, "Senator Bob
Dole would be the gold medal winner."[5] And it is true that the man
from Kansas had, throughout his long tenure in the Senate, been
known as one of that body's funniest members. Such Dole quips as
"I don't want to say that [Senator] Howard Baker is short, but last
week I saw him playing handball against the curb" were widely
quoted, as was Dole's comment when he saw a photograph of former presidents Carter, Ford, and Nixon standing next to each other
at a White House ceremony: "There they are. See no evil, hear no
evil, and evil." But there had sometimes been an overly hard edge
to his humor (including the last two witticisms). Some political pun-
dits had opined that the cutting aspect had in particular turned off
voters in 1976, when Dole unsuccessfully ran as the Republican vice
presidential nominee, and, apparently chastened by this defeat and
these remarks, Dole significantly softened his brand of kidding, and
the new version—with its heavy dosage of self-mockery—had become
to many people highly appealing.

Three days before Clinton's second inauguration, the incumbent
president presented the man whom he had defeated a presidential
Medal of Freedom. Dole's first words in his acceptance speech were,
"I, Robert J. Dole, do solemnly swear ... (pause) Sorry, wrong

speech." He then said that he had hoped that Clinton would be giving him the keys to the White House instead of the medal. Not long thereafter, he told a *New York Times* reporter regarding his being former White House intern Monica Lewinsky's next-door neighbor at Washington's elite Watergate, "I walk by fast. I don't want to be subpoenaed!"[6]

Two other political figures who came within striking distance of the White House should also be noted.

Morris Udall is one of them. Nurtured in the same Arizona desert that produced Goldwater, this cheerful Democrat was elected fourteen times to the U.S. House of Representatives and in 1984 was named the most respected and effective member of Congress by the full membership, Democrats and Republicans alike. He tried for his party's presidential nomination in 1976 and might well have gotten it had he not lost to Carter in the pivotal Wisconsin primary by a mere 5,000 votes out of 670,000 cast. Thereafter, until his death in 1998, he frequently quipped that he and Goldwater in tandem had made Arizona the only state in the union where mothers didn't tell their children that they could grow up to be president.

As good-natured as Goldwater, he took his Wisconsin defeat philosophically, telling reporters on the morning after it, "In the grand scheme of things, not everyone can be first. As you may recall, even George Washington, the father of our country, married a widow." He said that after his loss he felt like the missionary in one of Mark Twain's stories who tried to convert some cannibals, pointing out that Twain had written, "They listened with the greatest of interest to everything that he had to say. Then they ate him." He also sunnily drew upon the response that a former Alabama governor made to a reporter who had asked him what he'd do if elected to a third term: "Son, that's not what is bothering me. What is bothering me is what I'm going to do if I'm *not* elected to a third term." As for running for president again in 1980, he declared, "If nominated, I will run to Mexico; if elected, I will fight extradition."

A firm believer in the precept that putting oneself down was the best kind of humor ("it creates empathy, humanizes any message, and puts people at ease," he once wrote[7]), he often said that he was a "one-eyed Mormon Democrat from conservative Arizona. You can't find a higher handicap than that." He enjoyed telling crowds about the time during his 1976 presidential campaign in New Hampshire, when he stuck his head in the door of a barber shop and announced, "Mo Udall, I'm running for president," and the barber responded, "Yeah, I know. We were laughing about it just this morning." Asked by a journalist what had separated Carter from himself in that campaign, he said, "About seven hundred delegates."

He told as many stories, with an exquisite sense of timing, as anyone else portrayed in this volume: about the Death Row inmate, due to be executed by a firing squad, who when asked if he had a last request replied, "Yes. A bulletproof vest"; about the diner in a restaurant who, having hung his coat on a rack, saw a thief grab it and start to flee, got a policeman to join him in the chase and, after the thief had continued to run despite the officer's yell to him to stop, shouted to the policeman, "Shoot him in the pants!"; about the gay member of Congress who was asked if he was still a practicing homosexual and answered, "*Practicing*? No, I don't need to practice—I've been doing it long enough."

Lastly, Senator Edward Kennedy of Massachusetts, who arguably could have had the 1968 Democratic nomination for the asking in the wake of his brother Robert's assassination in June of that year (and also because of the huge lingering posthumous affection for another brother, JFK) but could not procure it when he did try for it—in 1980, eleven years after his watershed drive off the Chappaquiddick bridge with his passenger, Mary Jo Kopechne—warrants inclusion. He once remarked, "Frankly, I don't mind not being president. I just mind that someone else is." South Carolina Senator Ernest Hollings, who speaks with a heavy southern accent, is, Kennedy has said, "the only non–English-speaking candidate ever to run for president." In the Reagan era, Kennedy advocated that Reagan's controversial and tactless interior secretary, James Watt, believed to be a staunch enemy of conservationists, be thrown to the wolves "while there are still some wolves left."

Also an excellent storyteller, one of the personal tales that he often tells involves a widely watched Massachusetts television debate that pitted him against a more seasoned Republican opponent when he first ran for the U.S. Senate, as a wealthy thirty year old. The G.O.P. nominee announced to the viewers in no uncertain terms that "Mr. Kennedy has never worked a day in his life." The next morning, Kennedy was standing outside the factory gates in a central Massachusetts mill town, shaking the hands of the first shift workers as they arrived, when a grizzled old-timer looked the candidate right in the eye and said, "Mr. Kennedy, you ain't missed a goddamn thing."

His senatorial victory brought him to the nation's capital, which had at the time housed his presidential and attorney general brothers for two years. His first public speech there began, "Well, now that we are *all* here at home." In that same speech, he said that he had gone down to the White House to make some suggestions to his much older brother "but all I got from him was, 'Are you still using that greasy kid's stuff on your hair?'" Asked by a journalist in the audience, "Are you really independent?" he replied, "I'm independent. I've been helping him [JFK] for a number of years, and I think it's time he stood on his own feet."

We shall never know if any of these five men would have made a great national chief executive, or, what—if any—use each would have made of his pronounced sense of humor. All that can be said with certainty is that each had the potential to gain considerably from being able to see life, and himself, in perspective.

CHAPTER 7

THE LAST LAUGH:
CONCLUDING THOUGHTS
ON HUMOR

Testimonials to the positive contributions of humor are not in short supply. Art Buchwald, the greatly admired Pulitzer Prize winning humor columnist, sees a sense of the amusing as a personal lifesaver. Buchwald, whose mother was placed in a mental institution, where she was to stay for thirty-five years, shortly after he was born and who with his three sisters was first sent to New York's Hebrew Orphan Asylum and then assigned to a series of not always loving foster parents, says, "All I know is that I've survived my childhood … and ever since because I can see things humorously."

Humor to him isn't joke telling ("I'm not a joke teller at all") but putting everyday things together into a "humorous whole." "I just describe a situation," he says, "that you'd be familiar with yourself. For example, I walk down the street and see everyone on cell phones now. You think that they're yelling at you, but they're not. One guy is yelling at Arnie, in a business deal. So [in my column] I take his phone and yell back to Arnie myself." He also gets many of his professional ideas from the newspapers because what's on the front pages, he believes, is far funnier than anything that he could possibly make up. In the events surrounding the Clinton impeachment, for example, he viewed "everyone—Lewinsky, Tripp, Starr— as a character in a scene that had its very amusing aspects."

Buchwald thinks that it's a heady experience when you get people to laugh and says, "The day people stop laughing, you're in trouble." Humor is also, in the Buchwald scheme of things, "a great way to relieve a lot of tension." Perhaps above all, the use of humor can lead to personal likability: Buchwald says that he discovered at an early age that he could make kids laugh "and in exchange they would think that I was a nice person" and argues that "most people believe, with justification, that being seen as humorous and being a good guy go together." As for what's funny, he has one major rule: "If you think that it's funny, it's funny."[1]

Another critically acclaimed recipient of the Pulitzer Prize for humor, Dave Barry, believes that the possession of a funny bone "is probably innate to most people." In his opinion, "We have two major psychological responses. One of them is religion, which we need for solace—for a belief, for example, that it all doesn't end here. The other is laughing at the world. Having no sense of humor, especially if you have no religion, must be awful, because then you really have no outlet."

Barry shares the Buchwald likability hypothesis. He states just as unequivocally as his fellow humorist that "people like you better if you have a sense of humor" and points out that most great professional comedians have been eminently appealing, although he does recognize an occasional exception: "George, the character played by Jason Alexander in the "Seinfeld" television series, for example, was a total rodent and weasel and yet he was incredibly funny; maybe he got away with it because people realized that he was just acting the part."

"Humor," he points out, "clearly can't be used in all circumstances. When the plane is plunging—because of air pockets, turbulence, or whatever—you don't want to have the pilot make jokes." "But for most people," he argues, "the danger is that they don't use humor enough. Most people won't use it at a funeral, for example, whereas the widow might well be extremely grateful for it [in such a situation]."

Barry thinks that humor "is hard in both writing and in speaking, because it's the only kind of performance where you're promising a result, namely that people will find it funny and will laugh." He also believes that the funniest people he knows often achieve their comedic results through fear: "There's an honesty about them. They're not afraid of exposing their deepest fears. But difficult and even courageous as it may be to achieve real humor, every culture has it. It's a necessary part of being a human being."[2]

The most important prerequisite for seeing the funny side of life, in Barry's opinion, is the possession of perspective, which, he has declared, is a word derived from two ancient Greek words: persp, meaning "something bad that happens to somebody else," and ective, meaning "ideally somebody like Donald Trump." Although hardly preoccupied with the topic, he turns to funerals again for an example:

> Funerals are not funny, which is why we don't laugh during them unless we just can't help ourselves. On the other hand, if a funeral occurs way on the other side of the world, and it involves the late Mr. Ayatollah "Mojo" Khomeini, and the mourners are so upset that they start grabbing garments and souvenir body parts off the deceased to the point where what's left of him could be laid to rest in a standard Good & Plenty box, then we have no choice but to laugh until our dentures fall into our laps.[3]

Bob Orben, creator of the country's best-known humor newsletter and a man who has written literally thousands of gag lines not only for such comic luminaries as Red Skelton, Jack Paar, and Dick Gregory but—at the peaks of their respective careers—Gerald Ford and Barry Goldwater, says simply, "I'm afraid of people who don't laugh." Such people, he explains, "are wound up tighter than a spring. They're ready to do violence. I don't think, for example, that Hitler had a big sense of humor."

In Orben's opinion, humor reaches out to place a friendly and warm arm around an audience and say in effect, "I can understand you." It's a great bonding mechanism ("If you can laugh together, you can do many other things together") and is an excellent way to turn around a potentially unfavorable set of circumstances.

He believes that successful humor "overwhelmingly" has to be directed at oneself: "Self-deprecation," he says, "is a holy writ; it's a given." If the humor *is* about someone else, he feels strongly that "the someone else must be the victor." "Humble" humor, as Orben views matters, works much better than "attack" humor, and he sees few exceptions to this precept. One notable exception is Henry Kissinger, who "takes an imperious, all-knowing, all-powerful 'I am the man' approach and does it well." Orben is willing to give the public figure who has said that he "cannot be president because the United States Constitution disallows foreign-born, but says nothing about emperor" some credit.[4]

For those in the political arena, the potential benefits of humor are perhaps particularly large. The late Mo Udall, indeed, once deemed humor to be "possibly the most potent tool a politician can wield" and contended that anyone aspiring to elected office who failed to use it was "simply missing the boat."[5]

For one thing, as some of his previously offered words might imply, Udall thought that humor was "the best antidote for the politician's occupational disease: an inflated, overweening, suffocating sense of self-importance." Quoting with approval Konrad Lorenz's observation that "a man sufficiently gifted with humor is in small danger of succumbing to flattering delusions about himself because he cannot help perceiving what a pompous ass he would become if he did," he argued that "nothing deflates a pompous ass quicker than a well-placed barb."[6]

For another, he felt that people were drawn to, and reassured by, a politician who could poke fun at others and at himself. "Politics is a people business," he said, "and people crave laughter. Other things being equal, a droll politician will have an easier time than a dour one getting elected. Wit is an essential element of charisma, of leadership." Once a politician is elected, Udall declared, "humor becomes one of the most formidable tools he or she can wield in pursuit of ... goals. A savvy pol can use humor to disarm his enemies, to rally his allies, to inform, rebut, educate, console, and convince."[7]

Delaware Senator Thomas Carper is in general agreement and adds, "We're more of a television society today, where people can't see their political leaders in person nearly so much as they used to, in some cases because we're so [populous] a country and also, these days, for security reasons. One of the ways in which we humanize ourselves and relate to an audience is humor." Carper, his Democratic party affiliation notwithstanding, uses the G.O.P.'s Ronald Reagan as a solid example of what he means here. He especially admires the Gipper's outpouring of amusing remarks in the immediate aftermath of the assassination attempt, gives his highest praise to Reagan's "Please assure me that you are all Republicans" plea to his physicians, and asks, "How can you not like a guy like that?" He, too, sees a strong connection between being humorous and having personal appeal: "Part of getting people to go along with you, whether you're dealing with a legislative body or anything else, is to get the people to like you. Showing a sense of humor is very helpful in this regard."[8]

Massachusetts Congressman Barney Frank, whom many (including Carper) consider to be one of the funniest people in the current U.S. Congress, thinks that while humor is not a necessity for a successful political career (he points to Eisenhower and Nixon as examples of men who made it to the top without employing any humor at all), it can help in three important ways. He shares in the first

place the Buchwald-Barry-Carper opinion about being favorably
regarded: "Done right, [humor] is ingratiating. Likability is a major
prerequisite for success in politics." Second, in Frank's opinion,
humor "is a way to get attention for yourself. When you're dealing
with the press, humor can break through the clutter." Third, humor
can help you—and this is perhaps the most important of all—make
your points with the legislature and with voters. If you can successfully ridicule something, you've done it great damage. Humor is a
great deflator."[9]

Economist Galbraith believes that politicians who show humor
can establish their political identities in a highly appealing way, by
showing that they can separate themselves from the "grim ambition" that marks so many men and women who run for office.
("Humor in politics," he cautions, "is only possible for those who
are secure enough to detach themselves from politics.") A sense of
humor, he is also convinced, testifies to "a substantial measure of
intelligence. Then there is the further consideration that humor is
intimately associated with truth." By the same token, in Galbraith's
opinion, "nothing is so destructive as describing a person as humorless."[10]

It should be equally obvious, on the other hand, that the use of
humor can have its downside. George Shultz, who admiringly
observed Reagan at close range as the fortieth president's secretary
of State, says, "You have to be careful that people don't see you
using humor as a substitute for thought."[11] Reagan Defense Secretary Caspar Weinberger similarly warns that while "it's very justified
and legitimate for executives to use humor, it has to be sprinkled in
carefully, above all to make points. It can't be just a vaudeville routine."[12] While neither man even remotely faults Reagan's performance on this count, it is not irrelevant, of course, that some people
did.

It will be remembered that neither Lincoln nor Roosevelt
escaped entirely unscathed from criticism for their lightheartedness,
which was, in some quarters, at times considered highly inappropriate. Even Coolidge and Kennedy, as has also been pointed out,
had definite doubts about *their* respective uses of humor, with the
former harboring a belief (in his case, apparently quite unsubstan-
tiated) that whenever he indulged his funny bone it got him into
trouble, while JFK was avowedly afraid to be too funny and
restrained some of his humor at press conferences out of a fear that
some amusing remark would in cold print look unstatesmanlike.

At least two of the losing presidential candidates, too, found their talents to amuse to be mixed blessings. Stevenson, whom Arthur Schlesinger, Jr., has called "a truly serious man who expressed part of his seriousness in humor,"[13] was viewed with suspicion by sizeable portions of the electorate in both 1952 and 1956 partly *because* of his jocularity. He ran, in the eminently qualified Schlesinger's explanation, on both occasions "against a highly popular man [Eisenhower] who projected a seriousness, a gravitas—which is what the country wanted *then*, after twenty years of FDR and Truman, and all the tensions of the Depression, the war, and the postwar."[14] Dole's downside was probably no more controllable: memories of the earlier Dole and his less-benign wit—at times regenerated by tapes put on television by his opponents—persisted throughout the 1996 campaign. He was seen by many as having violated a cardinal principle of humor: to succeed, it should not be hurtful and should be aimed at oneself at least as much as it is aimed at other people.

Dole's experience in particular may be instructive. "Humor can be a very dangerous commodity," opines Douglas Dillon. "If you make fun of someone else or their problems, you can make an enemy for life. You have to refrain from doing it."[15] The former Kennedy and Johnson secretary of the treasury was presumably not thinking of Dole's "Howard Baker playing handball against the curb" or "See no evil, hear no evil, and evil" Carter-Ford-Nixon jokes when he offered this thought. But the two Dole comments are realistic examples.

The same might be said for many other cutting and widely reported remarks that the Kansas Republican made before his humor metamorphosis—from Dole's seemingly ill-natured jab at his blow-dried rival Jack Kemp, "Kemp wants a business deduction for hair spray" to a frequently repeated joke that Dole shared with his senatorial campaign audiences, "The good news is that a busload of supply-siders went over a cliff. The bad news is that there were three empty seats." "Partially of his own making," Dole's close friend (if ideological opposite) former Democratic National Committee Chairman Robert Strauss could say of the Kansan well before Dole's 1996 presidential race, "People see him as a fellow who has a sort of mean streak to him. He can be terribly cutting. He has a sense of humor that is sometimes not well understood."[16]

Humor consultant Landon Parvin advises that the *only* humor that should normally be used is that which pokes fun at oneself with grace and good nature. The Virginia speech writer, who before many of Reagan's public appearances was instrumental in putting together for him three to six pages of quips that relied heavily on self-parody, sees only two valid exceptions to this rule of self-deprecation. He cautions female clients that they should *not* put themselves down, however kiddingly, "for some in the audience will believe you, unless you're a Margaret Thatcher." He also feels that sharp humor sometimes, if rarely, does have a place: on those comparatively few occasions on which it is essential to attack the political or corporate competition. But in both the world of business and in politics, Parvin stresses—echoing a now-familiar theme—"the main rule of humor is to use the humor to be likable. The problem that most people run into in this area is that their humor comes across as too harsh. An audience responds more to how the speaker is perceived than to what he says."[17]

Among the men who actually served as U.S. president, Jimmy Carter perhaps personified what both Dillon and Parvin warn against as well as anyone. Prone to both arrogance and sarcasm, *his* concept of self-deprecating humor—at least as a well-circulated White House maxim had it—was to criticize his staff. When an unidentified journalist referred to him as a "cruel recluse," he publicly announced, "I have asked [Press Secretary] Jody Powell to find out who first used that phrase. He's interrogated all the White House correspondents and twenty-three White House staff members. If I find out who said it, I'll let you know. And if I'm not there, my *new* Press Secretary will let you know." At a Washington Press Club dinner, he ended an attempt at humorous remarks by declaring, "I told my staff I wanted them to prepare a talk for me to make tonight that was funny and they didn't get around to it."

He was no more gracious with nonstaff members. He once opened a press conference by informing those in attendance, "I'm not going to say anything terribly important tonight, so you can all put away your crayons." Not long after his 1976 defeat of incumbent Chief Executive Ford, he said at a New York City fundraising dinner, "On election night, when the returns came in from New York City and the former president, whose name escapes me—" At another fundraiser, this time in Hollywood, he announced to the large crowd of motion picture notables, "It's a real thrill to meet the famous people here tonight. I hope I don't get to know too much about you." On another occasion, he told a Democratic audience in reference to his vice president, "I am very grateful that my associate Walter Mondale is here. I've done the best I could to find something for him to do.... I would like to ask you to keep [him] from getting lonesome in the White House. He's given me a list of his projects and wanted me to call them out to you. If you have questions about the Concorde, Northern Ireland, abortion, gay rights, downtown parking..."[18]

There was, in short a sting to Carter's efforts to be funny that could quickly lead to a conclusion that he was *not* such a nice guy. While one can only conjecture as to how much, if any, of his decisive 1980 presidential race loss to the ever-amiable Reagan could be traced to a public perception of this factor, the idea certainly cannot be dismissed out of hand.

Lyndon Johnson, too, although his decision not to run for reelection in 1968 was at least primarily due to a credibility gap that he encountered as commander in chief in an intensely divisive Vietnam War, might conceivably have been able to surmount that problem had he been personally more attractive. Instead, he was viewed by many as a boorish, insecure, and insensitive chief executive—something that *his* attempts at humor did absolutely nothing to dispel.

In the words of Douglas Dillon, "Johnson had rough humor, if he had any at all. There was a lot of off-color stuff and not really any self-deprecation."[19] Johnson's own press secretary, George Reedy, believed that whatever humor his boss did have was "crude and coarse" and that while LBJ did have a good sense of mimicry "it was basically cruel." "To me," said Reedy, "a sense of humor is a sense of proportion and *that* he didn't have. Not in the sense that Stevenson and Kennedy had a sense of humor. If you examined the humor in his speeches you'd see they had one of two objectives—either to put a point across or as an expression of hate."[20]

Johnson was given to such indecorous statements as (in reference to speeches made by political opponents), "I may not know much, but I do know the difference between chicken shit and chicken salad" and (regarding the potential difficulty of getting rid of entrenched FBI Director J. Edgar Hoover), "Well, it's probably better to have him inside the tent pissing out than outside pissing in." Making a speech on economics was, in his opinion, "a lot like pissing down your leg.... It seems hot to you, but it never does to anyone else." He declared that Gerald Ford couldn't "fart and chew gum at the same time." (The comment was, understandably, widely reported to have been "*walk* and chew gum," but the sanitized version was, in many quarters, seen for what it was.) Once, as he stormed out of a party caucus that had treated him with what he thought was insufficient respect, he said, "Now I know the difference between a caucus and a cactus. With a cactus the pricks are on the *outside*." Most of these quips were made more or less in private ("He was," says newsman Sam Donaldson, "devoid of public humor"[21]), but they quickly received wide circulation.

Johnson regularly blasted members of his staff and joked about it: "There are no favorites in my office," he once said, "I treat them all with the same general inconsideration." On another occasion he asserted, "I don't have ulcers. I give em." The evidence confirms Dillon's assertion that Johnson totally lacked a willingness to engage in self-deprecation. If Kennedy was a master of putting himself down, the vain and boastful LBJ was a master at putting himself *up*. After he had reviewed some Marines who were headed for Vietnam, he headed for the wrong helicopter and was told by an officer, "That's your helicopter over there, Sir." He responded, "Son, they are all my helicopters." He is quite likely the only president to have referred to the "State of *My* Union address" in a speech. Informed that an address that he had just given had been interrupted by applause twelve times, he complained that there had been more applause than that—a statement that was correct, but only if one counted the clapping that had greeted him when he had been introduced and was again heard when he had finished.

Words such as "insensitive," "lacking in grace," "ill-natured," and "boastful" were never applied to the humor of Lincoln, Coolidge, Roosevelt, Kennedy, or Reagan. All five chief executives had a basic sense of security which let them laugh at themselves. Even the severest critics of these men, moreover, recognized that with rare exceptions their jocularity not only lacked both malice and pomposity but was delivered with a softness and selflessness that made it difficult to take personal offense.

Asked why he did not more frequently "turn the laugh" on Douglas, Lincoln explained that he refrained not only because his political opponent was "too much in earnest" but also because he doubted whether turning the laugh on anybody really gained any votes. The man who described himself as "only a retail dealer" in humor and deemed laughter "the joyous, beautiful, universal evergreen of life" by almost all accounts came across, when he told his humorous anecdotes and made his witty quips, as a kindly, sweet-tempered, and compassionate human being—a person who never seemed happier than when poking fun at himself.

His occasional tendency toward peevishness and marked Yankee reserve notwithstanding, Coolidge also exhibited a sense of humor that was entirely good-natured as he raised self-deprecation to an art form. "It's good for people to laugh," he said in words not inconsistent with Lincoln's, and he regularly succeeded in doing so with a deadpan comic gift that never had a harsh overtone. There was, as the prolific magazine writer of his day Bruce Barton once prophetically said of him, "a lovable side to Calvin Coolidge.... He was unique.... The nation will remember his personality and his dry humor long after it has forgotten most of the events of his administration."[22]

In announcing, "I have a cheerful disposition," Franklin D. Roosevelt was, if anything, engaging in understatement. He positively "radiated" cheerfulness, as M. S. Venkataramani wrote of him.[23] And, as this volume has shown, while much of his material was not especially funny, he achieved maximum mileage out of his thin stock through an affability that perhaps only Reagan among all U.S. presidents has come close to equaling on a consistent basis. A prime respecter of Parvin's main rule of humor, he brought about sustained laughter through his extraordinary personal charm as he delivered lines that, had they been dispensed by a less-engaging figure, might well have produced only an unsympathetic silence.

"More than any politician since F.D.R.," John Kenneth Galbraith wrote in his memoirs, "John F. Kennedy ... was completely content with his own personality. He never felt it necessary to say anything by way of self-enhancement."[24] If Kennedy's irony did at times have a bit of sharpness to it, these occasions were rare, and his chronically affable self-mockery more than made up for the lapses. Moreover, in Schlesinger's widely quoted words, "He was a man devoid of hatred. He detested qualities but not people."[25] As Lincoln, Kennedy believed in a short statute of limitations for staying angry, and even when his wit failed to mask an irritation on his part, he remained mad only briefly: "Calm would soon descend," Schlesinger has written, "and in time the irritation would become a matter for jokes."[26]

"Jackie once told me," Schlesinger said in a recent interview:

> that when Jack was a senator he'd come home and tell her that one fellow senator or another had let him down. She wouldn't speak to that person from then on, she said, but then she'd see Jack at a party smiling and chatting amiably with that same person. She'd tell [JFK] that she thought he was mad at that person; and Jack would say, "But that was three weeks ago."[27]

Kennedy Treasury Secretary Dillon thinks that JFK was "very good at recognizing that you can't hurt someone's feelings in your humor, that it can't be at the expense of anyone else."[28] More than this, unlike Johnson or Carter, Kennedy had—in the opinion of one of his closest aides—"no sensitive sore spots, no unhappy experiences that could not be laughed at later."[29]

Reagan, as the chapter devoted to him has stressed, could in some ways serve as a textbook example of the gains that can be registered when an eminently sunny outlook on life is combined with a talent for witty self-parody and first-rate raconteurship. The man whom Nixon described as possibly being "too nice to be president" often pushed the outer limits of the permissible in his joking and, thanks to both his visible abundance of good will and his clear willingness to laugh at himself at least as often as at others, came away fundamentally unscathed. Democratic Senator Sam Nunn once said that the Gipper "never believed his own press clippings"[30] and Reagan's national security advisor, Brent Scowcroft, believed that his boss was "a man who knows who he is and what he stands for and is comfortable with both."[31] Due by no means exclusively but certainly to some large extent to his comedic gifts, he was a personality whom it was almost—as his son Ron said of him—impossible to dislike.

All five of the featured presidents were, in short, highly appealing as individuals. Comfortable with themselves, they seemed to feel that, as Galbraith has phrased it, "They could risk humor from a secure position."[32] In a calling that has always been notorious for outsized egos, they viewed themselves with a vigorous detachment and saw the world in perspective. If, in all cases, displays of bad temper and pettiness documentably existed, and harsh personnel moves were occasionally made, such happenings were—for each of the five—relatively rare, certainly when stacked against the norm for White House occupants and, for that matter, when compared to the performances of most people. While presidents, as Schlesinger has pointed out, "can't afford to be nice guys all the time,"[33] Lincoln, Coolidge, Roosevelt, Kennedy, and Reagan did nothing significantly to disprove the maxim of humor scholar P. M. Zall, "To be genuinely funny, you really have to be a nice person."[34] Comparatively speaking, they all *were* nice people as well as secure ones, and their constant resort to the jocular only enhanced the public's appreciation of this fact.

Whatever the witticisms and storytelling may have cost each

man, the gains for all of them, both professionally and personally, appear to have been infinitely greater. They did, to paraphrase poet Marianne Moore, save steps—even years—through their use of humor, and their experiences in this regard deserve our attention.

NOTES

References are to sources in the Bibliography.

1. Abraham Lincoln

1. 5, pp. xvi–xviii.
2. 4, p. xiii.
3. 48, p. 145.
4. 26, p. 52.
5. 55, vol. 3, p. 301.
6. 59, p. 171.
7. 33, p. 473.
8. *Ibid.*
9. 53, p. 237.
10. 12, p. 3.
11. 31, p. 229.
12. 12, p. 14.
13. 50, p. 100.
14. 64, p. 3.
15. *Ibid.*
16. 2, p. 185.
17. *Ibid.*, p. 244.
18. 20, p. 12.
19. 47, p. 48.
20. 36, p. 117.
21. 29, p. 81.
22. 64, p. 47.
23. 25, p. 25.
24. 2, p. 31.
25. 36, p. 6.
26. 6, vol. 1, p. 142.
27. 3, p. 48.
28. 43, p. 153.
29. 219, p. 131.
30. 57, p. 116.
31. 5, p. 249.
32. 235, pp. 97–98.
33. 12, p. 6.
34. *Ibid.*, p. 25.
35. 235, p. 98.
36. 26, p. 49.
37. 17, p. 81.
38. 53, p. 216.
39. 33, pp. 429–30.
40. 64, p. 7.
41. 6, vol. 8, p. 420.
42. 36, p. 80.
43. 29, p. 315.
44. 64, p. 48.
45. 38, pp. 141–42.
46. 58, p. 83.
47. 53, p. 224.
48. *Ibid.*
49. 29, pp. 263–64.
50. 64, p. 41.
51. 17, pp. 129–30.
52. 23, p. 280.
53. 25, p. 75.
54. *Ibid.*
55. *Ibid.*
56. 42, pp. 17–18.
57. 4, p. 107.
58. 38, p. 133.
59. 228, p. 225.
60. 45, p. 163.
61. 17, p. 277.
62. *Ibid.*, p. 262.
63. 2, p. 438.
64. 29, p. 279.
65. 57, p. 475.

2. Calvin Coolidge

1. 89, p. 206.
2. 72, p. 498.
3. 71, p. 76.
4. Will Rogers, "How to Escape a Lecture," *Good Housekeeping*, Mar. 1925, p. 15.
5. *Ibid.*
6. 247, p. 178.
7. 78, pp. 154–55.
8. 89, p. 271.
9. 257, p. 233.
10. M. R. Werner, "The Prose of Presidents," *Progressive*, Aug. 1954, pp. 20–21.
11. 94, pp. 64–65.
12. 84, p. 25.
13. 78, p. 1.
14. *Ibid.*, p. 154.
15. 82, p. vi.
16. 84, p. 27.
17. *Ibid.*
18. George H. Mayer, "Calvin Coolidge," in *Presidents of the United States*. Chicago: Field Enterprises Educational Corporation, 1976, p. 812.
19. 95, p. 48.
20. 71, p. 74.
21. 94, p. 60.
22. 92, p. 232n.
23. 78, p. 157.
24. 92, pp. vi–vii.
25. 78, p. 159.
26. Interview with author, Mar. 11, 1999.
27. 82, p. 9.

28. *Ibid.*, p. 14.
29. *Ibid.*, p. 16.
30. 84, p. 36.
31. 72, p. 476.
32. 92, p. 273.
33. 89, p. 208.
34. 69, p. 172.
35. *Ibid.*, p. 187.
36. 78, pp. 158–59.

3. Franklin D. Roosevelt

1. 125, p. 615.
2. 121, pp. 165–66.
3. 111, p. 69.
4. 99, p. 202.
5. All quotations in this paragraph from 131, pp. 3–4.
6. *Ibid.*, p. 27.
7. 215, pp. 238–39.
8. 100, p. 274.
9. 134, p. 14.
10. 111, p. 23.
11. *Ibid.*, p. 56.
12. *Ibid.*
13. 99, p. 203.
14. 126, p. 322.
15. 116, p. 13.
16. 99, p. 235.
17. 235, p. 137.
18. 131, p. 7.
19. 235, p. 141.
20. 124, pp. 395–96.
21. 235, p. 144.
22. *Ibid.*, pp. 144–45.
23. 105, p. 558.
24. 127, p. 65.
25. 126, p. 151.
26. 129, p. 5.
27. 131, p. 12.
28. 123, pp. 233–34.
29. *Ibid.*, p. 192.
30. 129, p. 295.
31. 126, p. 321.
32. 235, pp. 138–39.
33. 128, p. 580.
34. 131, p. 29n.
35. 111, p. 66n.
36. 127, p. 66.
37. 132, p. vii.
38. 129, p. 2.

4. John F. Kennedy

1. 136, p. 54.
2. 149, p. 283.
3. 159, p. 20.
4. 141, p. 23.
5. 233, p. 216.
6. 169, p. 70.
7. This was almost verbatim a witticism that JFK's fellow Democrat had offered a Gridiron Club dinner audience in 1957. See 222, p. 574. Kennedy took them where he found them.
8. 144, p. 227.
9. 233, p. 226.
10. 169, p. 71.
11. 136, p. 11.
12. 159, p. 128.
13. 155, p. 483.
14. 233, p. 217.
15. 149, p. 260.
16. 170, p. 75.
17. 166, pp. 73–74.
18. Interview with author, Apr. 2, 1999.
19. Interview with author, Feb. 23, 1999.
20. Interview with author, Mar. 11, 1999.
21. 174, pp. 29–31.
22. 219, p. 305.
23. 137, pp. 18–19.
24. 174, p. 21.
25. 233, p. 231.
26. 167, p. 664.
27. 174, pp. 60–61.

5. Ronald Reagan

1. *New York Times*, June 28, 1986.
2. 182, p. 120.
3. *Philadelphia Inquirer*, Aug. 17, 1986.
4. *Washington Post*, Mar. 28, 1988.
5. 233, p. 50.
6. 180, p. 74.
7. 212, p. 56.
8. *Washington Post*, Nov. 8, 1981.
9. Interview with author, Feb. 10, 1999.
10. 180, p. 89.
11. Interview with author, Feb. 10, 1999.
12. 203, p. 98.
13. Interview with author, Feb. 10, 1999.
14. Author's interview with Weinberger, Feb. 10, 1999.
15. 185, p. 81.
16. 182, p. 125.
17. Garry Wills, *Reagan's America: Innocents at Home*, Garden City, NY: Doubleday, 1987, p. 2.
18. 212, p. 93.
19. 233, p. 21.
20. *Ibid.*, pp. 23–24.
21. *Washington Post*, Oct. 22, 1984.
22. 206, p. 57.
23. 183, p. 398n.
24. 205, p. 59.
25. 192, p. 59.
26. 185, p. 23.
27. *Time*, Apr. 13, 1981, p. 30.
28. *Washington Post*, Apr. 1, 1981.
29. 213, p. 121.
30. 209, p. 109.
31. 203, p. 272.
32. 182, p. 124.
33. 191, p. 33.
34. Interview with author, Feb. 8, 1999.
35. *Ibid.*
36. 229, pp. 95–96.
37. 178, pp. 76–77.
38. 185, p. 144.
39. 206, p. 55.
40. 213, p. 115.
41. 210, p. 109.
42. 189, p. 288.
43. 194, p. 157.
44. 233, p. 14.
45. 207, p. 382.

6. Presidential Candidates

1. Interview with author, Apr. 2, 1999.
2. 235, p. 258.
3. *New York Times*, Nov. 9, 1996.
4. *Ibid.*
5. 257, p. 148.
6. 229, pp. 181–82.
7. 257, p. 195.

7. The Last Laugh

1. Interview with author, Mar. 1, 1999.
2. Interview with author, Feb. 12, 1999.
3. 218, p. 7.
4. Interviews with author, Feb. 8 and 9, 1999.
5. 257, p. 190.

6. *Ibid.*, p. xiv.
7. *Ibid.*, pp. xiv–xv.
8. Interview with author, Mar. 5, 1999.
9. Interview with author, Feb. 22, 1999.
10. Interview with author, Apr. 2, 1999.
11. Interview with author, Feb. 10, 1999.
12. Interview with author, Feb. 10, 1999.
13. 167, p. 727.
14. Interview with author, Mar. 11, 1999.
15. Interview with author, Feb. 23, 1999.
16. 255, p. 4.
17. Interview with author, Feb. 10, 1999.
18. All quotations in this paragraph are from 233, pp. 74–76.

19. Interview with author, Feb. 23, 1999.
20. 233, pp. 171–72.
21. Interview with author, Feb. 8, 1999.
22. 81, pp. xii–xiii.
23. 131, p. 2.
24. 232, p. 373.
25. 167, p. 673.
26. *Ibid.*
27. Interview with author, Mar. 11, 1999.
28. Interview with author, Feb. 23, 1999.
29. 160, p. 406.
30. 192, p. 62.
31. *Ibid.*, p. 97.
32. Interview with author, Apr. 2, 1999.
33. Interview with author, Mar. 11, 1999.
34. Interview with author, Feb. 17, 1999.

BIBLIOGRAPHY

1. Abraham Lincoln

1. Adler, Bill, ed., *The Wit and Wisdom of Abraham Lincoln*. New York: Citadel, 1993.
2. Angle, Paul M., ed., *The Lincoln Reader*. New Brunswick, NJ: Rutgers University Press, 1947.
3. Arnold, Isaac N., *The Life of Abraham Lincoln*. Chicago: A. C. McClurg, 1884.
4. Ayres, Alex, ed., *The Wit and Wisdom of Abraham Lincoln*. New York: Meridian, 1992.
5. Basler, Roy P., ed., *Abraham Lincoln: His Speeches and Writings*. Cleveland: World Publishing, 1946.
6. Basler, Roy P., ed., *The Collected Works of Abraham Lincoln*. 8 vols. New Brunswick, NJ: Rutgers University Press, 1953.
7. Basler, Roy P., *The Lincoln Legend: A Study in Changing Conceptions*. New York: Octagon, 1969.
8. Bates, David Homer, *Lincoln in the Telegraph Office*. New York: Century, 1907.
9. Bishop, Jim, *The Day Lincoln Was Shot*. New York: Harper & Brothers, 1955.
10. Boritt, Gabor S., ed., *Lincoln's Generals*. New York: Oxford University Press, 1994.
11. Boritt, Gabor S., ed., *Of the People, By the People, For the People*. New York: Columbia University Press, 1996.
12. Boritt, Gabor S., ed., *The Historian's Lincoln: Pseudohistory, Psychohistory, and History*. Urbana and Chicago: University of Illinois Press, 1988.
13. Burlingame, Michael, ed., *An Oral History of Abraham Lincoln: John G. Nicolay's Interviews and Essays*. Carbondale and Edwardsville: Southern Illinois University Press, 1996.
14. Burlingame, Michael, and John R. Turner Ettlinger, eds., *Inside Lincoln's White House*. Carbondale and Edwardsville: Southern Illinois University Press, 1997.
15. Burlingame, Michael, *Lincoln Observed: Civil War Dispatches of Noah Brooks*. Baltimore and London: Johns Hopkins University Press, 1998.
16. Burlingame, Michael, *The Inner World of Abraham Lincoln*. Urbana and Chicago: University of Illinois Press, 1994.
17. Carpenter, F. B., *The Inner Life of Abraham Lincoln: Six Months at the White House*. Lincoln and London: University of Nebraska Press, 1995.
18. Charnwood, Lord, *Abraham Lincoln*. New York: H. Holt, 1916.
19. Cuomo, Mario M., and Harold Holzer, eds., *Lincoln on Democracy*. New York: HarperCollins, 1990.
20. Current, Richard N., *The Lincoln Nobody Knows*. New York: Hill and Wang, 1958.

21. Davis, William C., *Lincoln's Men*. New York: Free Press, 1999.
22. Dennett, Tyler, ed., *Lincoln and the Civil War in the Diaries and Letters of John Hay*. New York: Dodd, Mead, 1939.
23. Donald, David, *Lincoln*. New York: Simon & Schuster, 1995.
24. Donald, David, *Lincoln Reconsidered*. New York: Alfred A. Knopf, 1956.
25. Edwards, Herbert Joseph, and John Erskine Hankins, *Lincoln the Writer*. Orono: University of Maine Press, 1962.
26. Einhorn, Lois J., *Abraham Lincoln the Orator: Penetrating the Lincoln Legend*. Westport, CT: Greenwood, 1992.
27. Fehrenbacher, Don E., *Abraham Lincoln: A Documentary Portrait through His Speeches and Writings*. Stanford, CA: Stanford University Press, 1964.
28. Fehrenbacher, Don E., *Prelude to Greatness: Lincoln in the 1850s*. Stanford, CA: Stanford University Press, 1962.
29. Fehrenbacher, Don E., and Virginia Fehrenbacher, eds., *Recollected Words of Abraham Lincoln*. Stanford, CA: Stanford University Press, 1996.
30. Freeman, Andrew A., *Abraham Lincoln Goes to New York*. New York: Coward-McCann, 1960.
31. Garrison, Webb, *The Lincoln No One Knows*. Nashville, TN: Rutledge Hill, 1993.
32. Hanchett, William, *Out of the Wilderness*. Urbana and Chicago: University of Illinois Press, 1994.
33. Herndon, William H., *Life of Lincoln*. Cleveland: World, 1942.
34. Holzer, Harold, ed., *Dear Mr. Lincoln*. Reading, MA: Addison-Wesley, 1993.
35. Holzer, Harold, ed., *The Lincoln-Douglas Debates*. New York: HarperCollins, 1993.
36. Jennison, Keith W., *The Humorous Mr. Lincoln*. New York: Thomas Y. Crowell, 1965.
37. Kunhardt, Philip, Jr., Philip B. Kunhardt III, and Peter W. Kunhardt, *Lincoln*. New York: Alfred A. Knopf, 1992.
38. Lamon, Ward Hill, *Recollections of Abraham Lincoln, 1847–1865*. Chicago: A. C. McClurg, 1895.
39. Luthin, Reinhard H., *The Real Abraham Lincoln*. Englewood Cliffs, NJ: Prentice-Hall, 1960.
40. McPherson, James M., *Abraham Lincoln and the Second American Revolution*. New York: Oxford University Press, 1991.
41. Mearns, David C., ed., *The Lincoln Papers*. 2 vols. Garden City, NY: Doubleday, 1948.
42. Mitgang, Herbert, *Abraham Lincoln: A Press Portrait*. Athens and London: University of Georgia Press, 1989.
43. Neely, Mark E., Jr., *The Abraham Lincoln Encyclopedia*. New York: McGraw-Hill, 1982.
44. Neely, Mark E., Jr., *The Last Best Hope of Earth: Abraham Lincoln and the Promise of America*. Cambridge, MA: Harvard University Press, 1993.
45. Newman, Ralph G., ed., *Lincoln for the Ages*. Garden City, NY: Doubleday, 1960.
46. Nicolay, John G., and John Hay, *Abraham Lincoln: A History*. 10 vols. New York: Century, 1890.
47. Oates, Stephen B., *Abraham Lincoln: The Man behind the Myths*. New York: Harper & Row, 1984.
48. Oates, Stephen B., *With Malice toward None: A Life of Abraham Lincoln*. New York: Harper & Row, 1977.
49. Paludan, Phillip S., *The Presidency of Abraham Lincoln*. Lawrence: University Press of Kansas, 1994.
50. Peterson, Merrill D., *Lincoln in American Memory*. New York: Oxford University Press, 1994.

51. Phillips, Donald T., *Lincoln on Leadership*. New York: Warner, 1992.
52. Radford, Victoria, ed., *Meeting Mr. Lincoln*. Chicago: Ivan R. Dee, 1998.
53. Randall, J. G., *Mr. Lincoln*, ed. Richard N. Current. New York: Dodd, Mead, 1957.
54. Sandburg, Carl, *Abraham Lincoln: The Prairie Years*. 2 vols. New York: Harcourt, Brace, 1926.
55. Sandburg, Carl, *Abraham Lincoln: The War Years*. 4 vols. New York: Harcourt, Brace, 1939.
56. Steers, Edward, Jr., *Lincoln: A Pictorial History*. Gettysburg, PA: Thomas, 1993.
57. Thomas, Benjamin P., *Abraham Lincoln: A Biography*. New York: Alfred A. Knopf, 1952.
58. Warren, Louis A., *Lincoln's Youth: Indiana Years, 1816–1830*. Indianapolis: Indiana Historical Society, 1959.
59. Whitney, Henry C., *Life on the Circuit with Lincoln*. Boston: Estes and Lauriat, 1892.
60. Williams, Frank J., and William D. Pederson, eds., *Abraham Lincoln: Contemporary*. Campbell, CA: Savas Woodbury, 1996.
61. Williams, Frank J., William D. Pederson, and Vincent J. Marsala, *Abraham Lincoln: Sources and Style of Leadership*. Westport, CT: Greenwood, 1994.
62. Wilson, Douglas L., *Honor's Voice: The Transformation of Abraham Lincoln*. New York: Alfred A. Knopf, 1998.
63. Wilson, Douglas L., *Lincoln before Washington*. Urbana and Chicago: University of Illinois Press, 1997.
64. Zall, P. M., ed., *Abe Lincoln Laughing*. Knoxville: University of Tennessee Press, 1995.

2. Calvin Coolidge

65. Abels, Jules, *In the Time of Silent Cal*. New York: G. P. Putnam, 1969.
66. Booraem, Hendrik, V, *The Provincial: Calvin Coolidge and His World, 1885–1895*. Lewisburg, PA: Bucknell University Press, 1994.
67. Carpenter, Ernest C., *The Boyhood Days of President Calvin Coolidge*. Rutland, VT: Tuttle, 1925.
68. Commonwealth of Massachusetts, *Messages to the General Court, Official Addresses, Proclamations, and State Papers of His Excellency, Governor Calvin Coolidge, for the Years 1919 and 1920*. Boston: Commonwealth of Massachusetts, 1920.
69. Coolidge, Calvin, *The Autobiography of Calvin Coolidge*. New York: Cosmopolitan, 1929.
70. Coolidge, Grace, *An Autobiography*. Worland, WY: High Plains, 1992.
71. Fleser, Arthur F., *A Rhetorical Study of the Speaking of Calvin Coolidge*. Lewiston, NY: Edwin Mellen, 1990.
72. Fuess, Claude M., *Calvin Coolidge: The Man from Vermont*. Boston: Little, Brown, 1940.
73. Gilfond, Duff, *The Rise of Saint Calvin*. New York: Vanguard, 1932.
74. Green, Horace, *The Life of Calvin Coolidge*. New York: Duffield, 1924.
75. Griffin, Solomon Bulkley, *W. Murray Crane: A Man and a Brother*. Boston: Little, Brown, 1926.
76. Hennessy, Michael E., *Calvin Coolidge: From a Green Mountain Farm to the White House*. New York: G. P. Putnam, 1924.
77. Kent, Zachary, *Calvin Coolidge*. Chicago: Childrens, 1988.
78. Lathem, Edward Connery, ed., *Meet Calvin Coolidge*. Brattleboro, VT: Stephen Greene, 1960.

79. Lathem, Edward Connery, ed., *Your Son, Calvin Coolidge.* Montpelier, VT: Vermont Historical Society, 1968.
80. McCoy, Donald R., *Calvin Coolidge: The Quiet President.* New York: Collier-Macmillan, 1967.
81. McKee, John Hiram, *Coolidge Wit and Wisdom.* New York: Frederick A. Stokes, 1933.
82. Quint, Howard H., and Robert H. Ferrell, eds., *The Talkative President.* Amherst: University of Massachusetts Press, 1964.
83. Rogers, Cameron, *The Legend of Calvin Coolidge.* Garden City, NY: Doubleday, Doran, 1928.
84. Ross, Ishbel, *Grace Coolidge and Her Era.* New York: Dodd, Mead, 1962.
85. Shriftgiesser, Karl, *The Gentleman from Massachusetts: Henry Cabot Lodge.* Boston: Little, Brown, 1944.
86. Silver, Thomas B., *Coolidge and the Historians.* Durham, NC: Carolina Academic Press, 1982.
87. Slemp, C. Bascom, *The Mind of the President.* Garden City, NY: Doubleday, Page, 1926.
88. Sobel, Robert, *Coolidge: An American Enigma.* Washington, DC: Regnery, 1998.
89. Starling, Edmund W., *Starling of the White House.* Chicago: Peoples Book Club, 1946.
90. Stoddard, Henry, *As I Knew Them.* New York: Harper, 1927.
91. Washburn, Robert, *Calvin Coolidge: His First Biography.* New York: Small Maynard, 1923.
92. White, William Allen, *A Puritan in Babylon.* New York: Macmillan, 1938.
93. White, William Allen, *Calvin Coolidge.* New York: Macmillan, 1925.
94. Whiting, Edward Elwell, *President Coolidge: A Contemporary Estimate.* Boston: Atlantic Monthly Press, 1923.
95. Woods, Robert A., *The Preparation of Calvin Coolidge.* Boston: Houghton Mifflin, 1924.

3. Franklin D. Roosevelt

96. Asbell, Bernard, *The F.D.R. Memoirs.* New York: Doubleday, 1973.
97. Beschloss, Michael R., *Kennedy and Roosevelt.* New York: W. W. Norton, 1980.
98. Buhite, Russell D., and David W. Levy, eds., *FDR's Fireside Chats.* New York: Penguin, 1993.
99. Burns, James MacGregor, *Roosevelt: The Lion and the Fox,* vol. 1 New York: Harcourt Brace, 1956.
100. Collier, Peter, with David Horowitz, *The Roosevelts: An American Saga.* New York: Simon & Schuster, 1994.
101. Daniels, Jonathan, *White House Witness 1942–1945.* New York: Doubleday, 1975.
102. Farley, James A., *Jim Farley's Story: The Roosevelt Years.* New York: McGraw-Hill, 1948.
103. Flynn, John T., *Country Squire in the White House.* New York: Doubleday, Doran, 1940.
104. Flynn, John T., *The Roosevelt Myth.* New York: Devin-Adair, 1948.
105. Friedel, Frank, *Franklin D. Roosevelt: A Rendezvous with Destiny.* Boston: Back Bay Books/Little, Brown, 1990.
106. Gallagher, Hugh Gregory, *FDR's Splendid Deception,* rev. ed. Arlington, VA: Vandamere, 1994.
107. Gies, Joseph, *Franklin D. Roosevelt: Portrait of a President.* New York: Doubleday, 1971.

108. Gosnell, Harold F., *Champion Campaigner: Franklin D. Roosevelt.* New York: Macmillan, 1952.
109. Gould, Jean, *A Good Fight, The Story of F.D.R.'s Conquest of Polio.* New York: Dodd, Mead, 1960.
110. Graff, Robert D., and Robert Emmett Ginna, *F.D.R.* New York: Harper & Row, 1962.
111. Gunther, John, *Roosevelt in Retrospect.* New York: Harper & Brothers, 1950.
112. Harrity, Richard, and Ralph G. Martin, *The Human Side of F.D.R.* New York: Duell, Sloan and Pearce, 1960.
113. Hassett, William D., *Off the Record with F.D.R.* New Brunswick, NJ: Rutgers University Press, 1958.
114. Ickes, Harold L., *The Secret Diaries of Harold L. Ickes.* 3 vols. New York: Simon & Schuster, 1953 and 1954.
115. Lash, Joseph P., *Eleanor and Franklin.* New York: W. W. Norton, 1971.
116. Leuchtenburg, William E., *Franklin D. Roosevelt and the New Deal, 1932–1940.* New York: Harper & Row, 1963.
117. Lindley, Ernest K., *Franklin D. Roosevelt: A Career in Progressive Democracy.* Indianapolis: Bobbs-Merrill, 1931.
118. Maney, Patrick J., *The Roosevelt Presence.* New York: Twayne, 1992.
119. Moley, Raymond, *After Seven Years.* New York: Harper & Brothers, 1939.
120. Perkins, Frances, *The Roosevelt I Knew.* New York: Viking, 1946.
121. Rauch, Basil, ed., *Franklin D. Roosevelt Reader: Selected Speeches, Messages, Press Conferences and Letters.* New York: Rinehart, 1957.
122. Roosevelt, Eleanor, *This I Remember.* New York: Harper & Brothers, 1961.
123. Roosevelt, James, and Sidney Shallett, *Affectionately, F.D.R.* New York: Harcourt, Brace, 1959.
124. Rosenau, James N., ed., *The Roosevelt Tragedy.* Garden City, NY: Doubleday, 1951.
125. Rosenman, Samuel I., ed., *The Public Papers and Addresses of Franklin D. Roosevelt, 1938.* 13 vols. New York: Random House, 1938–1950.
126. Rosenman, Samuel I., *Working with Roosevelt.* New York: Harper & Brothers, 1952.
127. Ryan, Halford R., *Franklin D. Roosevelt's Rhetorical Presidency.* New York: Greenwood, 1988.
128. Schlesinger, Arthur M., Jr., *The Age of Roosevelt: The Coming of the New Deal.* Boston: Houghton Mifflin, 1959.
129. Tully, Grace, *F.D.R., My Boss.* New York: Charles Scribner's Sons, 1949.
130. Underhill, Robert, *FDR and Harry: Unparalleled Lives.* Westport, CT: Praeger, 1996.
131. Venkataramani, M. S., ed., *The Sunny Side of FDR.* Athens: Ohio University Press, 1973.
132. Ward, Geoffrey C., *Before the Trumpet.* New York: Harper & Row, 1985.
133. Ward, Geoffrey C., ed., *Closest Companion.* Boston: Houghton Mifflin, 1995.
134. White, Graham J., *FDR and the Press.* Chicago: University of Chicago Press, 1979.
135. Winfield, Betty Houchin, *FDR and the News Media.* Urbana and Chicago: University of Illinois Press, 1990.

4. John F. Kennedy

136. Adler, Bill, ed., *The Kennedy Wit.* New York: Citadel, 1964.
137. Ayres, Alex, *The Wit and Wisdom of John F. Kennedy.* New York: Meridian, 1996.

138. Bernstein, Irving, *Promises Kept: John F. Kennedy's New Frontier*. New York: Oxford University Press, 1991.
139. Berry, Joseph P., Jr., *John F. Kennedy and the Media: The First Television President*. Lanham, MD: University Press of America, 1987.
140. Beschloss, Michael, *The Crisis Years: Kennedy and Khrushchev, 1960–1963*. New York: HarperCollins, 1991.
141. Bradlee, Benjamin C., *Conversations with Kennedy*. New York: W. W. Norton, 1975.
142. Burner, David, *John F. Kennedy and a New Generation*. Glenview, IL: Scott Foresman, 1988.
143. Burns, James MacGregor, *John Kennedy: A Political Profile*. New York: Harcourt Brace Jovanovich, 1960.
144. Donald, Aïda DiPace, ed., *John F. Kennedy and the New Frontier*. New York: Hill and Wang, 1966.
145. Fairlie, Henry, *The Kennedy Promise: The Politics of Expectation*. Garden City, NY: Doubleday, 1973.
146. Fay, Paul B., Jr., *The Pleasure of His Company*. New York: Harper & Row, 1966.
147. Galbraith, John Kenneth, *Ambassador's Journal: A Personal Account of the Kennedy Years*. Boston: Houghton Mifflin, 1969.
148. Gardner, Gerald, *The Quotable Mr. Kennedy*. New York: Abelard-Schuman, 1962.
149. Giglio, James N., *The Presidency of John F. Kennedy*. Lawrence: University Press of Kansas, 1991.
150. Goodwin, Doris Kearns, *The Fitzgeralds and the Kennedys*. New York: Simon & Schuster, 1987.
151. Hamilton, Nigel, *J.F.K., Reckless Youth*. New York: Random House, 1992.
152. Kennedy, John F., *John Fitzgerald Kennedy: A Compilation of Statements and Speeches Made During His Service in the United States Senate and House of Representatives*. Washington, DC: U.S. Government Printing Office, 1964.
153. Kennedy, John F., *Profiles in Courage*. New York: Harper & Row, 1956.
154. Kennedy, John F., *Public Papers of the President of the United States, John F. Kennedy, Containing the Public Messages, Speeches, and Statements of the President, 1961–1963*. 3 vols. Washington, DC: U.S. Government Printing Office, 1962–1964.
155. Lasky, Victor, *J.F.K., Man and the Myth*. New Rochelle, NY: Arlington House, 1966.
156. Manchester, William, *One Brief Shining Moment*. Boston: Little, Brown, 1983.
157. Manchester, William, *Portrait of a President: John F. Kennedy in Profile*. Boston: Little, Brown, 1962.
158. Martin, Ralph G., *A Hero for Our Time*. New York: Macmillan, 1983.
159. Matthews, Christopher, *Kennedy and Nixon*. New York: Simon & Schuster, 1996.
160. O'Donnell, Kenneth P., and David F. Powers, with Joe McCarthy, *"Johnny, We Hardly Knew Ye."* Boston: Little, Brown, 1972.
161. Parmet, Herbert S., *Jack: The Struggles of John F. Kennedy*. New York: Dial, 1980.
162. Parmet, Herbert S., *JFK: The Presidency of John F. Kennedy*. New York: Dial, 1983.
163. Reeves, Thomas C., *President Kennedy: Profile of Power*. New York: Touchstone/Simon & Schuster, 1994.
164. Reeves, Thomas C., *A Question of Character*. Rocklin, CA: Prima, 1992.
165. Reeves, Thomas C., ed., *John F. Kennedy*. Malabar, FL: Robert E. Krieger, 1990.

166. Salinger, Pierre, *With Kennedy*. Garden City, NY: Doubleday, 1966.
167. Schlesinger, Arthur M., Jr., *A Thousand Days: John F. Kennedy in the White House*. New York: Greenwich House, 1983.
168. Sidey, Hugh, *John F. Kennedy, President*. New York: Atheneum, 1964.
169. Sorensen, Theodore C., *Kennedy*. New York: Harper & Row, 1965.
170. Sorensen, Theodore C., ed., *"Let the Word Go Forth."* New York: Dell, 1988.
171. Sorensen, Theodore C., *The Kennedy Legacy*. New York: Macmillan, 1969.
172. Whalen, Richard J., *The Founding Father: The Story of Joseph P. Kennedy*. New York: New American Library, 1964.
173. Wicker, Tom, *JFK and LBJ: The Influence of Personality upon Politics*. Baltimore: Penguin, 1970.
174. Wicker, Tom, *Kennedy without Tears*. New York: William Morrow, 1964.
175. Wills, Garry, *The Kennedy Imprisonment: A Meditation on Power*. Boston: Little, Brown, 1982.

5. Ronald Reagan

176. Adler, Bill, with Bill Adler, Jr., eds., *The Reagan Wit*. Aurora, IL: Caroline House, 1981.
177. Adler, Bill, and Bill Adler, Jr., eds., *The Reagan Wit*. New York: William Morrow, 1998.
178. Adler, Bill, ed., *The Uncommon Wisdom of Ronald Reagan*. Boston: Little, Brown, 1996.
179. Barrett, Laurence, *Gambling with History: Ronald Reagan in the White House*. Garden City, NY: Doubleday, 1983.
180. Bosch, Adriana, *Reagan: An American Story*. New York: TV Books, 1998.
181. Boyarsky, Bill, *Ronald Reagan*. New York: Random House, 1981.
182. Cannon, Lou, *President Reagan: The Role of a Lifetime*. New York: Simon & Schuster, 1991.
183. Cannon, Lou, *Reagan*. New York: G. P. Putnam's Sons, 1982.
184. Dallek, Robert, *Ronald Reagan: The Politics of Symbolism*. Cambridge, MA: Harvard University Press, 1984.
185. Deaver, Michael K., with Mickey Herskowitz, *Behind the Scenes*. New York: William Morrow, 1987.
186. Donaldson, Sam, *Hold On, Mr. President!* New York: Random House, 1987.
187. D'Souza, Dinesh, *Ronald Reagan*. New York: Free Press, 1997.
188. Dugger, Ronnie, *On Reagan: The Man and His Presidency*. New York: McGraw-Hill, 1983.
189. Edel, Wilbur, *The Reagan Presidency*. New York: Hippocrene, 1992.
190. Edwards, Anne, *Early Reagan*. New York: William Morrow, 1987.
191. Erickson, Paul D., *Reagan Speaks*. New York: New York University Press, 1985.
192. Felten, D. Erik, ed., *A Shining City: The Legacy of Ronald Reagan*. New York: Simon & Schuster, 1998.
193. Fitzwater, Marlin, *Call the Briefing!* New York: Times Books, 1995.
194. Hannaford, Peter, ed., *Recollections of Reagan*. New York: William Morrow, 1997.
195. Meese, Edwin, III, *With Reagan*. Washington, DC: Regnery Gateway, 1992.
196. Muir, William Kerr, Jr., *The Bully Pulpit: The Presidential Leadership of Ronald Reagan*. San Francisco: ICS Press, 1992.
197. O'Neill, Tip, with William Novak, *Man of the House: The Life and Political Memoirs of Tip O'Neill*. New York: Random House, 1987.
198. Pemberton, William, *Exit with Honor: The Life and Presidency of Ronald Reagan*. New York: M. E. Sharpe, 1997.

199. Reagan, Maureen, *First Father, First Daughter: A Memoir*. Boston: Little, Brown, 1989.
200. Reagan, Nancy, with William Novak, *My Turn: The Memoirs of Nancy Reagan*. New York: Random House, 1989.
201. Reagan, Ronald, *An American Life*. New York: Simon & Schuster, 1990.
202. Reagan, Ronald, with Richard Hubler, *Where's the Rest of Me?* New York: Dell, 1965.
203. Regan, Donald T., *For the Record*. Orlando, FL: Harcourt Brace Jovanovich, 1988.
204. Ritter, Kurt, and David Henry, *Ronald Reagan: The Great Communicator*. New York: Greenwood, 1992.
205. Ryan, Frederick J., Jr., ed., *Ronald Reagan: The Wisdom and Humor of the Great Communicator*. San Francisco: Collins, 1995.
206. Schaller, Michael, *Reckoning with Reagan*. New York: Oxford University Press, 1992.
207. Schieffer, Bob, and Gary Paul Gates, *The Acting President*. New York: E. P. Dutton, 1989.
208. Shultz, George, *Turmoil and Triumph: My Years as Secretary of State*. New York: Charles Scribner, 1993.
209. Speakes, Larry, with Robert Pack, *Speaking Out*. New York: Charles Scribner, 1988.
210. Stockman, David, *The Triumph of Politics: How the Reagan Revolution Failed*. New York: Harper & Row, 1986.
211. Van der Linden, Frank, *The Real Reagan*. New York: William Morrow, 1981.
212. Walsh, Kenneth T., *Ronald Reagan*. New York: Park Lane, 1997.
213. Weiler, Michael, and W. Barnett Pearce, eds., *Reagan and Public Discourse in America*. Tuscaloosa: University of Alabama Press, 1992.
214. Weinberger, Caspar, *Fighting for Peace: Seven Critical Years in the Pentagon*. New York: Warner, 1990.

Other

215. Allen, George E., *Presidents Who Have Known Me*. New York: Simon & Schuster, 1950.
216. Bailey, Thomas A., *Presidential Greatness: The Image and the Man from George Washington to the Present*. New York: Appleton-Century, 1966.
217. Barber, James David, *The Presidential Character: Predicting Performance in the White House*, 2nd ed. Englewood Cliffs, NJ: Prentice-Hall, 1977.
218. Barry, Dave, *Dave Barry Talks Back*. New York: Crown,1991.
219. Boller, Paul F., Jr., *Presidential Anecdotes*, rev. ed. New York: Oxford University Press, 1996.
220. Boller, Paul F., Jr., *Presidential Campaigns*. New York: Oxford University Press, 1985.
221. Bradford, Gamaliel, *The Quick and the Dead*. Boston: Houghton Mifflin, 1931.
222. Brayman, Harold, *The President Speaks Off-the-Record*. Princeton, NJ: Dow Jones Books, 1976.
223. Bremmer, Jan, and Herman Roodenburg, eds., *A Cultural History of Humour*. Cambridge, England: Polity, 1997.
224. Burns, James MacGregor, *Edward Kennedy and the Kennedy Legacy*. New York: W. W. Norton, 1976.
225. Caro, Robert A., *The Years of Lyndon Johnson: The Path to Power*. New York: Alfred A. Knopf, 1982.
226. Cormier, Frank, *LBJ: The Way He Was*. Garden City, NY: Doubleday, 1972.

227. Cunliffe, Marcus, *American Presidents and the Presidency*. New York: American Heritage, 1968.
228. DeGregorio, William A., *The Complete Book of U.S. Presidents*, 4th ed. New York: Barricade, 1993.
229. Dole, Bob, *Great Political Wit*. New York: Nan A. Talese/Doubleday, 1998.
230. Donovan, Hedley, *Roosevelt to Reagan: A Reporter's Encounters with Nine Presidents*. New York: Harper & Row, 1985.
231. Fields, Alonzo, *My 21 Years in the White House*. New York: Coward-McCann, 1981.
232. Galbraith, John Kenneth, *A Life in Our Times*. Boston: Houghton Mifflin, 1981.
233. Gardner, Gerald, *All the Presidents' Wits: The Power of Presidential Humor*. New York: Beech Tree Books/William Morrow, 1986.
234. Goldwater, Barry M., with Jack Casserly, *Goldwater*. New York: St. Martin's, 1988.
235. Harris, Leon A., *The Fine Art of Political Wit*. New York: E. P. Dutton, 1964.
236. Henggeler, Paul R., *In His Steps: Lyndon Johnson and the Kennedy Mystique*. Chicago: Ivan R. Dee, 1991.
237. Hoover, Irwin, *Forty-Two Years in the White House*. New York: Macmillan, 1948.
238. Kearns, Doris, *Lyndon Johnson and the American Dream*. New York: Harper & Row, 1976.
239. Krock, Arthur, *In the Nation: 1932–1966*. New York: McGraw-Hill, 1966.
240. Martin, John Bartlow, *Adlai Stevenson and the World: The Life of Adlai E. Stevenson*. Garden City, NY: Doubleday, 1977.
241. McCullough, David, *Truman*. New York: Touchstone/Simon & Schuster, 1993.
242. McFeely, William S., *Grant: A Biography*. New York: Norton, 1981.
243. Medved, Michael, *The Shadow Presidents: Top Aides in the White House from Lincoln to the Present*. New York: Times Books, 1979.
244. Murray, Robert, and Tim Blessing, *Greatness in the White House: Rating the Presidents from George Washington through Ronald Reagan*. University Park: Pennsylvania State University Press, 1994.
245. Neal, Steve, *The Eisenhowers: Reluctant Dynasty*. Garden City, NY: Doubleday, 1978.
246. Nevins, Allan, *Grover Cleveland: A Study in Courage*. New York: Dodd, Mead, 1933.
247. Parks, Lillian Rogers, *My Thirty Years Backstairs at the White House*. New York: Fleet, 1961.
248. Peskin, Allan, *Garfield*. Kent, OH: Kent State University Press, 1978.
249. Pollard, James, *The Presidents and the Press*. New York: Macmillan, 1947.
250. Ridings, William, Jr., and Stuart McIver, *Rating the Presidents*. Secaucus, NJ: Carol, 1997.
251. Ryan, Halford, ed., *U.S. Presidents as Orators*. Westport, CT: Greenwood, 1995.
252. Smith, Richard Norton, *An Uncommon Man: The Triumph of Herbert Hoover*. Worland, WY: High Plains, 1984.
253. Stevenson, Adlai E., *Major Campaign Speeches of Adlai E. Stevenson*. New York: Random House, 1952.
254. Thompson, Charles Willis, *Presidents I've Known and Two Near Presidents*. Indianapolis: Bobbs-Merrill, 1929.
255. Thompson, Jake H., *Bob Dole*. New York: Donald I. Fine, 1994.
256. Thompson, Kenneth W., ed., *Ten Presidents and the Press*. Lanham, MD: University Press of America, 1983.
257. Udall, Morris K., *Too Funny to Be President*. New York: Henry Holt, 1988.

258. White, E. B., *Essays*. New York: Harper & Row, 1977.
259. White, Theodore H., *The Making of the President 1964*. New York: Atheneum, 1985.
260. Wilson, Robert, ed., *Character above All: Ten Presidents from FDR to George Bush*. New York: Simon & Schuster, 1995.
261. Zall, Paul M., ed., *The Wit & Wisdom of the Founding Fathers*. Hopewell, NJ: Ecco, 1996.

INDEX